View across the Danube from the quayside at
Pest. On the far side of the river, the Royal
Palace ● *70* ▲ *190* can be seen as it was before
its restoration in the late 19th century; below
it are the arcades enclosing the palace gardens
▲ *182*.

At the end of the 19th century the Drechsler House ▲ *144* (opposite the State Opera House on Andrássy út) had a popular café on the ground floor. It is now the home of the Hungarian Ballet Institute.

Leopold Boulevard (Lipót körút) – now
St Stephen's Boulevard (Szent István körút)
▲ *164* – as it was in the late 19th century.
Houses were just beginning to be built
on Rózsadomb (Rose Hill) ▲ *211*, which
can be seen in the distance.

This photograph of a courtyard in the
Belváros district ▲ 116 was taken toward the
end of the 19th century. One of the twin
towers of the Inner City Parish Church ▲ 120
is just visible above the rooftops.

HUNGARY

BUDAPEST

All information contained in this guide
has been approved by the many specialists
who have contributed to its production.

ABOUT THE AUTHORS

MOHAMMED BANSAR
Art historian and journalist, graduate of Lóránd Eötvös University. Author of the Architecture section, and the pages on Parliament and the Király Baths.

BEATRIX BÁSICS
Author of the pages on the Hungarian National Museum.

SÁNDOR BODÓ
Director of the Budapest History Museum and author of the pages on the museum.

PÉTER BUZA (1)
Journalist and lecturer. He has published around twenty books on Hungary, mainly on Budapest. Author of the Buda itineraries.

LIVIA FUCHS (2)
Dance historian, senior lecturer at the Hungarian Academy of Dance, dance critic for the daily newspaper *Hungarian News.* Author of the spread on Hungarian dance.

MARIANN GERGELY AND ÁRPÁD MIKÓ
Authors of the pages on the Hungarian National Gallery.

ANNAMARIA KELLER (3) Author of the texts on the Academy of Music, where she is head of international relations.

SOPHIE KÉPÈS
Writer, translator (from Hungarian) and literary critic. Author of the pages on the Hungarian language.

ANTHONY KRAUSE (4) Graduate in history from the École Normale Supérieure in Paris, currently teaching at INALCO

(National Institute of Oriental Languages and Civilisations). Head of the book section in the cultural department of the French Embassy in Budapest (1992-4). Author of the Pest itineraries, 'The baths of Budapest' and 'Budapest, capital of the Hungarian cinema'.

FLORENCE LA BRUYÈRE (5)
Graduate of the Institute of Political Sciences (Paris) and the University of Cambridge (England), Hungarian correspondent for the French publications *La Croix* and *Libération,* and Radio France. Responsible for reading and updating the guide.

ANNA LAKOS
Involved in theater- and dance-related projects at the French Institute. Author of the spreads on 'Hungarian theater' and 'Opera in Budapest'.

GUILHEM LESAFFRE
Naturalist and co-author of the Nature section.

KATALIN MADAS (6)
Forestry engineer and PhD who worked for twenty years in the field of nature conservation in the Budapest region. She is currently involved in forestry management and planning in the Hungarian Forest Service. Member of the 'Joventry' committee of the Hungarian Academy of Sciences. Co-author of the Nature section.

MARCEL MARNAT (7) After studying sciences, Marcel Marnat made a name for himself writing articles on painting, cinema, fringe literature and especially records and music. He also broadcasts on radio and has published books on Mussorgsky, Stravinsky, Beethoven and Ravel. Between 1978 and 1992 he produced programs for France Musique. Author of the spread on 'Hungarian music'.

MIKLÓS MÁTYÁSSY (8) Born (1959) in Budapest, he has lived in Paris since 1981. Journalist and translator. Since 1994, he has edited the Central- and Eastern-European column of the French weekly, *Courrier international.* Author of the texts on 'Hungarian photographers', 'The Danube: banks and bridges' and 'Around Budapest'.

JUDIT PATAKI (9) Curator of the Museum of Applied Arts, she has written several publications or the museum, including a CD-ROM on 'Applied arts and crafts'. Author of the pages on the Museum of Applied Arts.

YANNICK PENAGOS (10) Multimedia writer-reporter who is particularly interested in tourism. He collaborated on the editing of the Practical Information section.

Pilot Committee chaired by György Ifju
(director of the Budapest Tourist Office):
Katalin Madas, Zsuzsa Medgyes, András Török, Agnès Vatin
(Hungarian Tourist Office).

KRISZTINA RÁDY (11)
Graduate of the universities of Budapest and Lisbon (Faculty of Arts), and the Institute of European Studies in Paris. Former head of artistic activities at the French Institute in Budapest and the Hungarian Institute in Paris. Author of the 'Specialties' spread.

GILLES SENSINI
Graduate of the schools of Architecture and Fine Arts in Versailles. Member of the Paris urban-development unit. Author of 'From houses to apartment blocks'.

VILMOS TÁTRAI (12)
Born (1946) in Budapest. Graduate in art history and classical philology from the Eötvös Lóránd University Arts Faculty, and assistant director of the Museum of Fine Arts in Budapest. He edited the museum's general catalogue on Italian, French, Spanish and Greek paintings. Author of the pages on the Museum of Fine Arts.

ANDRÁS TÖRÖK (13)
Author, lecturer, minister for culture. Former dissident who became assistant

minister for culture and president of the national-heritage department. He has founded a national photographic center, and an institute of modern art in Budapest of which he is also the president. Author of *Budapest: A Critical Guide.* Author of 'Profile of Budapest' and 'The café tradition'.

ANNAMÁRIA VÍGH (14)
Historian specializing in heraldry, head conservator of the Budapest History Museum and director of the Kiscell Museum. Author of the History section, and the pages on Heroes' Square and the Kiscell Museum.

JÓZSEF VINKÓ (15)
Journalist, playwright, translator, editor, producer. Author of the Óbuda itineraries.

PAULA ZSIDI
Graduate in art history and archaeology from the Budapest University Faculty of Arts. Director of archaeological excavations within the context of the project for the development of Roman Budapest. Director of the Aquincum Museum since 1989, and author of the pages on the museum.

EVERYMAN GUIDES

Published by Everyman Publishers Plc

Budapest: ISBN 1-84159-021-5

© 2000 Everyman Publishers plc
© 1999 Editions Nouveaux-Loisirs, a subsidiary of Gallimard, Paris.

First edition April 2000

TRANSLATED BY
Wendy Allatson

EDITED BY
Peter Leek

TYPESET BY
Adrian McLaughlin

SPECIAL THANKS TO
Zsuzsanna Ardó who helped to edit the English version of Budapest.

BUDAPEST
ARCHITECTURE: Bruno Lenormand
NATURE: Frédéric Bony
PHOTOGRAPHY: Éric Guillemot, Patrick Léger
EDITOR: Patrick Jézéquel
LAYOUT: Carole Gaborit
ILLUSTRATIONS: Marie-Amélie Béri
CONSULTANT: Yannick Penagos
UPDATING: Anne-Josyane Magniant
PRODUCTION: Catherine Bourrabier

ILLUSTRATIONS
COVER: Henri Galeron
NATURE: Jean Chevallier, François Desbordes, Claire Felloni, Catherine Lachaux, Alban Larousse, Pascal Robin
ARCHITECTURE: Philippe Biard, Philippe Candé, Jean-Marc Lanusse, Maurice Pommier, Claude Quiec, Jean-François Pénau, Christian Rivière, Jean-Sylvain Roveri, Amato Soro
ITINERARIES: Philippe Biard (Parliament, background illustrations), Jean-Marc Lanusse ('The Danube: banks and bridges'), Amato Soro ('Király Baths')
PRACTICAL INFORMATION: Maurice Pommier, Raymond Stoffel
MAPS: Édigraphie

WE WOULD ALSO LIKE TO THANK:
Lajos Menyhart, Agnès Vatin, György Ifju, Attila Laszlo, Krisztina Rády, Odile George, Annamária Vígh, Florence la Bruyère, Sophie Képès, Frédérique Hugot, Thierry Hugot, Ferenc Aczél, Réka Győrfi, János-Pál Hárricz, and finally Sandra Pisano.

EVERYMAN GUIDES
Published by Everyman Publishers Plc
Gloucester Mansions, 140a Shaftesbury Avenue, London WC2H 8HD

Printed in Italy by Editoriale Lloyd

CONTENTS

CONTENTS

BELVÁROS

ÚJLIPÓTVÁROS

TERÉZVÁROS

VÁROSLIGET

NAGYKÖRÚT

NAGYKÖRÚT

BUDA

ÓBUDA

Budapest's size and imposing character are due to the fact that it was conceived as the capital of a country much larger than present-day Hungary. Today around 20 percent of the country's population live in the capital, where the rate of unemployment is well below the national average. The 'Pearl of the Danube' is a microcosm of the country's geography. On the left bank of the Danube the lower town of Pest stretches to the edge of the Great Plain (Nagyalfőld), while on the right bank the steep hills of the upper town of Buda are the last bastions of the mountains of Transdanubia (Dunántúl).

FACTS AND FIGURES (1997)
Year of foundation: 1873 (following the unification of the towns of Óbuda, Buda and Pest ● 29)
Surface area: 203 square miles
Number of districts (*kerület*): 23
Population: 1,860,000 (declining rapidly)
Population density: 9,189 inhabitants / sq mile
Working population: 768,601

INDUSTRY Smoke from the factories of Csepel Island no longer drifts across the city. With their closure in 1989, Budapest's role in Hungarian industry was considerably reduced; shopping centers have been built on some of the abandoned industrial sites. The city now has a fast-developing service sector (especially information technology).

THE TWO FACES OF BUDAPEST
Although destined to become a major banking and financial center in the 21st century, the Hungarian capital has nevertheless managed to retain a certain provincial charm. Only a stone's throw from the city center you can go skiing or gather wild lilac.

14

> 'Budapest is the loveliest city on the Danube. It has a crafty way of being its own stage-set, like Vienna, but also has a robust substance and a vitality unknown to its Austrian rival.'
>
> Claudio Magris

A CULTURAL METROPOLIS

The Hungarian capital and state have always invested heavily in culture, both under the Stalinist regime and the more liberal dictatorship of the 1970s and 1980s. As a result, Budapest has 2 opera houses, 16 theaters and 4 European-level symphony orchestras. Today the city's cultural activities are supported by public funding, including its impressive network of 'art houses' and other non-mainstream cinemas ▲ 168, even though the American movies shown in the new multi-screen complexes account for 90 percent of the industry's revenue. Budapest is also a major center for avant-garde theater ● 42. Táncházak ('dance houses') are still a typical feature of the city; as popular today as they were thirty years ago, they ensure that the tradition of Hungarian and Slavonic folk dances is kept alive.

THE DANUBE
is 1,770 miles long and Europe's second longest river after the Volga. Called Duna in Hungarian, Donau in German and Czech, and Dunav in Serbian and Bulgarian, it flows majestically through Budapest for a distance of 17 miles, from north to south, between the hills of Buda and the steep-sided valley of Pest. Its width varies from 312 to 2,100 yards, its depth from 10 to 30 feet. The annual rate of flow amounts to 16 million gallons. The river's average temperature is around 52°F (11°C). During harsh winters, it freezes over.

PESTI EST
BUDAPEST
125 ÉVeS
Születésnapi
MULATSÁG
1998 június 20.

15

HOW TO USE THIS GUIDE

The symbols at the top of each page refer to the different parts of the guide.

■ NATURE SECTION

● ENCYCLOPEDIC SECTION

▲ ITINERARIES

◆ PRACTICAL INFORMATION

The mini-map locates the particular itinerary within the wider area covered by the guide.

The itinerary map shows main points of interest along the way and is intended to help you find your bearings.

● ▲ ■ ◆
The symbols alongside a title or within the text itself provide cross-references to a theme or place dealt with elsewhere in the guide.

★ The star symbol signifies that a particular area has been singled out by the publishers for its special beauty, atmosphere or cultural interest.

Where the layout permits the names of museums, squares, monuments etc. are in both English and Hungarian.

NATURE
**Katalin Madas,
Guilhem Lesaffre**

■ THE DANUBE

On leaving Austria, the Danube enters a narrow pass at Esztergom, before describing a huge meander and flowing south to Budapest. Here, despite its urban surroundings, it creates an attractive environment for wildlife – especially for birds, which vary according to the season. In particular, the river valley attracts the migratory birds that spend fall and spring on the eastern fringes of Europe, en route for their Mediterranean overwintering sites. During the winter months, when the region's lakes are frozen over, the Danube welcomes aquatic species; the broader stretches of the river, in places as much as 655 yards across, make an ideal habitat for waterfowl and divers.

COOT
Coots dive to find food on the riverbed. They "run" across the surface when taking off.

GRAY WAGTAIL
In winter this elegant and fairly tame member of the wagtail family frequents quays and embankments.

TUFTED DUCK
This small diver, with its characteristic two-tone plumage, is a winter visitor.

POCHARD
In winter these divers live in small groups on the river. They often remain submerged for half a minute or longer.

BLACK-HEADED GULL
In winter, when the Danube rings with its cries, this gull no longer has a black head, as it does during the mating season.

KINGFISHER
Kingfishers are most widely seen during the fall.

BREAM
In the evening bream can be seen feeding near the river banks.

CARP
The females lay their eggs on the underwater plants along the river banks.

CATFISH
Older specimens can reach lengths of over 6 feet.

The five islands of Budapest have retained some of their original appearance. You can explore them on foot, or take a boat trip round them. The best preserved of the five is Háros, although due to the partial silting of the Danube in the early 20th century, it is now a peninsula rather than an island. Its flood forest of willows and poplars is a designated nature reserve. Csepel, the largest of the islands, has several nature reserves; other interesting features include its 'floating marsh' – a thick raft of aquatic plants, in a bay on the 'Little Danube' – and the Tamariska dunes, with their rare plants.

Cygnet

Young bittern

GRAY HERON
When they are not fishing, herons perch in the trees along the river bank.

LITTLE BITTERN
This unobtrusive migratory heron hides in the reed beds.

MUTE SWAN
During the nesting season the male is extremely aggressive toward intruders.

BLACK POPLAR
Wet river valleys provide the ideal environment for this tree.

COMMON ASH
The ash can withstand floods and high water. It produces bunches of long winged seeds, or 'keys'.

WHITE WILLOW
This tree is named after the silvery white hairs that cover the new leaves.

Winter

Summer

GREAT CRESTED GREBE
This skillful diver lives mainly on fish.

MOORHEN
Its long toes prevent it from sinking into the mud along the river banks.

Male

Female

GOLDEN ORIOLE
This bird's piping song is heard from April onward. It lives mainly in poplar forests.

YELLOW WAGTAIL
The yellow wagtail feeds on insects found in the short grass.

SPARROWHAWK
The sparrowhawk's short wings enable it to fly through forests and among trees.

NIGHTINGALE
Its ringing song can be heard in the damp thickets that are its favorite haunt.

The seven large wooded parks and dozens of public gardens spared by the city's urban development cover a total area of several hundred acres. City Park (Városliget) ▲ *160*, where planting began in 1751, is one of the largest and is reputed to be the world's finest public park. Its green spaces harbor a wide variety of exotic and native trees, which attract many of the hundred or so bird species recorded in Budapest, especially woodland birds.

SYRIAN WOODPECKER

GREEN WOODPECKER

The area of distribution of this Central European bird is currently extending westward.

The green woodpecker is often seen on lawns, searching for ants, which form its staple diet.

GROSBEAK
Even the hardest seeds are no match for this bird's powerful beak.

FIELDFARE
This bird is seen mainly in winter. It eats the berries of ornamental bushes.

FIELD MAPLE
The field maple's smallish five-lobed leaves turn amber-yellow in the fall.

PEDUNCULATE OAK
This oak has long-stemmed (pedunculate) acorns and short-stemmed leaves.

BEECH
Beechnuts are one of the favorite foods of the red squirrel.

Female

Male

WHITE-COLLARED FLYCATCHER
These birds take over nesting holes abandoned by woodpeckers.

SERIN
The male's song is rapid and shrill. Its mating display takes the form of a slow circular flight.

SHORT-TOED TREE CREEPER
This little bird picks out insects and spiders from the tree trunks to which it clings.

TITMOUSE
The black-capped titmouse looks for food on leaves by hanging from twigs and small branches.

STONE MARTEN
Although primarily a nocturnal predator, the stone marten can sometimes be seen by day. It now has to compete with domestic cats that have become feral.

RED SQUIRREL
The parks of Budapest provide these little acrobats with all the food they need throughout the year. Although they mainly eats seeds, they sometimes take fledglings from birds' nests.

■ THE CAVES

These exquisite natural aragonite crystal formations are extremely fragile.

The rock underlying the Buda Hills is riddled with some 160 caves. Their galleries extend for a total distance of 12 miles or more. Although most of them are closed to the public, parts of the caves of Pálvölgy, Szemlő-hegy and Mátyás-hegy are open to visitors. Pálvölgy boasts the largest cavern in the world (about 4½ miles long); Szemlő-hegy's features include 'cauliflower' reliefs, bands of calcite and pisolite ('peastone') formations; and Mátyás-hegy has a lake that lies 300 feet below its entrance. The huge cave of József-hegy is interesting on two counts: as well as being rich in crystals, it contains the largest known underground cavern formed by thermal waters, approximately 230 feet long by 50 feet wide.

RECENT DISCOVERIES
For a long time the substratum of Buda's hills was literally *terra incognita*. The cave of Pálvölgy was discovered in 1904, Szemlő-hegy in 1930, and József-hegy in 1984.

Stalagmites (above and far right).

Stalactites on top of the 'great column' in the cave of Pálvölgy (top right).

Pisolite looks like lots of tiny marbles (bottom right).

HISTORY
Annamária Vígh

Sophie Képès

THE SITE OF BUDAPEST BEFORE THE ROMANS

Objects found during archeological excavations indicate that the site of modern Budapest has been inhabited continuously from the 4th millennium BC. Traces of Iron Age communities date from c. 900 BC, and *columbaria* – sepulchral buildings, rather like dovecotes, with dozens of small niches containing cinerary urns – have been unearthed at Békásmegyer and Pünkösdfürdő. Eraviscan (Celtic) settlements have been discovered dating from the late Iron Age (4th century BC). The *oppidum* (citadel) of the Celtic tribes was situated on what is now Gellért Hill ▲ 215. While the citadel was being built on the higher ground, settlements were also being established on the plain, on the right bank of the Danube.

THE ROMAN OCCUPATION (1ST CENTURY BC–5TH CENTURY AD)

In c. 10 BC the Eraviscan settlements came under Roman control, and in c. AD 90 a legionary camp was established at Óbuda. In 106 Aquincum (the Roman forebear of Budapest) became the capital of Pannonia Inferior, the eastern part of the Roman province of Pannonia, which lay on the route of continual Barbarian attacks and formed part of the line of defense that ran parallel to the border (*limes*). Hadrian was the first of several governors of Pannonia who went on to become Roman emperors. He had a palace built on Óbuda Island ▲ 226, and in 124 made Aquincum a municipium, an autonomous town under the jurisdiction of a praetor (senior magistrate). The legionary camp lay to the south of the Aquincum, its center occupying what is now Flórián tér (Flórián Square).

The population of the military town that developed around the *castrum* (camp) must have been in the region of 20,000. Beyond the main residential districts, laid out on a grid of streets at right angles, there were groups of villas, and farms dotted here and there along the major roads. Along the banks of the Danube stood a series of watchtowers punctuated by two forts: Trans-Aquincum – on what is now Dagály út (Dagály Street) – and Contra-Aquincum, on the east side of Március 15 tér ▲ 120 in Pest. These two forts protected the crossing points on the Danube: a permanent bridge built on piles near the modern Árpád Bridge, and a pontoon probably situated where the Elizabeth Bridge (Erzsébet híd) stands today. In 409 Aquincum fell to the Huns.

Left: Mithras slaying the cosmic bull (now in the Aquincum Museum ▲ 228).

THE MAGYAR CONQUEST

Following the establishment of the seven victorious Hungarian tribes in AD 896, the two chieftains Árpád (below) and Kurszán decided to settle on the site of what is now Budapest. Árpád's summer residence was on Csepel Island, while Kurszán's castle stood in the geographical center of the region, modern Óbuda.

THE KINGS OF THE ÁRPÁDIAN DYNASTY (1000–1301)

In the 10th century the center of power was moved to Esztergom ▲ 238, and neither Buda nor Pest featured among the *comitats* (counties) and archdioceses created by King Stephen I (István I) (1000–38), founder of the Christian state ▲ 203. Buda, the name of present-day Óbuda until the 13th century, established itself as the geographical and administrative center of the country.

This process was interrupted by the Mongol invasion of 1242, when the unfortified town fell and most of its houses were burned to the ground. The commercial town of Pest suffered the same fate. The construction of fortified towns and fortresses began during the reign of Béla IV (1235–70), who ordered the population living at the foot of the hill of Buda (1243) and in Pest (1247) to move to what is now Castle Hill (Várhegy) ▲ 190, probably uninhabited until then. This population consisted of two ethnic groups. The Germans from Pest settled around their church, Boldogasszony ('Our Lady'), now Matthias Church ▲ 202, while the Hungarians from the foot of the hill of Buda settled around their own church, of which the sole remnant is the Mary Magdalene Tower in Kapisztrán tér ▲ 205.

The construction of the fortified town and the royal palace could now begin. In spite of developing later than Buda, 13th-century Pest – rebuilt along the lines of the old town – became an important thoroughfare and market town. Its development was boosted by the king's decision to hold meetings of the Diet (the legislative assembly) in the fields alongside a nearby stream, the Rákos.

27

Sigismund of Luxembourg
orders a new royal palace
to be built in Buda

1308-82	1385	1418	1458-90	1526	154
The House of Anjou rules Hungary	Sigismund of Luxembourg marries Maria, daughter of King Louis I of Hungary and Poland, in Buda		Reign of Matthias Corvinus	The Hungarian army is defeated by the Turks at the Battle of Mohács	The Turks occupy Buda

THE HOUSES OF ANJOU AND LUXEMBOURG (14TH CENTURY)

The House of Árpád came to an end in 1301, when András III died without leaving an heir. The ensuing conflicts of succession ended with the accession of Charles Robert of Anjou who, as Charles I (1308–42), wanted to move the royal court from Visegrád ▲ 235 to Buda. For five years the inhabitants refused to let him enter the town. He finally gained access by subterfuge and, after executing the officials, had himself crowned king. He made Buda a 'place of call', which meant that, no matter where they came from, merchants had to stop there to sell their merchandise. A walled castle was built for the king and his court, and until the 14th century the royal residence remained within the city walls. The ramparts surrounding the new castle ran down to the Danube, which

greatly facilitated water supply, the mooring of boats and the operation of the water mills. At this time the Danube played a key role in the town's economy, so the castle and fortifications formed a cohesive system of defense.

The castle did not, however, satisfy the imperial requirements of Sigismund of Luxembourg (1387–1437 below). Gothic extensions were added at his instigation, then the royal archives and a treasury and treasurer's residence. Buda became the country's new capital. In 1406 Pest was granted the status of 'free town', and it soon became the country's second largest city. An enclosure wall punctuated by three gates was erected on what is now the Kiskörút (Little Boulevard) ▲ 123, and round bastions were built on the banks of the Danube. In 1355 Louis the Great of Anjou (1342–82) ▲ 199 made Óbuda the permanent possession of the queens of Hungary. It was given the status of 'market town', with lesser freedoms and rights than Buda and Pest. During the 14th century, which witnessed the founding of many universities in Central Europe, Hungary's second largest university (after that of Pécs) was founded at Óbuda, in 1395. King Matthias Corvinus (1458–90) ● 32 reaffirmed central power and established the seat of his government in Buda, which soon became famous throughout Europe.

The united Christian armies deliver Buda from Ottoman occupation				First legislative assembly, first representative government. War of Independence against the Habsburgs	
1686	**1703**	**1703-11**	**1795**	**1848-9**	**1867**
	Leopold I confirms the legal status of Buda and Pest by royal charter	War of Independence against the Habsburgs, led by Ferenc Rákóczi	Execution of the 'Hungarian Jacobins' at Vérmező		The Compromise: Austria-Hungary ruled by two governments

THE OTTOMAN PRESENCE: BUDA, A TURKISH TOWN (1541–1686)

On August 29, 1526 a 25,000-strong Hungarian army was annihilated by the Turks at the Battle of Mohács. The queen was in Buda when she learned of the defeat. She immediately abandoned the castle and fled to Pozsony (Pressburg, now Bratislava) with her entourage. Suleiman the Magnificent (1494/5–1566), Sultan of the Ottoman Empire (1520–66), entered Buda, where he had the royal treasure loaded into 7,000 leather trunks and transported to Istanbul. Then he crossed the Danube and plundered and burned the town of Pest. Although Buda did not fall into Turkish hands until 1541, the battle marked a turning point in the history of this hitherto flourishing town, which entered a long period of external attacks and internal conflict. Most of the population fled, and for almost 150 years Buda was a Turkish city, while Pozsony became the capital of the part of the country that remained under Hungarian rule. Apart from religious and military buildings, the Turks mainly built baths, to which the town's natural resources were ideally suited ● 62, ▲ 208. Buda was linked to Pest by a pontoon, and a toll was collected by the deputy of Buda's principal judge.

THE UNIFICATION OF BUDA, PEST AND ÓBUDA (1703–1873)

On September 2, 1686 Buda, which had been the stronghold of Turkish power in Hungary, fell to the Austrians. The former seat of the kings of Hungary was devastated; on the other side of the Danube, Pest was depopulated, too. When the fighting was over, Buda was rebuilt on its old foundations and repopulated by moving people there from other areas. In the early 19th century, Pest became the region's second largest market town after Vienna. The walls and gates of the city, which impeded expansion, were demolished between 1788 and 1808. After the extensive changes of the Age of Reform ● 34, Pest became the intellectual center of the 1848 uprising. The loss of the War of Independence merely postponed the unification of Buda, Pest and Óbuda, and their joint accession to capital status, by a few years. The Compromise (*Ausgleich*) of 1867 removed political obstacles, and the unification of the three towns was completed in 1873, with the creation of Budapest.

1868		1872		1887		1896		1914-

Introduction of trams
on the Nagykörút
(Great Boulevard)

Hungary fight
alongside Austria
in World War One

Nationalities Law paves
way for introduction of
Hungarian ● 38 as the
official language

Law instituting the
unification of Buda,
Pest and Óbuda to
create Budapest

Opening of the Földalatti (Underground
Railway ▲ 117, 145). Celebration of the
thousandth anniversary of the Magyar conquest

BUDAPEST DURING THE AUSTRO-HUNGARIAN MONARCHY

During the last thirty years of the 19th century Budapest, together with Vienna and Prague, became one of the great economic and cultural centers of central Europe. Its urban planning was developed by the Council of Public Works, which was inspired by other European models. Boulevards were built, and extensive investments made in the urban infrastructure. The city's traffic increased greatly and Margit híd (Margaret Bridge) was built, followed by the first Erzsébet híd (Elizabeth Bridge) ▲ 181 begun in 1897. In the course of its construction most of the old city center was demolished, including Pest's town hall, hitherto regarded as the symbol of the town. By 1900 the reformist dream had come true: Budapest had become the modern heart of Hungary. The 1000th anniversary of the foundation of the Hungarian state – the Millenium ▲ 150 – was commemorated by extensive celebrations in which the major event was the depositing of the royal crown in the Parliament building, still under construction, on June 8, 1896. The outbreak of World War One put an end to the long period of peace enjoyed by Hungary and its capital. As the nerve center of unoccupied Hungary, Budapest had to assume the heavy responsibilities of feeding its people and caring for the wounded.

Count Andrássy ▲ 140.

Queen Elizabeth ▲ 182, 240.

AN EXPANDING CAPITAL IN A DIMINISHED COUNTRY (1918–44)

The military defeat of 1918 led to the collapse of the Austro-Hungarian monarchy. Hungary, whose territory was reduced by two-thirds, became an independent state, and retained Budapest as its capital. During the ensuing period, under a succession of revolutionary and counter-revolutionary governments, the city was inundated by thousands of refugees from the ceded territories, plus around 100,000 demobilized soldiers returning from prisoner-of-war camps. The fact that in the 1920s less than 12 percent of the country's population lived in Budapest indicates the sharp rise in the number of inhabitants. The so-called 'Capital Law' of 1930, which created thirteen administrative districts (kerületke), adapted the structure of the city to the new demands being made upon it. During the interwar period Budapest became a major industrial city, and the suburbs and outlying districts developed accordingly.

In the second half of the 1930s, even though the city's administration was heavily influenced by Nazi and Fascist ideology, Budapest's Jewish community – which represented 20 percent of the city's population – was not forced to live in ghettos. However, in November 1944 a decree issued by the 'leader of the nation,' Ferenc Szálasi, a Nazi puppet and founder of the Fascist Arrow Cross Party, set up a ghetto (bounded by Dohány útca, Király útca and Károly körút), and concerted efforts were made to exterminate its inhabitants.

FEGYVERBE! FEGYVERBE!

1918	1919	1920	1941	1944	1956	1989

Hungarian Soviet Republic. On August 1 Romanian troops occupy Budapest

Treaty of Trianon: Hungary loses two-thirds of its territory

Hungary enters World War Two alongside Germany

Hungarian (anti-Stalinist) national uprising

The Republic of Hungary is proclaimed

Hungary declares independence, as a Republic, with Mihály Károlyi as president

Admiral Miklós Horthy becomes regent of Hungary

Budapest is occupied by German troops

BUDAPEST: 1945–89

Like Berlin and Warsaw, Budapest was almost completely destroyed by World War Two. In a pitched battle between Russian and German troops that lasted several months, 25,000 civilians died, all the bridges over the Danube were demolished, and three-quarters of the buildings were either destroyed or badly damaged. Immediately after the cessation of hostilities, the inhabitants and municipal authorities set about clearing and rebuilding their ruined city. After the elections in May 1949, a law for the creation of a 'Greater Budapest' was adopted, which officially incorporated 7 towns and 16 villages into the capital. At a stroke, the geographical area of the city was more than doubled and its population increased to 1.6 million. To meet political objectives, this development was subject to compulsory industrialization. In 1956 Budapest was once again under siege, this time by the tanks of the Soviet army ● 36. After the uprising of 1956 had been crushed, the city's political masters adopted a more pragmatic approach to theoretical problems, and the centralization of the municipal authorities under János Kádár had the effect of greatly limiting the

autonomous decision-making powers of the district councils. In accordance with the model of Socialist urban planning, apartment blocks were constructed and the older residential districts were allowed to decline. In 1989 the years of the so-called 'soft dictatorship' came to an end, when Budapest was once again the focus of political change. The first free legislative elections were followed by municipal elections, and the new multi-party city council initiated an extensive program of urban development on a truly European scale.

The People's Republic of Hungary lasted from August 1, 1947 until October 23, 1989, when the Republic of Hungary was proclaimed. Below: the funeral ceremony, in 1989, for those who died during the 1956 uprising.

ELŐRE A BÉKE ÉS A SZO AIIZM
IEJU HARCOSAINAK KONGRESSZUSÁ
1950. JUNIUS 17-18

THE REIGN OF MATTHIAS CORVINUS (1458–90)

Stove tile showing King Matthias on his throne, holding the royal orb and scepter.

In 1458 Mátyás (Matthias) 'Corvinus' Hunyadi, son of János Hunyadi, became king of Hungary at the age of fifteen. His foreign policy consisted of waging a defensive war against the Turks, on one hand, and attempting to annex Austria and Bohemia, on the other. His domestic policy was inspired by the Italian model (in 1476 he married Beatrice of Naples), and he made his court one of the cultural centers of Europe.

'BIBLIOTHECA CORVINIANA'

The library was housed in a wing of the palace overlooking the Danube, in two square vaulted rooms with astronomical frescos. The vault of one of the rooms was decorated with the king's 'birth sky'.

Bookcases embellished with marquetry stood against the wall, their shelves protected from the dust and light by gold veils.

'MATYAS REX MANU PROPRIA'

(signature of King Matthias) The library housed between 1,000 and 1,500 volumes containing some 3,000 contemporary scientific and literary works.

BUDA AND THE ROYAL PALACE AT THE END OF THE MIDDLE AGES

Brought up in the Humanist tradition, Matthias invited scholars, architects, artists and miniaturists from Italy and Dalmatia to transform the Royal Palace ▲ 190 in accordance with his tastes. In addition, he employed famous artists such as Botticelli, Mantegna and Filippo Lippi to work on his behalf in Italy.

KING MATTHIAS AND QUEEN BEATRICE
(manuscript from the Bibliotheca Corviniana)

ENI AD TVAM PRAE
STANTISSIMAM MA
I ESTATEM MATHIA
HVNGARORVM POTETIS
SIME REX ATQVE AD TE
BEATIX OMNI VIRTVTVM
GENERE ORNATISSIA REGINA

After Italy, Hungary was the next European country to embrace the Renaissance and Humanist movements. Buda's close links with Italy had already been forged during the Angevin dynasty. Matthias' accession to the throne made the Bibliotheca Corviniana – and Buda – the center of Humanism in Hungary.

MATTHIAS' ARMS CARVED IN RED MARBLE
Matthias was given the name 'Corvinus' by the Humanists because of the raven in the family coat of arms and a legendary Roman ascendancy.

MAJOLICA TILES
(opposite)
From the Royal Palace, Buda.

'There was a King who governed his affairs as wisely in times of peace as in times of war. Toward the end of his life, and seeing himself without enemies, he became an extremely pretentious and triumphant King in his house and gathered together a huge treasure of beautiful furniture and rings and services to decorate his house.'
Philippe de Commynes

MATTHIAS THE EDUCATIONALIST
In 1467, with the help of Hungarian and foreign Humanists, Matthias founded the University of Pressburg (now Bratislava). It was closed a few years later.

Between 1831 and 1848 what had previously been a group of feudal states was transformed into a nation-state. But major changes had been taking place in Budapest since the 1780s, when Joseph II (1780–90) transferred the most important administrative departments and law courts from Pozsony (now Bratislava) to Buda and Pest. To accommodate the vast body of employees, he distributed land and simultaneously levied a property tax. He was succeeded by Archduke Sándor Lipót who, as Leopold II (1790–2), moved into the castle in Buda, which had become the governor's seat.

PALATINE ARCHDUKE JOSEPH OF HABSBURG ▲ 199
The 'urban embellishment' committee set up in 1808 by Archduke Joseph (1776–1847), son of Leopold II, became the driving force behind Pest's development. Neoclassical palaces and public buildings, built according to the plans of the young architects József Hild and Mihály Pollack, reflected the aspirations of the city's new commercial classes: traders, industrialists and bankers. The Újváros ('New City') district – now Lipótváros – was the first fruit of this coordinated urban planning and became the economic heart of Pest.

Pest's neoclassical quay in 1834.

ISTVÁN SZÉCHENYI
In 1831 Count István Széchenyi (1791–1860) ▲ 185 suggested linking Buda and Pest to form the city of Budapest. The construction of the Széchenyi Lánchíd (Chain Bridge ● 74, ▲ 184) – the first permanent structure across the Danube – began in 1841. Designed by the English engineer William Tierney Clark, it was built under the direction of the Scottish engineer Adam Clark ▲ 183. The count also promoted the construction of a tunnel ▲ 184, and in 1845 he became president of the newly formed 'tunnel society'. The tunnel was built between 1853 and 1857.

LAJOS KOSSUTH
Hungary's economic crisis during the 1840s exacerbated social and national conflicts. Moderate opposition to the Conservatives focused on Széchenyi, more radical opposition on Lajos Kossuth.
Below: *Kossuth's electoral rally in front of the National Museum.*

● THE 1956 UPRISING

At 9.30pm on October 23, 1956 the statue of Stalin on Dózsa György út was overturned by the crowd.

Since 1945 Hungary has been shaken by a series of major revolutions. The Yalta agreements in 1945 placed Hungary within the sphere of Soviet influence. In 1947 the process of nationalization began in the fields of property, production and education. A policy of ultracentralized economic planning favored the development of heavy industry, of which the Soviet Union was the main beneficiary. Declining living standards and the development of a repressive police regime by the one-party government kindled widespread anger. On October 23, 1956 around 200,000 people took to the streets of Budapest.

THE BEGINNINGS OF THE UPRISING

After Stalin's death, in 1953, two main streams formed within the Hungarian Communist Party: the hardline Communists led by Mátyás Rákosi and the reformists led by Imre Nagy ▲ 151, former Minister of Agriculture. Nagy became prime minister in 1953, but was accused of 'deviationism' and removed from office, before being reinstated in 1956. It was the members of the Petőfi Circle ▲ 119 – a group of intellectuals and students – who began to demand radical reforms.
Left to right: Zoltán Tildy, Imre Nagy and Pál Maléter in the Hungarian Parliament.

IMRE NAGY, THE VOICE OF REFORM

In a radio broadcast on November 1, 1956 the prime minister, surrounded by representatives of the former coalition parties, announced Hungary's neutrality and secession from the Warsaw Pact.

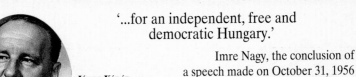

'...for an independent, free and democratic Hungary.'

Imre Nagy, the conclusion of a speech made on October 31, 1956

JÁNOS KÁDÁR

János Kádár, first secretary (1956–88) of Hungary's Communist Party, left Budapest and formed a new government under Soviet auspices.

THE FIRST RUSSIAN INTERVENTION

After forming a military committee, the Communist Party leaders called upon the commanders of the Soviet troops stationed in Hungary, in accordance with the Warsaw Pact, to reestablish order. On the night of October 24 Russian tanks entered Budapest. They were attacked by several thousand people: young workers, students and even schoolchildren, the 'urchins of Pest'.

THE REVOLUTION BETRAYED

During the subsequent street fighting and demonstrations, the opposition demanded political and economic reforms under an enlightened Socialist regime and the withdrawal of Soviet troops. The latter reoccupied Budapest at the request of the shadow government formed by János Kádár.

EXILE, IMPRISONMENT AND EXECUTIONS

200,000 Hungarians left the country at the end of December to escape the repression. Nagy was arrested and executed in 1958. Cardinal Mindszenty sought refuge in the United States Embassy... until 1971.

HISTORY OF THE HUNGARIAN LANGUAGE

Left: King Stephen I, with his son Imre (Emeric). Illustration from the *Gesta Hungarorum* (12th century), the first source of Hungarian historiography, written in Latin by the anonymous notary known as 'P. dictus magister' or 'Master P.'.

Most of the legends surrounding the origins of the Magyar people existed as an oral tradition only and have now been lost. When Stephen I (Saint Stephen) was crowned king in 1000, he forced the Magyar people to convert to Christianity. The earliest texts written in Hungarian, dating from the end of the 12th century, were translations of religious texts. With the development of the feudal system, 'Master P.' – alias 'Anonymus' (sic) – translated the most popular French chivalric novels. Then Latin was reinstated as the official language throughout the Gothic period.

Manuscript mixing Latin, German and Hungarian

THE FIRST HUNGARIAN GRAMMAR

The first Hungarian printing press was founded in Buda in 1472, during the reign of Matthias Corvinus ● 32, who introduced Humanism and other Renaissance ideas into his court. But it was the disciples of Erasmus who were responsible for the development of the Hungarian language. János Sylvester translated the New Testament, and wrote a Latin-Hungarian primer and the first Hungarian grammar (1539). 'If we do not hesitate to use our mother tongue,' he said, 'this treasure that has remained hidden from us until now but which we have just discovered, then from the poor people we once were we will soon become rich indeed.'

THE FIRST HUNGARIAN BIBLE

During the Reformation the use of Hungarian became widespread, since Martin Luther (1483–1546) wanted the Gospel to be preached in the language of the people. Gáspár Károlyi produced the first Hungarian translation of the entire Bible in 1590. Religious writers used the language for their treatises, hymns and history books to spread new ideas and denounce the feudal lords who oppressed the people. This period also witnessed the birth of Hungarian theater ● 42.

Although a native German speaker, at the age of thirty-six the minister Gáspár Heltai (1500–74) began to write in Hungarian.

Péter Bornemisza (1535–84) applied his talent to all types of prose: 'It is already a number of years since people began writing in Hungarian, and it falls to us to follow the example of Cicero and every civilized nation – to cultivate and enrich our own language.'

Bálint Balassi (1551–94), the first great Hungarian poet, wrote about love and religion, and abandoned melody as a concomitant of poetry to reinvent versification.

Left: *one of the earliest Hungarian manuscripts.*

> 'The fact that my mother tongue is Hungarian and
> that I speak, think and write in Hungarian is the most
> important event in my life, unique of its kind.'
>
> Dezső Kosztolányi

HUNGARIAN LITERATURE IN THE 17TH CENTURY

During the Baroque period the Puritan János Tolnai, inspired by the English model, demanded that Hungarian be used in public education. In 1655 János Apáczai compiled a Hungarian encyclopedia. The amount of literature written in Hungarian increased: Miklós Zrínyi (1620–64) created a politico-military genre, and Kelemen Mikes (1690–1761) adapted the style of literary correspondence developed in France by the Marquise de Sévigné. The exiled Ferenc II Rákóczi (1676–1735), on the other hand, had little choice but to write his memoirs in French. But Hungarian was then replaced by the 'popular Latin' used by Jesuit authors.

THE LINGUISTIC REFORM OF THE ENLIGHTENMENT

Toward the end of the 18th century Hungarian proponents of the Enlightenment launched a linguistic reform. György Bessenyei (1747–1811) noted: 'So far, no nation has been able to become cultivated other than through its own language. The first duty of any nation that wants to spread knowledge among its people, so as to contribute to their greater happiness, is to elevate its mother tongue to the level of perfection.' Because the language of the time had been the vehicle for religious and feudal ideology, the reformers felt it was unsuited to this mission. They therefore wanted to enrich it and make it more fitting for their vision of social progress and national identity, and were even prepared to impose it on the country's non-Magyar minorities. One leading writer of the day, Ferenc Kazinczy (1759–1831, right), translated many European classics into Hungarian and devoted his life to the movement. However, it encountered resistance from the Conservative nobility, and by insisting on German for official purposes Joseph II

provoked an energetic campaign of reform. This included launching twenty-three periodicals, creating lending libraries and a chair of Hungarian at the University of Pest (1791), and teaching the rural population to read and write. A colorful 'army' traveled the length and breadth of the country, delivering the message of nationalism and linguistic reform. Finally linguists developed the theory of the Finno-Ugric origins of the Hungarian language, which received recognition thanks to *Demonstratio. Idioma Ungarorum et Lapponum idem esse*, published by János Sajnovics in 1770.

Left: *Certificate of trading written in Hungarian (18th c.).*

NATIONALISM AND ROMANTICISM

The Hungarian language had become by 1825 a homogenous tool, purged of dialects and enriched with neologisms. The reforms ● 34 inaugurated by the Diet (legislative assembly) of 1825–7 favored using Hungarian as the official language. Then during the Diet of 1843–4 the Conservatives accepted a 'language law' advocating the introduction of Hungarian as the national language – thus arousing the hostility of the country's ethnic minorities, who demanded equal rights and linguistic autonomy. Finally on March 17, 1848 Ferdinand I, spurred on by the revolutionary momentum, appointed Lajos Batthyány head of the 'responsible independent Hungarian Ministry', and ratified the laws introduced by the Diet.

The Hungarian (or Magyar) language belongs to the group of Finno-Ugric languages, which form part of the larger family of Altaic-Uralic languages. Unlike the languages of its neighbors, Hungarian is therefore not of Indo-European origin but is related, if only distantly, to Finnish, Estonian and Lapp. It is the official language of the Hungarian Republic ◆ *254, 268.*

The alphabet contains the following vowels:
a – 'o' as in hot
á – 'a' as in father
e – 'ai' as in air
é – 'a' as in day
i – 'i'
í – 'ee' as in feet
o – 'o'
ó – long, closed 'o'
ö – 'ur' as in pleasure
∂ – like ö but longer
u – 'oo' as in pool
ú – long 'oo'
ü – 'u' as in tube
ű – long 'u'

Nyolc óra? Szórakozás!

The length and degree of openness of the vowels are extremely important, as they often make it possible to distinguish between certain words and phrases – for example, *örülök* (I am happy) and *őrülök* (I am going mad)!

The consonants are pronounced as follows:
b – 'b'
c – 'ts' as in roots
cs – 'ch' as in such
d – 'd'
f – 'f'
g – 'gu' as in go
gy – 'd' as in dew
h – aspirate 'h'
j – 'y', 'aïe'
k – 'k'
l – 'l'
ly – 'y' as in yellow
m – 'm'
n – 'n'
ny – 'n' as in new
p – 'p'
r – rolled 'r'
s – 'sh' as in wash
sz – 's' as in sat
t – 't'
ty – 't' as in tube
v – 'v'
z – 'z'
zs – 's' as in casual

The very marked tonic accent is placed on the first syllable of the word. The Hungarian language can sound rather monotonous because of the vowel system, which only uses front (i, í, e, é, ő, ö, ű, ü) or back (a, á, o, ó, u, ú) vowels in a word. Although disconcerting, its structure has very regular forms. An agglutinative language, it adds 'affixes' to a usually monosyllabic root and uses 'post positions' rather than prepositions – so the literal meaning of *ház-am-ban* is 'house-my-in'.
Also, in Hungarian:
◆ The verb 'to be' lacks a third person singular – so 'the boy is tall' is rendered as *a fiú magas* ('the boy tall').
◆ There is no gender. On the other hand, there are nine local suffixes. Two conjugations (objective and subjective) are used, depending on the nature of the complement of the direct object.
◆ Word order, which is extremely flexible, can be utilized to convey subtle shades of meaning.
◆ Given its aptitude for coining neologisms, the vocabulary is virtually unlimited.

There are about 11 million Hungarian speakers in Hungary, plus those who live in neighboring countries and other parts of the world. Not surprisingly, they are immensely proud of their language, which, despite a national history marked by oppression, has successfully resisted dilution by the Germanic, Slavic, Turkish and Latin languages.
Top: *'Eight o'clock? Relax!' (from an advertising poster).*

ART AND TRADITIONS

● HUNGARIAN THEATER

Considered 'unperformable', Imre Madách's
The Tragedy of Man (1861) was staged for the first
time, by Ede Paulay, on September 21, 1883.

One of the most memorable events in the history of Hungarian theater was the famous Budapest tour of the László Kelemen theater company in October 1790. In a manner of speaking, it marked the birth of professional Hungarian-language theater. Of course, theater existed in Hungary before Kelemen, but his performances had all the value of a political event, since they represented a decisive stage in the fight for national and linguistic independence. Between 1880 and 1905 many theaters were opened in Budapest, as its population rose from 400,000 to 1 million. In 1949 theaters were nationalized, as the new (Communist) government took control of all aspects of Hungarian culture. Hungarian theater eventually managed to free itself from its ideological shackles – partially during the early 1960s, and completely since 1989.

THE HUNGARIAN NATIONAL THEATER (NEMZETI SZÍNHÁZ)

In September 1935 the authorities of the comitat (county) of Pest gave Mátyás Zitterbach the task of building a national theater.

The new building was inaugurated on August 22, 1837 with a play by Mihály Vörösmarty (1800–55 ▲ 116). The theater's aim was to present classics plays by Hungarian and foreign playwrights. Such works as *Csongor and Tünde* by Mihály Vörösmarty and *The Tragedy of Man* (*Az ember tragédiája*) by Imre Madách (1823–64) featured regularly on the bill. Below: scene from István Örkény's *Catsplay*.

VÍGSZÍNHÁZ
The Vígszínház (Comedy Theater) opened in 1896 and became the theater of the new bourgeoisie that was developing along with the city. Initially it was devoted to French comedy, but subsequent directors also staged works by contemporary Hungarian playwrights such as Sándor Bródy, Ferenc Molnár and Zsigmond Móricz.

Ferenc Molnár
(1878-1952)

KATONA JÓZSEF SZÍNHÁZ ▲ 121

Between 1951 and 1982 the Katona József Theater occupied the small auditorium of the Hungarian National Theater. However, thirty or so actors gave up the privilege of performing in the National Theater to work under the directorship of Gábor Székely and Gábor Zsámbéki, who wanted to work outside the official program. The new Katona József Színház acquired an international reputation for its performances of Chekhov, Bulgakov, Gogol, Shakespeare, Molière, Jarry and György Spiró. Below: poster for a production of György Spiró's *Csirkefej*.

MOLNÁR, VÁRKONYI, ÖRKÉNY

Ferenc Molnár was one of the leading playwrights of the Vígszínház in the 1920s. His career reached its peak in 1910 with *Liliom*. Although he had refused Puccini permission to turn *Liliom* into an opera, it was later made into the famous musical *Carousel* by Rodgers and Hammerstein. In 1962 Zoltán Várkonyi took over the directorship of the theater and, as well as his own plays, staged the works of other contemporary Hungarian writers, including Gábor Thurzó, Gyula Illyés, Károly Szakonyi and Tibor Gyurkovics. István Örkény (1918–79) was extremely popular at the Vígszínház in the 1970s.

TRAFÓ ▲ 174

On October 5, 1998 the opening of the Trafó (Contemporary Arts) Theater in a power station built at the turn of the century was a first for Budapest. The theater does not have a permanent company, as its aim is to promote experimental theater.

During the first half of the 19th century the Hungarian National Theater gradually opened its doors to a new genre: operetta. The German Theater in Pest acquired the rights to perform the operettas of Offenbach and the genre became so popular that the Municipal Operetta Theater was opened in Pest in 1875. It performed the works of Johan Strauss, Franz von Suppé, Offenbach and József Konti, the master of Hungarian operetta.

Lehár Ferenc

FRANZ (FERENC) LEHÁR (1870–1948) was born in Komáron, into a family of French origin (his great-grandfather's name was Le Harde). He studied at the conservatory of Prague before joining his father in Vienna.

JACQUES OFFENBACH (1819–80) At the turn of the century, when the literary and musical life of Budapest was in a state of flux, a great many theaters were opened. In 1903 the Király Színház (Royal Theater), the temple of Hungarian operetta, opened on Király út with a performance of the *Golden Flower* by Jenő Huszka (1875–1960).

IMRE KÁLMÁN (1882–1953) After studying under János Koessler at the Academy of Music ▲ *146*, Kálmán became music critic for Pesti Napló and, between 1904 and 1908, held the post of *répétiteur* at the Vígszínház ● *42*. In 1908 he had his first major success with the operetta *Tatárjárás* (*The Gay Hussars*). From 1910 onward most of his works were performed abroad.

RÓBERT RÁTONYI
After World War Two, the Municipal Operetta Theater of Budapest continued to promote this highly distinctive genre. The individual style and charismatic performances of such great operatic stars as Hanna Honthy, Kálmán Latabár, Kamill Feleki and Robert Rátonyi ensured the success of the theater's productions.

HANNA HONTHY IN 'THE MERRY WIDOW'
Franz Lehár became a violinist in the military orchestra conducted by his father. From 1890 he led the military orchestras of several Austro-Hungarian towns (Losonc, Trieste, Budapest and Vienna).
In November 1906 his famous operetta *The Merry Widow* was performed at the Magyar Színház; in March 1907 it celebrated its 100th performance.

During the period of Socialist Realism the performances and personality of stars like Rátonyi and Honthy evoked a bourgeois era that had vanished.

Rátonyi (Ákos) and the merry widows.

HANNA HONTHY
(1893-1978)
Hanna Honthy began her singing career in 1912 at the municipal Operetta Theater and by 1916 was one of the young stars of operetta. In the 1930s she played the leading role in many major operettas and was idolized by her fans. She had her greatest success after World War Two, in Kálmán's *The Csárdás Princess*.

● TRADITIONAL HUNGARIAN MUSIC
FOLK, RELIGIOUS AND COURTLY MUSIC

Flute player.

The Hungarian musical tradition originated among the Finno-Ugric and Altaic tribes, and was inspired by pentatonic (five-note) scales. In this respect it was essentially different from the Italo-Germanic music that dominated the rest of Europe. Over the centuries this oriental characteristic – apparent in all aspects of a flourishing popular tradition, from children's nursery rhymes to battle songs and funeral dirges – has remained untainted by foreign influences, even surviving the conversion to Christianity. Only the clergy and nobility were affected by Western influences. Thus, at the end of the 19th century János Erdélyi, Gábor Mátray and István Bartalus (1821–99) were able to compile remarkable collections of unpublished traditional music.

ETHNO-MUSICOLOGISTS

The early transcriptions of Hungarian folk music, which had inspired many researchers, were soon challenged by Béla Vikár, who replaced the romantic approach of his predecessors with more scientific methods. In 1905 Zoltán Kodály ● 50 started to compile an authoritative record of this corpus of traditional music, using a phonograph, and in 1906 he was joined by Béla Bartók.

Page from a late-15th-century antiphonary.

Violin and *gardon* players.

RELIGIOUS MUSIC

In addition to Hungary's very fertile folk tradition, more cosmopolitan forms of music developed in more formal environments. The Church was the prime example of this 'westernization', since in spreading the Gregorian tradition it ignored national boundaries and local traditions. The older monasteries (Esztergom ▲ 238, Vác ▲ 235) disseminated a plainchant tinged with popular influences (*Antiphonary of Graz*), whereas the Hungarian people did not adapt their music to meet the needs of religion until the *Codex of Nádor* (1508).

THE SHADOW OF THE REFORMATION

Paradoxically the Reformation, which revitalized music in the rest of Europe, was disastrous for Hungarian music. Wars, invasions, divisions and secessions divided a country that had hitherto been united, especially by its language. Right: fragment from a 15th-century stove.

The *Chronicle* of András Farkas, which included Hussite (Bohemian Reformation) and Franco-Flemish polyphonic songs, gives some idea of this heterogeneity, whilst the *Chronicle* of Sebestyén Tineodi (mid 16th century) tried to provide a synthesis of the heroic genre, folk music and biblical psalmody.

COURTLY MUSIC

The nobility resolutely copied Western customs, and in the 15th century Matthias Corvinus ● *32* filled his court with troubadours, minnesingers and other poet-musicians from France, Italy and Germany. From this point on, institutionalized Hungarian music disdained local tradition and aspired to cosmopolitanism.

Pipe and bagpipes.

INTERNATIONAL RENOWN

The court of Prince Ferenc II Rákóczi (1676–1735) was renowned for its secular vocal and instrumental music – for example, the *Rákóczi March* ◆ *283*, which Berlioz included in his *La Damnation de Faust* (1846) and which later became a symbol of Franz Joseph's Vienna.

REVIVAL UNDER THE COUNTER-REFORMATION

The Counter-Reformation saw an increase in religious music (*Cantus catholici*), written both by anonymous composers and by masters such as Ferenc Szegedy, Iván Nagy and János Kusser. Poets were often musicians and vice versa – for example, Bálint Balassi and Péter Bornemissa or, a century later, Prince Pál (Paul) Esterházy (1635–1713), who wrote *Harmonia coelestis*, a collection of fifty-five short cantatas covering the religious year. This courtly art also produced an increasing number of famous musicians, such as the lutenist Bálint Bakfark and the organist János Kajoni.

Hungary's best-known composers are Joseph Haydn (1732–1809) and Franz Liszt (1811–86). Haydn was born in Hungary and spent most of his working life in Eisenstadt, the home of the descendants of Prince Pál Esterházy. Liszt, who was born near Sopron – not far from Eisenstadt – was, by contrast, much more cosmopolitan. He led an itinerant existence, drawing on the elements of Italian and French music that inspired the more flamboyant music of such German composers as Robert Schumann and Richard Wagner. Faced with this increasingly varied input, the wave of nationalism that followed the Napoleonic wars gave rise to the vogue for a specifically Hungarian genre, the *verbunkos*. This rousing 'recruitment music' was exploited by wealthy families to recruit their militias.

THE 'VERBUNKOS' formed a diptych of dances, initially slow (*lassu*) and becoming very fast (*friss*). It was originally vocal, but soon used instruments (violins) and even reinstated traditional instruments such as the dulcimer (a tuned percussion instrument comprising a set of strings of graduated length stretched over a sounding board and struck with two hammers). The *verbunkos* was quickly adopted by the Hungarian gypsies (right) and even inspired Liszt's famous *Hungarian Rhapsodies*.

Military musicians

'ALLA HUNGARESE' The *verbunkos*, which appeared at the end of the 18th century, inspired the phrase *alla hungarese* used by Haydn, Schubert and, until the late 19th century, Liszt, Wagner, Brahms and Dvořák. For a century the international acclaim given to the *verbunkos* eclipsed all other forms of traditional Hungarian folk music.

> 'But the murderer of pianos [Liszt] infected his compatriots with a national fever, for this Parisian from Italy had the idea of glorifying Hungarian gypsy music. He ended his first concert with a transposition of the *Rákóczi March* that held his audience spellbound.'
>
> Guy de Pourtalès

FERENC ERKEL (1810–93)

The operas of Ferenc Erkel are still popular in Hungary, despite the dated political content of some of the librettos; musically speaking, they are elegant syntheses of various genres. *Bátori Mária* (1840), *Hunyadi László* (1844) – a veritable anti-Austrian manifesto – and *Bánk Bán* (1852–61) ▲ *142* were crowned by such historical works as *István Király* (*King Stephen*, 1885). Erkel's contribution to Hungarian music is immense: not only did he compose the Hungarian national anthem, but he also founded the Budapest Philharmonic Society, in 1853. Under his direction, the city's new bourgeoisie was introduced to the latest trends in European music. One of his sons, László, taught Béla Bartók.

THE BARYTON

Geographically isolated near Eisenstadt and making little use of traditional sources, Joseph Haydn (1732-1809) was only able to become the initiator of the extremely cosmopolitan Viennese classical style thanks to his own genius and the prestige of his music teachers. Haydn composed a total of 175 pieces for the baryton, a now obsolete cello-like instrument.

FRANZ (FERENC) LISZT

Having reached the pinnacle of his art, Liszt set about illustrating the most outstanding aspects of his country's music ◆ *282*. He did not hesitate to combine classical Hungarian and gypsy music, *verbunkos* and folk music. However, his use of strange harmonies in his later works, such as *Cszardas macabre* (1882), detracted from his immediate influence to the extent that, under Habsburg pressure (left, Liszt playing in front of the imperial couple), late-19th-century Hungarian music became increasingly subject to German influence. This was mainly transmitted by the Hungarian Academy of Music and its teachers, who were among the best instrumentalists of the period ▲ *146*.

In the early 20th century the dominant esthetic influences in Budapest were those of the German composers Richard Wagner and Richard Strauss and, in a wider sense, of the Western symbolists. However, from 1905 the two great masters of the new Hungarian school, Kodály and Bartók, followed in the footsteps of Béla Vikar ● 46 and began to explore the roots of traditional Hungarian music. The eloquence of the material they discovered significantly revitalized the work of both composers.

KODÁLY ZOLTÁN MAGYAR NÉPZENE

TWO BRILLIANT ETHNO-MUSICOLOGISTS: KODÁLY (1882–1967) BARTÓK (1881–1945)

For thirty years this brilliant duo overcame many difficulties and pursued work that was probably unique in the field of ethno-musicology.

From 1925 Bartók published 350 popular Hungarian melodies according to an entirely new method of classification.

The years 1936, 1951 and 1958–70 saw the complete publication of a huge body of work, which was pursued by teams of ethnological composers trained in the methods of their predecessors László Lajtha and Bence Szabolcsi. Under the postwar leadership of Kodály, the popular foundations of Hungarian music were taught from primary school onward, to a nation that already had a highly developed love of music.

ZOLTÁN KODÁLY
● 46 ▲ 148 ◆ 282

Kodály based many of his compositions on folk music – initially rediscovered in a series of enchanting pieces of chamber music (such as his *Sonata for Cello solo*, 1915), then further developed in a number of lively orchestral works (*Dances of Marosszék*, 1927–30; *Dances of Galánta*, 1933; *Variations on a Hungarian Folksong, The Peacock*, 1939). He also produced a great many vocal and choral works.

'Bartók presented an austere, forbidding front to the world, and even in those years, when he was still in his mid-forties, his reputation was daunting. [...] We music students knew exactly how important he was, and we revered him. We were fully aware that there was an authentic genius teaching at our academy.'

Sir Georg Solti

'THE SZÉKELY SPINNING-ROOM' 1932) In his choral works Kodály treated the popular origins of Hungarian music extremely elaborately (for example, in *Psalmus Hungaricus* 1923) and in various religious pieces 1930–40). His comic opera *Háry János* 1926) is also deliberately rustic.

BÉLA BARTÓK ▲ *146*
Bartók was first noted for works inspired by a fascinating blend of Straussian esthetics and French symbolism – such as his two *Pictures* (for orchestra, 1910), his magnificent one-act opera *Duke Bluebeard's Castle* (1911) ▲ *143*, his first string quartet (1909) and his extremely expressionist ballet *The Miraculous Mandarin* (1918–19, below). When Hungary gained independence from Austria after World War One, Western influences – especially the neoclassical dogmas illustrated by Stravinsky – led Bartók to combine the strictness of form inherited from Haydn ● *48* with a series of themes that, although not used directly, were inspired by central European folk music. The use of this 'fictionalized folklore' dominated most of his work up to his death. He died in exile, in New York, at the end of World War Two.

Bartók Béla

The various political upheavals since the 1930s resulted in periodic 'diasporas' of Hungarian artists (writers, film directors and especially musicians), who emigrated to other parts of Europe or, more frequently, to the United States. Furthermore, the ascendancy of serial (twelve-note) music during the postwar period favored the international revival of Hungarian music. Thus, while such composers as György Kurtág (b. 1926) and György Ligeti (b. 1923) were heavily influenced by Bartók in their early careers, they subsequently evolved a personal style based on the post-Webernian mold.

MUSIC ON THE AIR
Radio, which has always been more important than television in Eastern European countries, is the principal broadcasting medium for the Hungarian Radio Orchestra. 'Bartók', one of the few national channels to broadcast on FM, plays mainly classical music, jazz and traditional music.

THE BENEFITS OF COLLECTIVISM

One of the benefits of the Communist regime was the *carte blanche* given to Kodály to organize the theoretical and practical teaching of music from nursery school onward. Another was that a number of state-owned recording companies (such as Hungaroton, bought back by a consortium of artists in the 1990s) were able, in the absence of commercial competition and with the help of technically first-class recordings, to build up a catalog of Hungarian music that constituted a vast system of artistic reference. Hungary was also one of the few countries in Central Europe to have a musical publisher – EMB (Editio Musica Budapest) – with an extensive catalog.

MÁRTA AND GYÖRGY KURTÁG
György Kurtág studied under Sándor Veress in Budapest, and under Darius Milhaud and Olivier Messiaen in Paris. Although his references to Hungarian folk music are indirect, Kurtág has – with pieces such as *The Sayings of Péter Bornemissa* (for voice and piano, 1963–8) – established himself as one of Hungary's leading modern composers. He teaches composition in Budapest.

'The technique of Ockeghem – in vogue in the late 15th century – uses varietas: although there are rules, they do not observe a strict form. It is a magnificent example of ordered disorder.'

György Ligeti

SOME CELEBRATED MUSICAL ÉMIGRÉS
It is important to remember the Hungarian origins of such soloists as the pianists György Cziffra (above) and György Sebők, the cellist János Starker, the violinists Joseph Szigeti and Ede Zathurecsky, and conductors such as Fritz Reiner, Antál Doráti, George Szell, Eugene Ormandy and Georg Solti (right). Solti, a pupil of Kodály, is buried between his former teacher and Bartók in the Farkasréti Temető ▲ 217 in Buda.

GYÖRGY LIGETI
Ligeti became an expatriate in early 1956, after teaching at the Franz Liszt Musical Academy ▲ 146. He appears to have welcomed the changes of the period, and his music – multidimensional and unpredictable – is a skillful combination of extreme musical sophistication and openly aggressive experimentation. The 'nationalist' works written for choir and piano (1946–55) were followed by two string quartets (1954–68), *Atmosphères* (1961), *Aventures and Nouvelles Aventures* (1962–5), *Requiem* (1963–5), *Lontano* (1967), *Continuum* (for harpsichord, 1968), *Horn Trio* (1982), *Viola Sonata* (1994) and *Études* (for piano, 1985–95).

Costume design for
The Wooden Prince.

The Opera House is still the 'mecca' of classical dance in Budapest. Its 100-strong *corps de ballet* has an international reputation, acquired primarily through the productions of the choreographers Gyula Harangozó and László Seregi. Modern dance made its debut in Budapest in the 1930s, when a group of dancers founded the first modern-dance dance schools and independent dance troupes based on the German model. At the same time there was a renewed interest in the origins of traditional Hungarian dance, as a result of the collection of historical documentation – especially films of peasant dances.

INNOVATIONS IN DANCE
In the 1980s talented young dancers developed a new form of dramatic expression and experimented with a new body language. This in turn gave rise to a new form of minimalist choreography that combined innovation with elements of traditional folklore. This modern trend produced the choreographer Joseph Nadj and the soloist and innovative post-modern artist Yvette Bozsik (below).

CLASSICAL DANCE
In the 1930s Gyula Harangozó's spirited ballets raised the status of the Budapest Opera troupe to that of a national ballet company. From the 1960s Hungarian ballet acquired another innovative choreographer, László Seregi, who made his debut with *Spartacus* (1968). He reached the pinnacle of his career with three ballets inspired by Shakespearean plays: *Romeo and Juliet, The Taming of the Shrew* (above) and *A Midsummer Night's Dream.*

Gyula Harangozó's interpretation of *The Miraculous Mandarin.*

In the 1950s Russian-style professional folk groups used ethno-musicological research to enhance the authenticity of their productions.

FOLK DANCING
The revival of authentic traditional Hungarian dancing dates from the 1970s. Previously it had mainly been presented on stage, whereas it now began to form the basis of folk evenings and was restored to its natural function. Today the *táncházak* ('dance houses') still help to promote a sense of national identity among the young, while making a valuable contribution to traditional festivals.

Every week in Budapest dancers aged from seven to seventy-seven take part in Hungarian, Greek, Irish, Jewish and Transylvanian *táncház* evenings.

CONTEMPORARY DANCE
The expressive power of Hungarian folk dancing has provided a source of inspiration for contemporary dance. In particular, a number of young Hungarian choreographers have drawn upon the rich national heritage. The most representative creations of this new wave are those of Gerzson Péter Kovács and Csaba Horváth.

● THE CAFÉ TRADITION

The first coffee shops in Budapest were opened by the Turks and reserved exclusively for Turkish customers. Cafés made their debut in Pest in 1714, and soon after in Buda. One hundred years later they had become a favorite meeting place for students and intellectuals. The golden age of Hungarian cafés was between 1890 and World War One, as evidenced by the words of Dezső Kosztolányi: 'After its Turkish baths, the Hungarian café is the most oriental feature [of Budapest]. It is where we spend our lives' (1914).

CAFÉ GERBEAUD
▲ 117
The Café Gerbeaud, which has remained open since it was founded 140 years ago, is a fine example of the 'tearoom' tradition. It comprises several buildings (with a single entrance, on Vörösmarty tér), and each of the rooms is different. Like the Café New York, the Gerbeaud is a popular tourist venue.

'AT THE CAFÉ'
(January 1940)

Table decorated with portraits of its 'regulars'.

MEETING AT THE CAFÉ PILVAX IN 1848
The original Café Pilvax, the focus of the 1848 uprising ▲ 119, has disappeared. Its modern namesake stands about 100 yards from the original site.

That cafés became a social phenomenon was partly due to inadequate living conditions, which prevented 'bohemians' and even members of the bourgeoisie from inviting friends into their homes. As a result, the café became a sort of forum or universal meeting place.

56

LITERARY REVIVAL

Attempts are being made to keep alive the tradition of literary cafés such as the Café Eckermann (next to the Goethe Institute), which now offers free Internet connections in the afternoon, or to revive it with the reopening of cafés such as the Central.

CAFÉ NEW YORK ● 77 ▲ 167
In the late 1940s cafés were converted into sports shops, libraries, post offices or self-service restaurants. When the New York reopened in 1954, a popular actor is said to have exclaimed: 'Waiter, bring me a pair of tennis shoes!' The New York is also a restaurant, with evocative menus (right).

Among today's most fashionable cafés is the Vian, whose premises were occupied by a dry cleaner's until 1977. A plaque informs us that Allen Ginsberg used to bring his dry cleaning here...

'NYUGAT' READER ON THE TERRACE OF THE NEW YORK (1917)
Opened in 1894, the Café New York rapidly became the refuge of Hungary's new young literary movement. It was here that the legendary periodical *Nyugat* ('The West') ● 97 was launched in 1908. In the 1910s, as well as the local and international newspapers, some 400 Hungarian periodicals were among the reading matter devoured at the café.

Why Hungary should have produced so many 'classic' photographers, both in the early days of photography and later, is still a mystery. But the fact remains that Daguerre and Niepce soon found a following, with the result that the face of the poet Sándor Petőfi ▲ *119* was immortalized in 1848 shortly before his glorious death. In the following decades, at the Universal Exhibitions held in Paris Hungarians won awards for their technical inventions. In the early 20th century photography was regarded as a 'good career' in Hungary, and Budapest had over 300 photographic studios, plus numerous amateur clubs.

aul Almásy, Brassaï,
Robert Capa, Emeric
ehér, Lucien Hervé,
László Moholy-Nagy,
Martin Munkácsi,

André... All these
photographers had
their own individual
style, and one thing in
common: they were

were Rudolf Balogh,
Károly Escher, Iván
Vidarény, Kata
Kálmán and József
Pécsi, but the latter

Hungary and are less
well known in other
countries.

F rom the end of
the 19th century
until 1920 the main
photographic trend
was 'pictorialism': a
style of photography
that imitated fin-de-
siècle academic
painting. It used
such techniques as
placing gauze over
the lens, soft focusing
touching up, and
printing on grainy
paper.

1. Rudolf Balogh :
Snow in Budapest,
c. 1920.
2. Károly Escher :
Hail in Budapest, 1928
3. Iván Vydarény :
The Tabán District.
4. János Reismann :
Buda Hill, 1970s.
5. André Kertész :
Spring Shower, 1920.

	4
1	
2	3	5

In the 1920s photography became a means of expression in its own right and assumed different forms, from reportage and sociological studies to avant-garde art. 'Hungarian' photography was very much in vogue in the interwar period, when many Hungarian artists such as Brassaï and Robert Capa (whose real names were Gyula Halász and Endre Ernö Friedmann) pursued their careers abroad.

6

Once established the new discipline was constantly being regenerated, both in the field of 'reporting' (Tamá Féner, György Lőrinczy, Péter Korniss), in the broadest sense, an its purely artistic a experimental form (Tibor Hajas, Tan Baranyai, János V Lenke Szilágyi, Ág Eperjesi, Tibor Várnagy). To thes names should be added those of No Dumas (Nóra Kelenföldi Telkes Árpád Szélpál anc Lucien Hervé (Lá Elkán) – the Hungarian founde of the Keystone, Dephot and Raph agencies – and An Krazna-Krausz, founder of Focal Press publications The Hungarian Museum of Photography in Kecskemét contai a wealth of histori and modern documentation, a exhibits the work of contemporary photographers. Ir 1995 a gallery nan after Manó Mai, t photographer of t imperial court, wa opened next to th museum. The gall (Mai Manó ház) is located at 20 Nagymező utca ▲

1. Robert Capa:
Váci út, 1940.
2. Károly Hemző:
Holy Trinity Squar
1990.
3. Miklós Rév:
Aerial View of Parliament, 1970.
4. Zoltán Zajky:
On Gellért Hill, 19
5. József Pécsi :
Ruins in Budapest,
1945.
6. Miklós Rév :
Elizabeth Bridge at Night, 1970.

THE BATHS OF BUDAPEST

KIRÁLY GYÓGYFÜRDŐ ▲ *208*
'A huge lion tirelessly spews water into
the pool, whose water reflects the colored
light and softens it into shadow. From time
to time, bodies pass through these areas of
blue or red or sunshine yellow...'

Julien Green

The Rác Baths
in the late
19th century.

Since the Romans built their *thermae*
at the foot of the Buda Hills, Budapest's
hundred or so hot springs have made
it the most beautiful spa town in Europe;
and it may be the last. Rediscovered by the
Turks in the 16th century, and later by the
Edwardian bourgeoisie, the baths combine
sumptuous architecture with a sophisticated
use of light. Today they are still very much a
part of the city's everyday life. Whether you
want a treatment for rheumatism, a massage,
to play chess or discuss politics, or simply
to relax, you can choose the more muted
ambience of the Rudas Baths, the neo-
Baroque radiance of the Széchenyi Baths,
or the Art Nouveau elegance of the Gellért
Baths.

**RUDAS GYÓGYFÜRDŐ
ÉS USZODA** ◆ *261*
Many of the city's
public baths were
built by the Turks,
to observe the rituals
of the Muslim
religion and cure
certain ailments.
The Rudas Baths,
built in 1566 by
the pasha of Buda,
are among the
most beautiful.
A magnificent
interior vault inlaid
with shards of colored
glass (as in the Király
Baths) filters and
tints the light above
an octagonal central
pool fed by three
springs. These baths
are for men only.

The dome of the
Király Baths.

Chess players at the
Széchenyi Baths.

'At Királyfürdő, a 16th-century bath built by
a padishah of uncertain memory, the light falls
from a dome of multicolored glass, producing
an effect worthy of *The Arabian Nights*.'

Julien Green

GELLÉRT GYÓGYFÜRDŐ ▲ *216*

The Hotel Gellért,
with its beautiful
Art Nouveau façade,
was built in 1914.
In 1934 an indoor
pool was installed in
the old conservatory,
beneath the
magnificent metal-
and-glass dome,
which was retained.

The central pool
is surrounded by
Rococo cabled
columns, a mosaic
floor, and flower-
filled balconies below
the glass roof. The
outdoor 'wave pool',
with its rocky setting,
is a favorite with
children in summer.

SZÉCHENYI GYÓGYFÜRDŐ ▲ *160*

These are incontestably the largest baths in
Europe. In summer sunshine or winter snow,
Hungarians come to the vast open-air pool
with its grandiose neo-Baroque setting, to
play chess or relax in water temperatures
of around 100°F.

LUKÁCS GYÓGYFÜRDŐ ÉS USZODA ▲ *210*

These beautiful 19th-
century baths are
situated more or less
on the boundary of
Óbuda. This is the
capital's most
restrained but also its
most comprehensive
baths complex: as
well as three warm
springs and twenty-
three hot springs,

with temperatures
varying between
60°F and 120°F (17°C
and 50°C), it offers
massages and mud
baths. In the 1970s
and 1980s it was a
favorite meeting
place for they city's
dissident intellectuals.

Left: votive plaque.

AZ ÉG ÁLDÁSÁT KÉREM
E NAGYSZERÜ HATÁSU FÜRDŐRE,
MELYBEN SULYOS BAJOMTÓL
GYORSAN SZABADULTAM MEG.
1902 AUGUSZTUS 5.

REISMANN JOZEFA
TASNÁD.

● FOOD
CHICKEN PAPRIKA AND 'GALUSKA'

Chicken paprika *(paprikás csirke)* is one of Hungary's most popular dishes ◆ *268*. It is prepared like a stew *(pörkölt)*, with a sauce that should be neither too thick nor too thin. The only difference between this dish and an ordinary *pörkölt* is the addition of fresh sour cream. *Galuska* (pronounced 'galooshka') are small dumplings rather like gnocchi.

INGREDIENTS FOR THE CHICKEN
– 1 chicken cut into small pieces
– 2 small onions
– 1 green pepper
– 2 tomatoes
– 1 tbsp mild paprika
– ⅓ cup lard or pork fat (or olive oil)
– 10 fl oz fresh sour cream
– salt

INGREDIENTS FOR THE 'GALUSKA'
– 3 cups flour
– 5 eggs
– salt

(CHICKEN) 1. Slice the tomatoes and pepper, and chop the onions.

2. Lightly brown the onions in the fat.

3. Add the chicken pieces, and brown to seal in the juices.

4. Sprinkle the chicken pieces with paprika, and lightly brown. Stir.

5. Add the sliced tomatoes and pepper. Add a little water, so that the chicken cooks in a very thick sauce. Season, cover, and leave to simmer gently.

6. Stir in the sour cream, to obtain a thick creamy sauce.

'GALUSKA' I. Put the eggs and flour into a mixing bowl. Mix together using a wooden spoon, adding enough warm water to form a dough.

II. When the mixture has a dough-like consistency, use a wooden spatula to press it slowly through a large-holed sieve (the Hungarians have a special utensil for this). Drop the pieces of dough into boiling water.

III. Alternatively, roll the dough out onto a pastry board and chop it into small pieces (about the size of a teaspoon), then drop them into boiling water. Don't make too many galuska at a time.

IV. Remove the pieces immediately with a slotted spoon. Rinse, drain, and reheat in butter or lard. Season to taste before serving.

Chicken paprika is traditionally accompanied by *galuska*, but can be served with steamed or boiled potatoes. A green salad goes well with it.

SPECIALTIES

HEREND PORCELAIN AND ZSOLNAY VASE ▲ *136, 172*
These are the jewels in the crown of Hungarian craftsmanship. They are sold in a number of shops and at the Museum of Applied Arts.

PAPRIKA GARLANDS ◆ *268*

In rural areas, the red pimentos are hung up to dry on the fronts of houses.

'FOIE GRAS'
Hungarian *foie gras* is spread on bread, salted and eaten with sweet onions.

RIBBONS
The markets sell embroidery at very reasonable prices. Avoid buying it in city-center shops.

WINES
Bull's Blood of Eger *(Egri bikavér)* is so called because of its color and strength. *Tokaji aszú* is made from very sweet grapes harvested in October, when almost dried, in baskets known as *puttony*.

The more *puttonyos* (specified on the label of a bottle of *Tokaji aszú*), the sweeter the wine.

CDs ● *52* ◆ *282*
Hungaroton's catalog offers a wide range of musical styles. In Hungary, its CDs are reasonably priced.

THE GERBEAUD PATISSERIE
was founded more than a century ago by a master Swiss chocolate maker. It is renowned both for its patisserie ▲ *117* and for its morello cherries in brandy *(konyakos meggy)*.

DRIED PAPRIKA
The Great Plain is the favored home of the red pimento. Szeged is the town for paprika.

SALAMI
Hungarian salami is traditionally eaten at breakfast and tea time. The best salami is the *pick téliszalámi*, made from well-seasoned pork and pieces of bacon.

ARCHITECTURE
Mohamed Bansar, Iván Bojár

The rich colors of Budapest reflect the diverse influences that have shaped the city's development. And yet these vibrant colors combine to create an impression of harmony in which their individual brightness is softened by the overall effect. For this reason, all that the eye retains of the extravagance of detail and the bold use of contrasting colors is the impression of a dominant color that varies from district to district: the ocher tones of Baroque Buda, the white and green-ocher of neoclassical Pest, the multicolored Art Nouveau style of the newly unified Budapest...

BAROQUE BUDA
The buildings of Baroque Buda are mostly built of brick and the rather crumbly limestone (*méskő*) quarried in the Buda Hills. The originally white or yellow-ocher façades are today decorated in a much richer range of colors (1). Doors and windows are highlighted with hard gray or beige stone (2, 3) or a plain white band that creates a trompe-l'œil effect (6). Window lintels of Hungarian marble (*süttő*), from the Esztergom region, are decorated with the sculpted heads (4) characteristic of the *copf* style (a variation of Rococo) ▲ 231. The pure, simple lines of the façades are embellished by outlines, set-backs and square corbeled balconies that catch the light and create the typically Baroque chiaroscuro effect (5).

PEST: NEOCLASSICISM AND ROMANTICISM
Between the early 1800s and 1867 the architecture in the center of Pest evolved from neoclassicism to historicism. Its public buildings were built of stone, and the white façades of the brick apartment blocks were highlighted by stone

details (7). The vast inner courtyards were paved with pink *süttő* marble. Today white has been largely replaced by greens and ochers (8, 9).

PEST: ECLECTICISM AND ART NOUVEAU
From 1867, with the rise of the bourgeoisie, stone and colored façades were the order of the day at a time when decoration was deemed more important than the quality of the materials (12). There was an increase in richly decorated architectural features – domes (13), spires (14), towers (11, 15) and turrets – and façades were stuccoed (17, 18), painted and decorated with mosaics.

Around 1880 the Zsolnay ● *66,* ▲ *136, 172* manufactory developed a range of glazed ceramic tiles that the best Hungarian architects – Ödön Lechner, Miklós Ybl and Imre Steindl – used for polychrome roofs (10) and the decoration of façades (20).

MODERN BUDAPEST
After 1918 the development of materials and the appearance of concrete resulted in simple monochrome decoration, highlighted by the geometric effects of light and shade (21, 22). Today the use of brick (23, 24) marks a return to natural materials.

AN EYE FOR DETAIL
Whatever the style, Budapest has always had a remarkable eye for detail that makes close examination well worthwhile.

69

● Baroque architecture

Baroque architecture appeared in Hungary around 1620. It became very popular from the end of the 17th century, and reached its peak in the 18th century. The Turks, driven from Hungary in 1686, left nothing but ruins in their wake. The establishment of the Austrian Habsburg dynasty in Hungary and the extensive Jesuit influence gave rise to intense architectural activity, especially in Buda and Pest. Although initially religious in nature, it was soon emulated by the nobility, impressed by the examples of Italian Baroque architecture introduced into Hungary via Austria.

St Anne's Church ▲ 207
(1740–62, Kristóf Hamon and Mátyás Nepauer)
The Baroque façade of St Anne's Church (Szent Anna templom) is marked by an interplay of vertical and horizontal lines. Its two slender towers seem to rise from ground level, giving the structure a vertical dynamic – tempered by the horizontal lines, which divide the building into three equal sections and reestablish its equilibrium. The God's-eye motif dominate the composition of the tympanum.

God's-eye motif The triangular God's-eye motif (above) represents the Holy Trinity. This Baroque motif was widely used in the 18th century.

The Royal Palace of Buda ▲ 190
(1753, Pacassi; 1765, Hillebrandt). The construction of the Baroque palace on the ruins of its Gothic predecessor had a symbolic and moral significance. After the departure of the Turks and Hungary's incorporation into the Holy Roman Empire, it was important to reaffirm the status of a site that was, ironically, unsuitable. Situated on a rocky spur, it would be impossible for it to fulfill the traditional function of royal palace and residence. The new U-shaped building had a central dome dominated by a watchtower, a feature inspired by northern Italian architecture.

'The 100-year-old Restaurant'
(Százéves Étterem, 2 Pesti Barnabás utca) (1755, Mayerhoffer)
The projecting central section is all that remains of this two-story building, which originally had two wings, forming a U-shape Built for János Péterffy, it is a fine example of secular Baroque architecture.

MANSIONS (Erdődy Palace ▲ *204*)
In the 18th century the mansions of Budapest had a single upper story (the piano nobile) above a massive bossed base (Italian influence). The ornamentation was not excessive and focused on the projecting central section of the façade. The entrance, which is surmounted by a balustraded balcony, has a tympanum above it.

HOUSES IN BUDA (Bécsi kapu tér ▲ *205*)
From left to right: houses by Appel, Grigely and Seth. Built according to individual Gothic designs, they have no gardens. The assortment of façades resulted from lack of an urban planning program.

THE HOLY TRINITY COLUMN
▲ *202*, left. Surmounted by the Holy Trinity, decorated with an image of the Virgin Mary, this column (1710–13) stands on a plinth surrounded by the city's patron saints.

COUNTRY RESIDENCE (Gödöllő Palace)
(1744–9) Unlike the Royal Palace of Buda, the residence built by Count Grassalkovich ▲ *240* was part of an integrated plan (courtyard, building and park). It represented the ideal aristocratic Hungarian country residence. It has a compact façade with five projections, forming a U-shape, a central pavilion with an elaborate entrance surmounted by a double-pitched dome, and a piano nobile.

FROM HOUSES TO APARTMENT BLOCKS
VARIATIONS ON A THEME

Recessed seat in the entrance passage at 2, Országház utca ▲ *204*, in Buda.

One of the main features of Budapest's apartment blocks is that they are arranged around a central courtyard, a characteristic inherited from rural architecture. In the farms of the Danube plains living accommodation and outbuildings are arranged around an open central courtyard. The more compact urban version, rationalized and developed over three centuries, is still based on the same layout.

THE GOTHIC TOWN

Because Budapest was so often devastated by war, there are not many courtyards that offer a glimpse of the Gothic town. The houses had an overhanging upper story pierced by two (often double) windows, a façade that did not face the street, and an arched entrance passage large enough to accommodate horse-drawn vehicles.

A STONE STREET FAÇADE

Gothic urban housing echoed the farm layout. However, the building was unified by the addition of a stone street façade. An arched entrance passage, with a recessed seat in the middle of the wall, gave access to the courtyard.

FARM ON THE DANUBE PLAIN

BUDA, 2, ORSZÁGHÁZ UTCA

TRADITIONAL LAYOUT OF THE FARMS OF THE CENTRAL PLAINS

'...the houses are all equidistant from and back onto the outer wall...the windows are set in a single arcaded façade. Thus, each house has its own courtyard and enjoys perfect privacy.'

Le Corbusier

A BAROQUE 'VENEER'

The façade, refurbished in the Baroque style (with bosses, capitals, and pilasters framing the windows), conceals the typical Gothic structure of the building.

72

RATIONALIZATION OF THE COURTYARD AREA
Baroque buildings rationalized the courtyard and service area. From the entrance a flight of steps led to landings that gave access to the buildings at the rear. The reception rooms of the piano nobile overlooked the street.

BUDA, 11, ORSZÁGHÁZ UTCA

PEST, 25, KIRÁLY UTCA

PEST, AN EXPANDING CITY
In the early 19th century the suburbs of Pest expanded into the open spaces surrounding the city. Neoclassical architecture retained the traditional two-story building; the larger plots of land made more spacious, planted courtyards feasible.

MODERN APARTMENT BLOCKS
These blocks reflect the rapid expansion of Budapest. Although they stand on a geometrical grid of streets and have three to six floors, they have retained the traditional layout around a central courtyard.

PEST, 6, OKTÓBER UTCA

73

NEOCLASSICISM

Detail from an entrance porch on Apáczai Csere János utca.

From the 1820s onward Hungary experienced a period of prosperity known as the Age of Reform ● 34. It was during this period that Pest began to acquire public and cultural buildings (museums, baths, theaters, hotels). Characterized by a style that is both rigorous and majestic, these buildings reflect the aspirations of a new bourgeoisie that wanted an architecturally homogeneous city. Baroque was abandoned in favor of neoclassicism, and official monuments and apartment blocks alike were built in neoclassical style. Despite differences of form and function, they all shared the same clean, harmonious lines and carefully balanced symmetry.

THE HUNGARIAN NATIONAL MUSEUM ▲ *123, 124* ◆ *265*

(1837–44, Mihály Pollack) This is one of the best examples of neoclassical Hungarian architecture in the early 19th century. The long rectangular building has a sculpted tympanum, a central portico, derived from the Erechtheion in Athens, with eight Corinthian columns, and a base supporting two rows of symmetrical windows. The epitome of gravitas and restraint.

PLAN OF THE NATIONAL MUSEUM

Mihály Pollack adapted the plan for the ideal museum described by J.N.L. Durand in 1801. He divided the building in two to create twin courtyards and placed his rotunda near the entrance, instead of in the center.

THE CHAIN BRIDGE
(1839–49, Adam Clark and William Tierney Clark ● 35, ▲ *183, 184*) The first stone bridge built across the Danube, the Chain Bridge is symbolic of the city's development. Previously Buda and Pest had been linked by two wooden bridges that suffered damage every winter. The chains that give the bridge its strength are suspended from two piles, each with its base resting on the river bed and an upper section resembling a miniature triumphal arch. The bridgeheads are guarded by apotropaic lions.

CHURCHES

Religious architecture was also influenced by the dominant architectural style. The Lutheran Church (1799–1809, plans by János Krausz) on Deák Ferenc tér ▲ 123 was completed by Mihály Pollack, the great 'planner' of neoclassical Pest. The façade overlooking the square has a portico with four Doric columns supporting an architrave decorated with a simple frieze.

THE FORMER GYÜRKI MANSION

(1814–15 and 1855, plans by József Hofrichter) Placed under the protection of the gods of Olympus – the head of Zeus is sculpted above the entrance – this four-story building (at 5, Apáczai Csere János utca) is a model of neoclassical symmetry.

DECORATION OF THE GYÜRKI MANSION

The stone arcature decorating the ground floor of the mansion is surmounted by medallions featuring heads inspired by figures from Greco-Roman mythology.

A UNIFORM STYLE

Apartment blocks and official buildings received identical treatment. The neoclassical façade of the Tänzer apartment block (left), dating from 1836, has a central six-columned balcony supporting a tympanum. The same 'truncated portico' is found at the center of the façade (below) of Pest County Hall (Pest Megyei Önkormányzat, ▲ 121), built between 1838 and 1841.

HISTORICISM AND ECLECTICISM

HEROES' SQUARE ▲ *150*
At the base of the column are equestrian statues of Árpád ● *27* conquering and the other six Magyar chiefs. On top i the Archangel Gabriel.

Historical events tend to be reflected by architecture. In the mid 19th century Hungary freed itself from Habsburg (Austrian) rule, and welcomed the neo-Gothic influence of Western Europe with great enthusiasm. It reinvented its past by drawing esthetic references from the great 'historical' styles of Europe (Romanesque, Gothic, Renaissance) and developed a 'Hungarian line' by using iconographic motifs from its own history. The architecture of this period was dominated by Miklós Ybl.

OFFICIAL ARCHITECTURE (Parliament building: 1880–1904, Imre Steindl ▲ *127*)
The magnificent 290-yard neo-Gothic façade overlooking the Danube is reminiscent of the Houses of Parliament in London. Sculpted figures of Hungarian kings, princes and historical figures look out over the river. The official entrance is on the opposite side of the building.

REFERENTIAL ARCHITECTURE
(Hungarian State Opera House: 1875–84, Miklós Ybl ▲ *141, 142*)
The façade of this elaborate neo-Renaissance building, based on the Opéra Garnier in Paris, is decorated with statues of Liszt, Mozart, Verdi and Puccini.

ST STEPHEN'S BASILICA
▲ *136* (1851–1905, József Hild and Miklós Ybl) Dedicated to Saint Stephen ● *27, 38*, the first king of Hungary, the basilica has a central Renaissance-style dome. Its twin towers are reminiscent of St Paul's in London.

Details of the Fishermen's Bastion (Magyar soldiers) ▲ 203.

MILLENNIAL ARCHITECTURE

The Fishermen's Bastion (right), the Matthias Church (left) and Heroes' Square (top left) were the architectural *tours de force* of the town-planning project that commemorated the thousandth anniversary of the founding of the Arpadian dynasty. The neo-Romanesque Fishermen's Bastion (1899–1905) was built on the city's medieval ramparts. A little further on, the Matthias Church, founded in the 13th century by Béla IV, was extended and refurbished as part of the same project. In Pest, Heroes' Square marked the limit of the new urban development to the east.

SYMBOLIC IMAGE

This statue of the architect Imre Steindl, dressed in medieval costume and holding the plans of the Parliament building, is highly symbolic. When Pest freed itself from Habsburg rule, it invented a past that gave its Parliament a precedence free from Austrian influence.

ECLECTIC ARCHITECTURE

(New York Palace: 1891–5, plans by Alajos Hauszmann ▲ 167) This five-story building combines neo-Renaissance and neo-Baroque architectural elements to produce a truly eclectic style. The façade is decorated with towers, spires, corner domes, a great many windows, balustraded balconies, Ionic columns and statues. On the ground floor, the Café New York ● 56 has frescos signed by Lotz, Eisnhut and Magyar-Mannheimer.

77

THE ROMANTIC MOVEMENT
THE FIRST 'HUNGARIAN STYLE'

In the 1860s, while still under Habsburg (Austrian) rule, Budapest was seeking to establish its identity. It preferred Romanticism to the neoclassical style that was still very much in vogue, since it offered greater creative freedom. Architects sought to develop a specifically Hungarian style, that would be distinct from other 'historical' styles, by infusing them with Hungarian symbolism and idealism.

THE GREAT SYNAGOGUE (Zsinagóga) ▲ 166 (1854–9: plans by Ludwig Förster, elevation by Ignác Wechselmann) Hungary's growing Jewish population led to the construction of many synagogues throughout the country. Although ostensibly eastern, the Great Synagogue, in Pest, reflects other architectural styles: the two minaret-like towers surmounted by onion-shaped domes are certainly reminiscent of the columns of the Temple of Solomon in Jerusalem, but they also echo the twin towers of Western European churches. The multicolored glazed bricks of the façade were an innovation. The synagogue's remarkable longitudinal plan, supported by a metal frame, is reminiscent of Christian churches – hence its nickname, the 'Jewish cathedral'.

THE VIGADÓ, PEST

(1860–5, plans by Frigyes Feszl ▲ 118) Built as a ballroom and concert hall, the Vigadó is one of the supreme achievements of the Hungarian Romantic movement. In this instance, the 'Hungarian style' asserts itself via a Moorish theme – with high arcades, inspired by Venetian Orientalism, and Islamic-style geometric friezes referring to the eastern origins of the Hungarian people.

HISTORY CARVED IN STONE

The statues of great Hungarian leaders, such as kings Matthias Corvinus and Béla IV, that grace the Vigadó's façade proudly recall Hungarian history. In addition, allegories of dance and music allude to the building's function.

Details from the bas-reliefs decorating the façade of the Vigadó.

THE ROOTS OF HUNGARIAN ROMANTICISM

Hungary was affected by the revolutionary fervor that swept across Europe in the 1840s. But the uprising of 1848 was suppressed by the Habsburgs, and the Emperor Franz Joseph incorporated Hungary into a unified empire. The Hungarians opposed this enforced integration with a cultural resistance in which architects played a major role, investing their monuments with the spirit of Hungarian nationalism.

THE PÉKARY HOUSE

(1847–8, Ferenc Brein) This mansion (5, Király utca) is a fine example of the stylistic amalgam favored by Hungarian Romanticism. In niches on either side of the central balcony, two Magyar warriors recall the ancient origins of the Hungarian nation. The stylized lines of the doors (left) were later echoed by the architectural Cubism of Prague (1910–20).

● HUNGARIAN ART NOUVEAU...

Finial from the former Post Office Savings Bank (1899–1901, Ödön Lechner ▲ 136) in Pest. The finials of the towers framing the main façade have winged serpents, symbolizing renewal.

On the eve of the 20th century the revival of Hungarian nationalism found expression in the unprecedented use of forms and techniques manifested by the 'explosion' of Hungarian Art Nouveau. Ödön Lechner, the uncontested master of this innovative period, defined the archetypes of a 'language of national forms' that successfully combined oriental references and images of Hungarian folklore to produce a strongly individualistic style.

MUSEUM OF APPLIED ARTS (1893–6, Ödön Lechner and Gyula Pártos ▲ 171, 172) It was designed to demonstrate the extraordinary richness of Hungarian decorative and applied arts. Inside, oriental elements and folkloric motifs are incorporated into the fabric of the building. When it was opened, some people derisively referred to it as the 'gypsy palace'.

THE VOGUE FOR POLYCHROME TILES
The façade and roofs of the Museum of Applied Arts are entirely covered with polychrome tiles – an inexpensive and waterproof material – from the Zsolnay manufactory. Above: the central lantern.

FROM HOUSES AND VILLAS...
(Villa Egger: 1902, Emil Vidor ▲ 149) Initially the new stylistic freedom found expression in the design of private houses. This villa was the first to be built entirely in Art Nouveau style.

...TO GRANDIOSE OFFICE BLOCKS
(Gresham Palace: 1905–7, Zsigmond Quittner and the Vágó brothers ▲ 138) This lavish building, originally the offices of the London-based Gresham insurance company, is typical of the Hungarian Secessionist style. At first the authorities disapproved of this type of Art Nouveau, and refused to finance Ödön Lechner's work because they regarded his style as Secessionist. Nevertheless, Lechner's ideas soon triumphed and greatly influenced the architecture of Budapest.

HYBRID STYLE
(Entrance of the
Sonnenberg Mansion:
1904, Albert Körössy
▲ *148*) An example
of a hybrid style: Art
Nouveau (wavy lines)
and Baroque
(chiaroscuro effects).

**HISTORICISM AND
ART NOUVEAU**
(Former Turkish Bank:
1906, Ármin Hegedűs,
Henrik Böhm ▲ *121*)
This is a fine blend
of the Hungarian Art
Nouveau and
historicism that
coexisted until 1914.
The glass and steel
façade are surmounted
by a wavy-edged
tympanum decorated
with a large mosaic of
Hungaria, the symbolic
representation of
Hungary.

FORMER TURKISH BANK

THE ART OF DETAIL
The key materials of Hungarian Art Nouveau
were tiles and wrought iron. Above, the
polychrome ceramic tiles with stylized motifs
used on the façade of the Gresham Palace,
and the wrought-iron gates decorated with
a peacock design. The building has such a
wealth of decorative detail that its restoration
is proving an extremely delicate undertaking.

GRESHAM PALACE

Art nouveau, Hungarian Secession, Art deco

ART NOUVEAU CAPITALS
From left to right: Gresham Palace ▲ *138,* Hotel Gellért and the apartment block at 18, Szent Gellért Rakpart (St Gellért Quay).

TOWARD GEOMETRIC STYLIZATION

(Institute for the Blind: 1905–7, Béla Lajta ▲ *113*) The building is amazingly avant-garde and "European" in style. A sober façade of dark-red brick attests to a Scandinavian influence. The only 'decorative' feature is the parabolic arch of the entrance porch and, on a reduced scale, over some of the windows. Folkloric motifs, combined with biblical scenes, reaffirm the national identity.

A NEW DECORATIVE VOCABULARY

(Hotel Gellért: 1912–18, Ármin Hegedűs, Arthur Sebestyén, Izidor Stark ▲ 216) The influence of Ödön Lechner ● 80 is no longer apparent in this jewel of spa architecture, fashionable in the early 20th century: the floral motifs inspired by Hungarian folklore that embellish the building have become geometric, while the richly detailed decoration, typical of late Art Nouveau, is combined with a neo-Baroque style (see the domes). There is also an underlying reference to Roman baths.

HOTEL GEL

SYMBOLIC FORM
(Porch of the Hospital of Neurosurgery: 1908–11, Béla Lajta)
The parabolic form of this porch, decorated with Hebraic motifs and scenes from the Old Testament, was favored by Béla Lajta, for whom it symbolized Hungary's architectural heritage.

JOZSEF RIPPL-RÓNAI
A member of the French Nabis group, this artist created the stained-glass window on the staircase of the Ernst Múzeum (8, Nagymező utca).

TOWARD ART DECO
(Porch of Calvinist Church and details: 1911–13, Aladár Árkay ▲ 112)
The massive porch of the Calvinist Church (at 5–7, Városligeti fasor) is an amazing example of late Art Nouveau. It is decorated with magnificent ceramic tiles in subdued colors (ochers, golds and blacks) and uses geometric rather than figurative motifs.

83

Modernism did not become firmly established or conquer the public domain until a few years before World War Two, despite the fact that the character of certain early 20th-century architectural works (the forerunners of Art Deco) had fore-shadowed functionalism. In the early 1920s an attachment to traditional values placed the emphasis on historicism and neo-Baroque, postponing the development of Modernism until the 1930s.

STRUCTURE EXPOSED TO VIEW
(Rózsavölgyi building: 1911–12, Béla Lajta) The dual purpose (public and private) of this building is immediately apparent: the glass façade of the lower floors marks the office area, while the residential upper floors are characterized by judiciously positioned traditional windows. The structure of the building is visible on the ground floor.

TOWARD MODERNISM
(Új Színház: 1909; Béla Lajt ▲ 144) This committedly A Nouveau theater building foreshadows the Modernis that came into vogue twent years later. The Art Nouvea angels contrast with the sta grayish-white marb façade.

Villa no. 2 of the Napraforgó utca housing estate: 1931, Gyula Wälder. Based on the principle of a square within a square. The function creates the form.

MODERNIS AND FUNCTIONALIS
Modernism, with it intellectual, avant-gard connotations, prove unsuccessful within the contex of the grave economic and moral crisis that followed World War One. However, a smal group of architects provided fresh impetus t innovation by creating the Napraforgó utca housin estate (1931), applying the functional concepts o Modernism inspired by the Bauhaus. These principle (economy and clarity of form, linear precision, simplicity o interior spaces) are also evident in the Villa Zenta (above, 1933)

GEOMETRIZATION

(Rózsavölgyi building)
Modernism
abandoned decoration
to highlight structure.
Nevertheless, the
Hungarian love
of decoration has
survived in this
building, where the
horizontal strata
of the façade are
emphasized by
ornamental friezes,
with geometrized
motifs (above)
foreshadowing
Art Deco.

MINIMALIST DECOR

(Átrium Cinema:
1935, Lajos Kozma)
The emphasis
on structure is
immediately
apparent in
Budapest's first
Modernist building.
Color, the ultimate
decorative medium, is
employed to highlight
function and use of
materials: white for
walls, black for fixed
metal frames, and red
for mobile frames.

CONSTRUCTIVISM

A constructivist composition
(1923), signed by the architect,
features on the wall of the entrance
hall of this residential building
(1937) in Trombitás utca. Farkas
Molnár, one of the first Hungarian
architects to apply Bauhaus
concepts to architecture, was the
leader of the Hungarian
Modernist movement.

ITALIAN MONUMENTALISM

(Városmajor Church: 1932–3, Aladár & Bertalan Árkay)
The travertine cladding used for the exterior of this
church softens the complex interplay of space. Bertalan
Árkay had just returned from Italy, and the design
reflects the influence of Northern Italian rationalism;
it is in effect a contemporary
adaptation of a basilica.

THE WAR YEARS

(Apartment block in
Szent István Park: Béla
Hofstätter and Ferenc
Domány, 1941 ▲ 139)
Modernism, for a long
time criticized for its
starkness by the
authorities and the
bourgeoisie, was
perfectly suited to the
war years and the great
urban development
project for the left
bank of the Danube.
Its lack of decoration,
rationalism and use of
inexpensive materials
made quick, efficient
construction possible.

85

The Yalta agreements placed Hungary within the Eastern bloc, under the aegis of the Soviet Union. Nevertheless, this rebellious country, brought sharply to heel in 1956 and ostensibly subjected to the Stalinist architectural model, succeeded in expressing its determination, often very subtly, to create an authentically national architectural style. It was this spirit of nationalism that sometimes managed to modify the unprepossessing appearance of Communist architecture.

POSTWAR RATIONALISM (LEFT)
(Apartment block on Lakóház út: 1948, MATI)
In the period immediately after World War Two priority was given to reconstruction and local authority housing projects, which as a logical consequence of Modernism still observed the principles of functionalism.

MODERNIST CONTINUITY (RIGHT)
(Deák Ferenc tér bus station: 1949, István Nyíril ▲ 123) In the early years of Communism Modernism accommodated Socialist ideology, and the great Modernist architects continued to express themselves via public buildings such as this dynamic, functional bus station.

INTERNATIONAL MODERN (ABOVE) (Mémosz: 1947–50, MATI). Born of Modernism, the International Modern style enjoyed widespread success. An example is this trade-union building – although it also contained the first iconographic representations of Socialist Realism, in the form of sculptures of manual workers in the assembly hall. The façade (above) displays a kinship with ones designed by Le Corbusier.

tails of bas-reliefs, Budapest Technical University.

IMPLICIT PROTEST
(School of Applied Arts: 1935, Zoltán Farkasdy)
The return to neoclassicism under the Soviet regime had a symbolic, 'anti-propagandist' significance – since classical elements such as the portico and tympanum were associated with Athens and democracy.

EDIFYING ARCHITECTURE (RIGHT)
(Entrance to the Technical University; 1955; Gyula Rimanóczy)
The pure Socialist Realism of this building (right) constitutes a celebration of manual labor. The images of manual workers in the bas-reliefs (left and top right) on either side of the entrance have a nobility reminiscent of classical sculpture. The classical reference is also reflected in the form of the tympanum and its decorative frieze of Greek motifs.

THE RETURN TO NEOCLASSICISM (LEFT) (Town Hall of the District II)
The Communist dictatorship, which condemned Modernism as an embodiment of Western bourgeois decadence, demanded a break with the immediate past and imposed neoclassicism as the expression of Hungarian national style.

SOCIALIST REALISM HUNGARIAN-STYLE (BELOW)
(OTP Bank: 1963, Zoltán Gulyás)
The post-Stalinist era of the 1960s reestablished links with Modernism, a concept that incorporated Western influences – in this instance, those of New York – and, with its emphasis on essentials and people's needs, aspired to a more 'human' scale. Here the spaces are clearly defined: the ground floor is opened up by a central patio, while the two towers are devoted to offices.

● CONTEMPORARY ARCHITECTURE

Plan for the renovation
of the ING Bank, 1994.

Certain aspects of Budapest's modern
architecture can be ascribed to the ecological
considerations being taken into account throughout Europe.
In addition, as well as respecting the urban landscape and the
environment, it aims to preserve the city's rich monumental
heritage. When it is not an amalgam of materials and
references, it tends toward an organic style that reflects the
individuality found throughout Budapest's architectural history.

(ABOVE) INTEGRATED ARCHITECTURE
(Ferenc Cságoly and Richárd Hönich 1993)
The apartments of this architectural complex on the western slope of Gellért Hill ▲ *215* are, literally, incorporated into the hillside. Instead of interrupting the natural contours of the hill, the S-shaped complex blends into them and complements them with its roof gardens.

RENOVATION (RIGHT)
(ING Bank: 1994, Erick Van Egeraat)
A historical façade, dating from 1883, conceals the very modern offices of the ING Bank. The glass roof above the courtyard incorporates a highly original caterpillar-like conference room.

SEARCH FOR IDENTITY (BELOW) (Church of the Hungarian Saints, 1996, Ferenc Török and Mihály Balázs)
This building sets out to create a sense of identity. It combines a wide range of materials (copper, glass, wood, granite, brick) and a variety of features that refer to the past: the dome provides a reference to Budapest's Turkish baths, while the central plan is inspired by Baroque

ORGANIC ARCHITECTURE (BELOW)

Organic architecture is not so much a collection of architectural principles as a way of perceiving architecture. It aims to codify the spatial relationship between human beings and nature according to criteria that focus on people within an environment, rather than on stylistic considerations.

BUDAPEST
AS SEEN BY PAINTERS

> 'From there, I crossed the Danube and entered Buda, the most beautiful town in Hungary. There is a large and magnificent palace... And I was told the Emperor Sigismund began it.'
>
> Bertrandon de La Brocquière

Under Matthias Corvinus ● *32*, he Royal Palace had become the symbol of Buda throughout Europe. During the Turkish occupation artists continued to paint its awesome battlements, as can be seen from the painting [1] by an anonymous Hungarian artist (c. 1664). However, the citadel – very much in the background – merely serves to identify the figure in the foreground: the Hun chieftain Buda. The reconquest of 1686 gave military

engineers the opportunity to record the battles, with a view to informing the general public of the most decisive events. Their drawings inspired a number of artists, including the Flemish painter Frans Geffels, whose *Siege of Buda* (1686) [3] was probably commissioned by the Duke of Mantua. After the duke was exiled, his collection was dispersed and a few works found their way to Budapest. As well as being highly evocative, its topographical detail is extremely accurate:

Óbuda, Castle Hill, Gellért Hill, Margaret Island and the small town of Pest are all clearly recognizable. It is easy to understand how, after such a formidable siege, Buda was completely devastated and took over a century to become a capital once again. A painting by Charles Herbel (c. 1659–1702) inspired Heinrich Faust's *Triumph of the Duke of Lorraine on the West Slope of the Castle of Buda* (1694) [2]. This unrealistic Roman-style victory, with Castle Hill

relegated to the distance, is in effect an allegorical celebration of the glory of Charles, Duke of Lorraine, whose victory over the Turks enabled the Hungarians to turn once more toward Europe after a century and a half of Turkish rule.

	2
1	
	3

Work carried out to regulate the Danube in the late 19th century had major repercussions for the city's development. Public buildings and private mansions were built in an eclectic style on the reclaimed land, masking the traditional houses that stood near the river. These buildings on the riverfront of Pest were closely monitored by a committee formed under the aegis of the Palatine Archduke, Joseph of Habsburg (1776–1847) ● *34*, to ensure that they presented an overall architectural unity. Visitors were captivated by the majestic image of Pest and wanted to immortalize their impressions. This period of urban development and prosperity corresponded to the golden age of *vedute* (topographically accurate landscape paintings). The most talented of the *vedutisti* was the Transylvanian artist Miklós Barabás (1810–98) ▲ *212*, who painted *Quay on the Danube at Pest, from the North* [1] in 1843 and *Quay on the Danube at Pest, from the South* [2] in 1842. Although Antal Ligeti (1823–90) did not paint many views of Budapest, scenes such as *Budapest from József-hegy* (1884) [3] were among his most accomplished works.

| 1 | 2 |
| 3 | |

'The hotel entrances were on Mária-Valéria út,
while their terraces stretched beneath the awnings
of the Duna korzó, the promenade overlooking
the loading platforms of the Danube.'

John Lukacs

'My Hungarians took great pride in their appearance. They were veritable dandies in this respect, and dressed carefully in outdated English style; but they were not in the least offended by the coarseness of my apparel.'

Patrick Leigh Fermor

This aquatint [3] of the Franciscans' Square (Ferenciek tere) in the 1840s was the work of two artists: Josef Kuwasseg 1799–1859) did the ink drawing, and Frederick Martens (c. 1809–75) did the painting. The formality of the buildings is offset by the relatively naïve depiction of everyday scenes. In 1884 the city of Budapest organized a competition to revive the genre of *veduta*, which had fallen into disuse. It was won by two architects: Róbert Nádler and Albert Schickedanz (1846–1915) ▲ *148, 150*. The authorities also saw this as a way of compiling an artistic record of the city's monuments. The painting [2] by Albert Schickedanz (1884) shows Holy Trinity Square (Szentháromság tér ▲ *202*, formerly Market Square) before the restoration of the Matthias Church. It includes the Holy Trinity Column ● *71*, and the old town hall of Buda (on the right). The competition judges awarded third place to József Molnár (1821–99) for his study of Calvin Square (Kálvin tér). Molnár was then commissioned to produce an oil painting on the same theme: *Kálvin tér, Pest* [1]. It shows the Pest Savings Bank on the right and the National Museum ▲ *124* in the center. (The Danubius Fountain was resculpted and placed in Elizabeth Square (Erzsébet tér) in 1959, after being badly damaged in World War Two.) The competition attracted a number of artists. However, in the end the municipal committee for the arts decided to promote photography, and the photographer György Klösz (1844–1913) was commissioned to create a photographic record of Budapest's principal monuments.

| 1 |
| 2 | 3 |

Painting by József Rippl-Rónai (1861–1927) ● *83*, ▲ *176* of the coronation of the last Habsburg emperor, Charles I (Károly IV), on December 30, 1916, in the Matthias Church ● *77*, ▲ *202*.

BUDAPEST
AS SEEN BY WRITERS

*A*ttila József (1905-1937), one of the greates
Hungarian poets of the 20th century, was born i
Budapest. Central themes in József's poems ar
poverty, loneliness and suffering, and although ofte
melancholic, they also express the author's faith i
life's essential beauty and harmony.

I sat there on the quayside by the landing,
a melon rind was drifting on the flow.
I delved into my fate, just understanding:
the surface chatters, while it's calm below.
As if my heart had been its very source,
troubled, wise was the Danube, mighty force.

Like muscles at work, when lifting the axe,
harvesting, welding, or digging a grave,
so did the water surge, tighten, relax
with every current, every breezy wave.
Like Mother, dandled, told a tale, caressed,
laundered the dirt of all Budapest.

A drizzle started, moistening the morning
but didn't care much, so it stopped again.
And yet, like someone who under an awning
watches the rain – I gazed into the plain:
as twilight that may infinitely last,
so grey was all that used to shine, the past.

The Danube flowed, and like a tiny child
plays on his musing, lively mother's knee,
so cradled and embraced and gently smiled
each playful wave, waving hallo to me.
They shuddered on the flood of past events
like tombstones, tumbling graveyard monuments.

ATTILA JÓZSEF, *BY THE DANUBE* (EXCERPT),
TRANSLATED BY PETER ZOLLMAN, IN *IN QUEST OF THE 'MIRACLE STAG'.*
THE POETRY OF HUNGARY, ADAM MAKKAI (ED.), ATLANTIS-CENTAUR INC.
CHICAGO; M. SZIVARVANY, BUDAPEST; CORVINA, BUDAPEST, 1996.

*H*ungarian-born author and journalist Arthur Koestler (1905–83), is the best known
political refugee and prisoner of his time. His experiences as a political
correspondent, Communist party member and prisoner of war are described in Scum
of the Earth (1941), *and they provide the background for his first novel in English,*
Arrival and Departure (1943). *In the following excerpt, taken from his autobiography,*
Arrow in the Blue, *Arthur Koestler discusses the life and work of his poet friend, Attila
József.*

[...] Though in his native Hungary Attila József is posthumously regarded as the
greatest poet the nation has produced, his name is still virtually unknown in the
West. This may justify the pages that follow – quite apart from my personal feelings
for a dead friend.

Attila József committed suicide at the age of 32; both his work and his personal
fate were a terrifying symbol of our time. He was a contemporary Villon, whose life
and poetry revolved around the two treacherous poles of this age, Marx and Freud,
and who died a victim of both.

Attila was born in 1905, the son of a day-labourer and of a charwoman. His
father disappeared when he was three, and until his seventh year Attila was
brought up in an orphanage. He earned his living while at school as a movie-usher,

ewsboy and night-waiter; and at college as a railway porter, Danube sailor, dock-
orker, office-cleaner and private tutor.

His first poems were published in the leading Hungarian literary magazine,
Nyugat ('Occident') when he was sixteen. One year later, in 1922, *Nyugat* printed
is poem 'Innocent Song' which caused a nation-wide scandal, and his expulsion
rom the University of Szeged. 'Innocent Song' was acclaimed as a kind of
manifesto of the Central European post-war generation.

INNOCENT SONG

I have no God, I have no King,
my mother never wore a ring,
I have no crib or funeral cover,
I give no kiss, I take no lover.

For three days I have chewed my thumb
for want of either crust or crumb.
Though I am twenty, strong and hale –
my twenty years are up for sale.

Should there be none who wish to buy
The Devil's free to have a try;
then shall I use my commonsense
and rob and kill in innocence.

Till, on a rope, they hang me high,
and in the blessed earth I lie –
and lush and poisoned grasses start
rank from my pure and simple heart.

...] When I met Attila in 1933, we were both twenty-seven. He was of pure-bred
Magyar, rural stock: of medium height, lean, sparse, sinewy, he carried his body
like a regimental sergeant-major. He had a narrow face with a high forehead, calm
brown eyes, and calm, regular features to which a certain dash and enterprise was
added by a trim moustache with pointed ends. It was a handsome and manly, but
quite unremarkable face that could have been a ladies' hairdresser's; nothing in its
unruffled appearance suggested that its owner had spent several months in a
mental hospital, suffering from delusions, and was heading for the final break-up.

...] At the time of our friendship, however, Attila was an extremely amiable and
amusing, though somewhat exhausting, companion. He had his moments of
exuberance and would write drinking songs – 'O wine, milk of virile men..' – though
he drank rarely. He also wrote a congratulatory poem to his own birthday – the
thirty-second and last:

Thirty-two and very wise –
this poem shall be a surprise
    and so pret-
    ty-pretty.

A gift that shall the spirits rouse
of the lonely guest in the coffee-house:
        my-
        self.

Thirty-two, what an event,
and never enough to pay the rent,
    and always hungry
    in Hung'ry...

He had moments of a classical and festive mood: his poem of welcome to Thoma
Mann, on the occasion of Mann's visit to Budapest, has the beautiful closing lines:

> ... We shall listen to you and some
> will just gaze at you in joy, for it delights
> us to have you here: a European among the Whites.

Arthur Koestler, *Arrow in the Blu*
First published by Collins with Hamish Hamilton Ltd, 195

The following excerpts are taken from Paul Hoffman's book The Man Who Love
Only Numbers – *the story of the Hungarian mathematical prodigy, Paul Erdő
(1913-1996). The details of Erdős's life are related against the historical and cultura
backdrop of his native Budapest.*

The Budapest of Erdős's birth was a sophisticated modern city, home of the large
stock exchange in Europe and the most grandiose parliament building in the worl
Budapest rivaled Paris and Vienna in first-class hotels, garden restaurants and late
night cafés, which were hothouses of "illicit trading, adultery, puns, gossip an
poetry, the meeting places for the intellectuals and those opposed to oppression
It was also an Old World city, its women praised for their beauty and its men fo
their chivalry. Budapest "has never been an agreeable town. But desirable, yes: lik
a racy, full-blooded young married woman about whose flirtations everyone know
and yet gentlemen are glad to bend down and kiss her hand," wrote Gyula Krúd
an acclaimed writer of Magyar prose, who moved from the Hungarian provinces t
Budapest, in 1896, the year the city's subway system opened, the first in Europe
Krúdy's enthusiasm for Budapest was irrepressible:

> Here the dancing in the theaters is the best, here everyone in a crowd
> may think that he is a gentleman even if he had left jail the day before;
> the physicians' cures are wonderful, the lawyers are world-famous, even
> the renter of the smallest rooms has his bath, the shopkeepers are
> inventive, the policemen guard the public peace, the gentlefolk are
> agreeable, the streetlights burn till the morning, the janitors will not
> allow a single ghost inside, the tramcars will carry you to the farthest
> places within an hour, the city clerks look down on the state employees,
> the women are well-read from their theater magazines, the porters
> greet you humbly on the street corners, the innkeeper inquires of your
> appetite with his hat in hand, the coach drivers wait for you solemnly
> during an entire day, the salesgirls swear that your wife is the most
> beautiful of women, other girls in the nightclubs and orpheums hear out
> your political opinions politely, you find yourself praised in the morning
> newspaper after you had witnessed an accident, well-known men use
> the spittoons in the café gardens, you are being helped into your
> overcoat, and the undertaker shows his thirty-two gold teeth when you
> take your leave from this city forever.

[...] Death and tragedy have long been part of the Hungarian character. Accordin
to the historian John Lukacs, on All Soul's Day in Erdős's youth, "thousands o
people streamed toward the cemeteries of Budapest, with flowers in their hand
on that holy day which is perhaps taken more seriously in Hungary than anywher
else because of the national temperament. *Temetni tudunk* – a terse Magyar phras
whose translation requires as many as ten English words to give its proper (an
even then, not wholly exact) sense: 'How to bury people – that is one thing w
know.'" The phrase was coined long before Hungary had experienced th
devastation of the two world wars, whose carnage would come disproportionatel
from within its borders.

Few countries have had as violent a history as Hungary. In the ninth century, nomadic Magyar warriors from the steppes of Eastern Europe crossed the Carpathian Mountains and, renouncing their peripatetic way of life, settled in the middle Danube basin at the heart of what is now Hungary. The Magyars, also known as the On-Ogurs ("people of the ten arrows"), were skilled archers and javelin throwers who raided their neighbors, plundering Germany from Bavaria to Saxony. Recent converts to Christianity, the Magyars had to defend their own territory against a series of invaders. They held their own until 1241, when several hundred thousand Mongol horsemen from Genghis Khan's empire slaughtered half the Magyar population and enslaved much of the rest, a bloodbath from which the country barely recovered. "The problem with Hungary," Erdős once joked, reflecting on his country's history, "is that in every war we chose the wrong side."

PAUL HOFFMAN, *THE MAN WHO LOVED ONLY NUMBERS*,
PUBLISHED BY IN FOURTH ESTATE LIMITED, 1998

Acclaimed travel writer Jan Morris is an honorary D. Litt. of the universities of Wales and Glamorgan and a Fellow of the Royal Society of Literature. In one of her many volumes of collected travel essays, she offers her own observations of the city of Budapest.

[...] the Hungarian Rising was the most tragically heroic event of the entire Cold War between capitalism and Communism [and] Budapest was just the place for it.

It does not seem to me a very lovely city, as the tourist brochures claim, but it is made for glory. On the right bank of the Danube is piled the old capital of Buda, with its royal castle and cathedral resplendent at the top; on the left bank extends the mass of Pest, all grand boulevards, parks and church steeples, running away to the horizon in a flatland of suburbs, and fronted on the river bank by the grotesque and mighty Parliament. Six bridges connect the two halves of Budapest, and the whole city suggests to me a figure of lapidary pride, commemorating always the sieges, battles, rebellions, and miscellaneous splendours of its history. By and large modern Hungarians may look about as ordinary as the rest of us, but in my romantic way I like to fancy in them the spirit of the Magyar horsemen who ride in sculpted bronze about the national memorial in Heroes' Square: haughty magnificent noblemen, ineffably proud on their caparisoned horses as they ride at a leisurely pace into the city, their kingly leader looking majestically in front of him, his companions glaring this way and that from beneath their feathered helmets like presidential security men.

And in 1956, as it happened, my fancy proved to be true: the people of Budapest, ancients to schoolchildren, rose in fury against their oppressors as the Magyar manner born. How I would love to have been there!

JAN MORRIS, *THE WRONG STORY*
IN *FIFTY YEARS OF EUROPE: AN ALBUM*
PUBLISHED BY PENGUIN BOOKS, 1997

Sir Cecil Beaton (1904-1980), English scenery and costume designer, photographer, writer and painter, also wrote and illustrated many books. In his autobiographical The Wandering Years, Diaries 1922–39, *he describes his experiences of Budapest by night.*

By the time we staggered to our beds at dawn, we felt as though we'd already spent a week sightseeing and living in Budapest. Many impressions had been gathered. A letter of introduction provided us with a willing escort, who promptly guided two eager foreigners and showed them every aspect of night life. We ate Hungarian food in enormous quantities including a kind of salmon-trout from Lake Balaton. Gypsy orchestras serenaded us. In the huge inferno-nightclub *Arizona*, spectacle vyed with spectacle. There were revolving dance floors and cabaret that went on from ten o'clock until three in the morning. The walls had breathing shells; balconies suddenly shot ceilingwards on the trunk of a palm tree; stars flashed and chorus girls, suspended by their teeth, twirled at the ends of ropes. To Miss Arizona, once a beauty and now the singer-wife of the proprietor, were allotted the big 'production numbers'. Her entrances were spectacular accompanied by every variety of dog, or riding an elephant.

SIR CECIL BEATON, *A NIGHT OUT IN BUDAPEST, 1936*
IN *THE WANDERING YEARS, DIARIES 1922–39,* 1961

József Gvadányi (1725-1801), was a poet in close contact with the writers of his age, and he embarked on a literary career with occasional verses. His long narrative poem, *A Village Notary's Journey to Buda*, which appeared anonymously in 1790, contrasted a naive provincial hero and the urban sophistication of the Hungarian capital. His hero sets out for Buda in order to study the public policies of Emperor Joseph II. Part one depicts the vicissitudes of the notary on his trip. It is always the simple people who rescue him from trouble. In part two, however, he becomes the mouth-piece of Gvadányi himself and passes judgment on contemporary morality. He finds the chief source of trouble not in the political oppression of the day but in the people's tendency to ape foreign customs.

He was praised for his attempts at purifying the language and for his ability to strike a chord of popular sentiment. His language is simple and expressive, and his earthy humor won him many devoted readers. In the 19th century this story was adapted for the stage by József Gaál (1811–66).

I thought to view the comeliness
of freely chosen Magyar dress,
of scarlet velvets without flaw
and sables from Siberia.

I looked for capes, for cloaks of fur,
for trousers fine from belt to spur,
new girdles gay with golden threads
and sable calpacks on their heads.

Red riding-boots should grace their shins,
their backs be hung with leopard skins,
their caps be plumed, while greet the ears
their jingling jewelled bandoliers.

I thought: their long hair graceful flies,
while sabre-scabbards smite their thighs:
with battle-axe or mace they play
or dress in armour for the fray.

JÓZSEF GVADÁNYI, *ON THE DRESS OF THE HUNGARIANS*,
(EXCERPT FROM *A VILLAGE NOTARY'S JOURNEY TO BUDA*), TRANSLATED BY
WATSON KIRKCONNELL IN *IN QUEST OF THE 'MIRACLE STAG': THE POETRY OF
HUNGARY*, ADAM MAKKAI (ED.), ATLANTIS-CENTAUR INC., CHICAGO; M.
SZIVARVANY, BUDAPEST; CORVINA, BUDAPEST, 1996

Claudio Magris, scholar and critic specialising in the field of German literature and culture, was born in Trieste in 1939. After graduating from the university of Turin he lectured there in German Language and Literature from 1970 to 1978. He is the author of novels, plays and works of literary criticism and has translated Ibsen, Kleist and Schnitzler. In his book, Danube, *from which the following excerpts are taken, Magris embarks on a journey through the history and culture of the Danube lands. His observations here are of Budapest.*

The day is generous with undulating lines and sensual pleasure. At 9 Fortuna utca it even offers us the compliant breasts of the goddess Fortuna, carved by the not very famous Ferenc Medgyessy in 1921: they are tender models of the curvature of the earth. At No. 4 in the same street there was once the Fortuna Inn, which now houses the Hungarian Museum of Commerce and Catering. Clearly inspired by this name, Amedeo, who, like Monsieur Teste, goes through life classifying, begins to expound a theory concerning the connection between erotica and the art of travelling. He subdivides it into a number of sections: eros and coaches, eros and post-houses, adventures in trains, licentious cruises, the customs of ports and of inland cities, the differences between capital cities and provincial towns, the aeroplane and sexual inactivity (imputed chiefly, but not solely, to the brevity of air trips and the constant interruption to which one is subjected).

The *Musée de l'Hôtellerie* appeals to gluttony rather than to lasciviousness. It displays posters for historic pastries such as Joseph Naisz's creation which promised maraschino from Zara, Curaçao, Anisette and Tamarind: it shows majestic cakes like towering temples, reproduces sweetmeats of illustrious memory, figures once fashioned of chocolate and cream, Gâteau d'ananas à la Zichy, Fruits entiers à la Duchesse Gisèle. Gluttony ogles other pleasures in the Pain de Framboises à la Leda, a pyramid of temptations, a dish supporting a naked woman in a shell, who appears to be offering herself to a swan: the bird, who looks equally delicious, is stretching out his neck to her. These dainties end up by making one feel slighty sick, like every kind of affectation. But in the reconstruction of an older-days pastry-shop, the knobs on the drawers are exactly the same as those in use in Fiume and Trieste forty years ago: the tiniest indications of a domestic Mitteleuropa, mysterious treasures of childhood, the distant feel of home.

We stop at Margaret Island where, according to the proverb, love begins and ends. This transience of the heart and senses was made much of in the Hungarian novels of the 1930s, that production line of books entitled *The Most Beautiful Woman in Budapest* or *Meeting at Margaret Island*, which seemed to match the caressing, stereotyped aura of these burgeoning flower-beds, parks, hotels and *belle époque* pavilions, with fountains playing among the roses. But even this allurement touches the soul, like some tired old waltz, and is a little promise of happiness: it induces the melancholy associated with any meditation on joy. And that love can end is always a thought that wrings the heart, even if expressed in the banal refrain of a popular song. That evening, at the *Matthias*, a gypsy fiddler plays the *Pacsirta*, the skylark. All this is still "décor" of the beginning of the century, the style of the superannuated gentry who liked Hungarian gypsy music, which was really neither Hungarian nor gypsy. But the *Pacsirta* is a lovely song, the violinist plays it in a masterly style and, at least for this evening, love is not over. Even on an ordinary evening it can happen that one finds real life in something false.

[...] The buildings of Budapest are eclectic, given to historical posturing, weighty in themselves and often adorned with heavy decorations; their non-style occasionally appears as some bizarre face of the future, the sort of backward-looking yet futuristic townscape of the cities posited in science-fiction films such as *Blade Runner:* a future that is post-historical and without style, peopled by chaotic, composite masses, in national and ethnic qualities indistinguishable, Malay-Redskin Levantines who live in shacks and

kyscrapers, twelfth-generation computers and rusty bicycles fished up from the
past, rubble from the Fourth World War and superhuman robots. The
architectural townscape of this metropolitan future is archaic-futuristic, with
skyscrapers kilometres in height and temples in the *kolossal* style like Milan
Station or Grand Central. The eclecticism of Budapest, its mixture of styles,
evokes, like every Babel of today, a possible future swarming with the survivors of
some catastrophe. Every heir of the Hapsburg era is a true man of the future,
because he learnt, earlier than most others, to live without a future, in the absence
of any historical continuity; and that is, not to live but to survive. But along these
splendid boulevards, in a world as lively and elegant as this, a world which does
not display the melancholy of the Eastern Bloc countries, even survival is
charming and seductive, magnanimous and maybe, at times, almost happy.

CLAUDIO MAGRIS, *DANUBE*, PUBLISHED BY THE HARVILL PRESS, 1999

*Sir Georg Solti, one of the leading conductors of the century, relives, in his memoirs,
an unparalleled musical life. His musical education began in his native Budapest,
and he went on to serve as musical director with orchestras in Munich, Frankfurt,
London, and Chicago, and performed all over the world. He made 250 records and
CDs, including more than forty operas. Here he recounts some of his experiences
whilst attending the Liszt Academy.*

...] When I was fifteen or sixteen, Professor Székely caught pneumonia, and we
pupils were told that during his absence his lessons would be given by Professor
Bartók. Although Béla Bartók was a fine pianist and needed to teach in order to
earn a living, the obvious question remains: Why was he teaching piano instead of
composition? The answer is he believed that composition cannot be taught. He
was absolutely right. One does have to learn the elements of composition, such as
harmony, counterpoint, and form, but one can't be taught how to to compose
anything worth hearing; one either does or does not have a talent for composing
music.

Bartók presented an austere, forbidding front
to the world, and even in those years, when he
was still in his mid-forties, his reputation was
daunting. Until Székely became ill, I had seen Bartók
only in the Liszt Academy's corridors, and I had never
exchanged a word with him. I can say with absolute honesty, and
without leaning on hindsight, that although he had received little
official recognition and was widely regarded as a raving radical, we
music students knew exactly how important he was, and we revered
him. We were fully aware that there was an authentic genius
teaching at our academy.

When I learned that I would have to play for him, I felt terribly
fearful. Bartók kept our class separate from his own; we spent several
hours with him twice a week throughout the six weeks of Székely's
illness. Seventy years have elapsed since
then and I do not remember much about those sessions, but I
do recall that at every lesson each pupil played parts of
The Well-Tempered Clavier for Bartók. I also played some

Debussy preludes for him. During one of the first lessons, I made a terrible faux pas: I sat down to play his *Allegro barbaro*, for piano solo. When he saw me set the music on the stand he became quite upset. "No, no, not that!" he said. "I don't want to hear that!" It was stupid of me to have thought that he might have enjoyed hearing an immature pupil play one of his compositions, but my intentions had been good: I had wanted to show my love and respect for him.

After I left Bartók's class, I never again had significant personal contact with him. There was an occasional "Good morning, Professor," when I passed him in a corridor, but that was all. I attended many of his recitals, at which he played Scarlatti and Liszt (I particularly remember some of the less freqently performed pieces from the *Années de pèlerinage*), Haydn, Mozart, Schubert, Debussy, and even Schoenberg, whose music was as much disliked in Hungary as elsewhere in those years. I never heard him play Beethoven or Brahms, but I did hear him perform many of the pieces from his own *Mikrokosmos,* for which he favored a crisp staccato articulation. Bartók was a marvelous pianist who took practicing seriously, but his playing was somewhat dry, not at all Romantic. He opted for a rather hard but extraordinarily clear sound, and he used less pedal than most pianists – very little even in Debussy.

Horthy and his supporters eventually forgave Kodály his Communist sympathies, but they never forgave Bartók, who had a much more uncompromising character. And yet, however isolated he may have been within the Hungarian musical milieu, his situation became even more difficult when he emigrated. The story of his departure at the beginning of World War II, and of his struggle for survival in the United States, where he died in 1945, is well known. Since his death, he has been recognised as one of the great composers of the century. In Hungary, he posthumously became a national hero: Most cities and towns have streets or squares named after him, and what used to be called the Franz Lizst Academy is now the Franz Liszt-Béla Bartók Academy.

I don't remember the name of my first teacher of musical theory at the Liszt Academy, but when, at the age of thirteen or fourteen, I won a prize in a piano competition promoted by a Budapest politician, one of the pieces I played was my own. My mother, convinced that I was a second Mozart, persuaded the politician to write a letter of recommendation on my behalf to the academy's best-known composition teacher, Zoltán Kodály.

Kodály, then in his mid-forties, was a brilliant man who went through some very bad years, on the verge of madness. There was something of the fanatic in him, and back then his youthful, ascetic face and Lenin-style beard gave him a somewhat Christ-like appearance. He believed in an almost messianic form of communism, and he became a disciple of an extremist "healthy life" cult that called for a severe form of vegetarianism, cold-water cures, and going barefoot. There was a period when he even came to the academy shoeless. His wife, Emma Sándor, the sister of a wealthy liberal member of parliament, was no beauty, but she was highly ntelligent, and gifted as a composer, pianist, poet, and translator. Her wealth allowed Kodály to spend time composing and carrying out his research into folk music, which he wouldn't have been able to do so freely if he had had to teach full time.

I don't know how my mother had the courage to take me to a man of such prestige as Kodály, but there we were one day in his studio at the academy. Such was her naivete in political matters that she didn't realize that the politician who had written the letter she handed him was right-wing; Kodály was left-wing. "My son composes and has brought along some little pieces that he has written," she said. "Would you like to listen to them?"

I am sure that the pieces were terrible, but Kodály listened patiently. "The boy certainly has talent," he told my mother, "but he must finish his education. Bring him back to me when he is eighteen, and we'll discuss the matter again." This was a fair remark, but my mother was deeply offended: How had Kodály dared to turn down her little Mozart? Instead of following his advice, she took me immediately to Albert Siklós, the other principal composition professor at the academy; he listened to my pieces and accepted me as a pupil.

[...] Composition exams were held twice a year; we were given blank music paper early in the morning and had to produce a certain type of composition by noon. Together, Siklós and Kodály looked at each student's work and graded it. On those occasions – and there were at least eight such tests over a four-year period – Kodály never gave the slightest indication that he recognized me. He always graded my work fairly, but he never said a word to me. I finished the course successfully and wrote a string quartet as a graduation piece, thereby ending my career as a composer. Kodály handed me my diploma, but not even then did he say a word to me.

One evening, a few years after my graduation, when I was a coach at the State Opera, I was sitting in my usual place in the opera house's restaurant before a performance of Kodály's *The Transylvanian Spinning Room*. The director came in with Kodály and asked me to show the composer the way to his box. As we walked, Kodály turned to me and said, "You see, you didn't need that letter of recommendation. You've made your way without it."

"Professor, do you remember that?"

"Oh yes," he said softly.

I didn't see him again for about thirty years. At Salzburg in 1964, after a performance of Mahler's First Symphony that I had conducted, an usher came to my dressing room and said that Professor Kodály wanted to see me. Kodály entered with his new, young wife – his first wife had died – and made the following astonishing remark: "I must apologize to you for the time I was so unfriendly to your mother," he said, "but, you see, the man who had written that letter of recommendation was my political enemy."

Sir Georg Solti, *Memoirs*,
PUBLISHED BY
Alfred A. Knopf, Inc., 1997

Patrick Leigh Fermor is one of the finest travel writers of his generation. In Decemb
1933, he set out to walk from Rotterdam to Constantinople and his book, A Tim
of Gifts, *from which the following excerpt is taken, is the account of his journey as fe*
as Hungary.

[...] There was a lull in the air. Holy Saturday, with its lamps out and shrines emp
and the distant tolling over the fields, cast a spell of catalepsy and suspense. It wa
a time of sealed tombs and sleeping sentries with the Protagonist of the week
drama deep underground harrowing Hell... There was not a fisherman on the rive
not a peasant in the fields, nothing but those little volecatchers and skimmin
wagtails, the waterbirds and the massed larks and the frogs, whose steady diurna
croak, though universal, seemed milder than the full-moon brekekekexing the nigl
before. A thrown stick could silence an acre for several seconds. The flecks of du
on the current and the spinning fluff suggested midsummer. I ate my bread an
cheese on the shady side of a rick and fell asleep. (Hay-ricks are conica
hereabouts, cleverly stacked round a centre pole and when most of the hay ha
been sliced away for fodder, the sun catches the shorn planes as if lopsided obelisl
had been erected in the fields.) I awoke later than I had intended. The woods, fu
of rooks and wood-pigeons, were sending long shadows over the grass. I drank at
brook, sloshed some water on my face and tidied up. Civilization lay ahead.

Far away on the other bank I could see my destination: it had been growin
steadily in size since my first glimpse that morning. A cliff loomed over a lon
sweep of the river and on this ledge was perched a white fane that resemble
St.Peter's in Rome. A light circle of pillars lifted a gleaming dome into the sky.
was dramatic, mysterious, as improbable as a mirage and unmistakable as
landmark for many miles across the desert of liquid and solid. The Basilica o
Esztergom, I knew, was the Metropolitan Cathedral of all Hungary, the large
religious building in the Kingdom and the archiepiscopal See of the Cardina
Prince-Archbishop: the Hungarian equivalent, that is, of Rheims, Canterbur
Toledo, Armagh, and old Cracow. The Basilica, though spectacular and splendid,
not old: little in that part of Hungary was spared the ravages of the Tartars and th
Turks; after the Reconquest everything had to begin again. But the town – th
Latin Strigonium and the German Gran – is one of the oldest in the country. Eve
since the first Apostolic King of Christian Hungary – the conquering Árpad
descendant, St Stephen himself – was born and crowned in Esztergom, history ha
been accumulating here and entwining itself with myth. From my footpath, th
Basilica was the only building in sight. The monasteries, the churches, the palace
and the libraries that encrust the steep little town were all in baulk. The great pil
with its twin cupola-topped belfries, its ring of pillars and its great nacreous dom
hovered above water and timber and fen as though upheld, like a celestial city in
painting, by a flurry of untiring wings.

PATRICK LEIGH FERMOR, *A TIME OF GIFT.*
FIRST PUBLISHED BY JOHN MURRAY, 197

IN AND AROUND BUDAPEST

▲ White Cross Inn (now the *Casanova* night club)

◀ Statue Park ◆ *266*

▼ City Park and Heroes' Square ● *76* ▲ *15*

Vajdahunyad Castle (City Park) ▲ *161*   ▼ Ibusz building (Ferenciek tere) ▲ *121*

▲ Mosaic by Miksa Róth with Hungarian motifs ▼ Academy of Music ▲

▲ Calvinist Church (Városligeti fasor) ● 83 ▼ Former Post Office Savings Bank ● 80 ▲

PEST
Anthony Krause

'Vörösmarty tér is Pest's best known, friendliest and most pleasant square. Here you'll find the Hungaroton record store and the Luxus fashion boutique, where the staircase has Art Nouveau handrails and painted mirrors. Talking of staircases, you must try the elevators found in most buildings at least once. They are a sort of service lift that never stops and which you have to jump into and out of while it's moving...'

Dominique Fernandez

ART NOUVEAU FOUNTAIN
(end of Deák Ferenc utca) Don't leave the square before you've seen the atlantes supporting the domes at no. 3, designed by Korb and Giergl (1911) in typically Art Nouveau style.

When Budapest was unified, in 1873, it was the lower town of Pest that gave it its air of a fully fledged active, modern, cosmopolitan city. From then on, it was on a par with Prague and Vienna. It was unusual in that it was a city where architectural eclecticism and pastiche flourished (in the 1870s it acquired a neo-Gothic Parliament building and a medieval City Park); but it was also a fin-de-siècle city that welcomed new European architectural styles, and it was further embellished by the dazzling Hungarian Secessionist style ● *80, 82*. Pest can easily be divided into clearly defined districts: the old historic center; the elegant Andrássy út and the City Park; the grand boulevards of the commercial district; and the working-class districts of eastern Pest. The city's landmarks are also easily distinguishable. Many of them bear the stamp of the 19th-century imperialism and classicism that still marks the central districts of Pest. Most of the districts are named after the Habsburg emperors and empresses: Terézváros (Maria Theresa), Józsefváros (Joseph), Lipótváros (Leopold). Of all the cities of Central Europe, probably to an even greater degree than Vienna, the Hungarian capital is characterized by a sense of calm and reverie – evoked by the gentle harmony of the Danube plain, the secret magic of its passages (*gang*) and courtyards, the treasures of its old Jewish quarter, and its shady parks and beautiful cemeteries.

VÖRÖSMARTY TÉR, THE HEART OF BELVÁROS

The Belváros ('inner city') district corresponds to the site of the old medieval town before its walls were demolished to make way for the 19th-century urban development program ● *29, 34*. Nowadays the line of these walls is represented by Deák Ferenc utca to the north, the boulevards of Károly körút and Múzeum körút to the east, and Vámház körút to the south. Today the historic heart of Pest, which lies within the arc of the Kiskörút (Little Boulevard) ▲ *123*, is still the busiest part of the city. It is centered on Vörösmarty tér and the famous Váci utca pedestrian precinct ▲ *235*, and bisected by Kossuth Lajos utca. This is a district of cafés, restaurants, banks, businesses, boutiques and stores (including bookstores and souvenir shops). Its narrow pedestrianized streets and unrivaled views of the Buda Hills provide an ideal setting for city walks. For most of them Vörösmarty tér, the large square named after the 19th-century Romantic poet Mihály Vörösmarty, makes a convenient starting and finishing point.

GERBEAUD The Gerbeaud Cukrászda is Budapest's most famous patisserie ● 56. It was founded in 1858, and in 1884 was bought by the Swiss patissier Émile Gerbeaud. The Viennese-style tearooms, with their luxurious Baroque decor and green velvet drapery, are one of the capital's most prestigious meeting places. Visitors from Vienna and Milan come here to soak up its early-20th-century atmosphere. Here customers, served by white-booted waitresses, can sample the famous *pogácsa* (savory cakes made with bacon and cumin), *kifli* (croissants which can be filled with poppy seeds and nuts) and *Dobos torta* (thin layers of cake with mocha cream between them, sprinkled with nuts and coated with a brittle caramel glaze).

THE 'YELLOW METRO' In front of the patisserie is the entrance to Budapest's most popular subway (*metro*) line. The yellow (no. 1) line, known locally as the Kis Metro ('little subway'), was opened in 1896, four years before the Paris Metro. It runs the length of Andrássy út ▲ 140 to the Széchenyi Baths ● 62, ▲ 160.

LUXUS AND HUNGAROTON On either side of the square stand time-honored institutions. The first is the fashion boutique Luxus – in the period before 1989, during the Kádár regime ● 31, 37, the showcase of Western fashion and symbol of Hungary's opening up to the free market economy. The second is the now privatized Hungaroton record company ● 52, ◆ 282. Next door is the main sales point for tickets for concerts and other cultural events.

GERBEAUD TEAROOMS Next door to Gerbeaud's tearooms (on the corner) you can buy cakes at the patisserie's annex, the Kis Gerbeaud.

Vörösmarty (then Gizella) tér around 1890, including the building that houses the Gerbeaud patisserie.

PESTI VIGADÓ ● 79
The original Vigadó
(1859–65), designed
by Frigyes Feszl in
Romantic style, was a
prestigious concert
hall where Liszt ● 48,
Brahms, Debussy and
Bartók ● 51, 52
performed. It was
rebuilt after World
War Two and is today
a major venue for
concerts, shows and
other cultural events.

**GREEK ORTHODOX
CHURCH (Görögkeleti
templom)**
The city once had a
flourishing Greek
community. Pest's
Greek Orthodox
Church has a beautiful
painted wood
iconostasis (1797) by
the Serbian sculptor
Miklós Jankovitch.

VIGADÓ TÉR

Deák Ferenc utca runs from
Vörösmarty tér, past the
splendid BANK PALACE (built
in 1915), which now houses
the Budapest Stock Exchange
(right), to the VIGADÓ CONCERT
HALL. Vigadó tér opens onto
the DANUBE CORSO (Duna
korzó), the magnificent
pedestrianized embankment that

runs alongside the Danube between Chain Bridge ▲ 183 and
Elizabeth Bridge ▲ 181. In summer there is a continuous
stream of people strolling along the quays, eating in the
restaurants and sitting at the café terraces. In the evening the
Corso offers an enchanting view of the Royal Palace and the
illuminated Buda Hills. It is bordered by a number of luxury
hotels, including the BUDAPEST MARRIOTT HOTEL (the 10th-
floor Bellevue tearooms and terrace are well worth a visit).
Today floating casinos and restaurants are moored beside the
quays for the benefit of tourists. This is also the departure
point for cruises to the Danube Bend (Dunakanyar) ▲ 230.

PETŐFI TÉR

Continue southward to PETŐFI TÉR, with its
statue of Sándor Petőfi (1823–49), the poet-
hero of the 1848 uprising. Petőfi is seen
here (opposite) reciting his *Nemzeti Dal*
('National Song'), with its famous line 'Rise
up Hungarians!' Each year on March 15,
the date that marked the beginning of the
uprising against Austrian (Habsburg) rule,
the statue is covered with flowers and flags.
On October 23, 1956 thousands of people
gathered here, at the instigation of the Petőfi
Circle ● 36, to demonstrate against the
Soviet occupation. To the left of Petőfi 's
statue is the late-18th-century GREEK
ORTHODOX CHURCH (Görögkeleti templom).
Its Rococo façade was redesigned by Miklós
Ybl ● 76 in 1872.

he Petőfi Museum of Literature
situated at no. 16 Károlyi Mihály
ca ◆ 264.

'Europe is calm, calm once again.
Its revolutions have swept by like a whirlwind.'

Sándor Petőfi, early 1849

Anyone who was there in 1956 will never forget how in the days
following March 15 the ground around the statue was littered
with tiny burnt paper flags, soaked by the rain and tattered by
the wind. March 15 had become an official day of remembrance,
when young people (even children) were allowed to file past the
statue of Sándor Petőfi, each holding a paper flag. In 1956 the
unofficial demonstrations that had taken place there year after
year developed into a protest against the totalitarian regime.

THE POET
Petőfi's first poem
was published in 1842.
His humor and
powerful imagery
created a new
language that elevated
the ordinary to the
realm of poetry. He
was an epic poet who
presented popular
tales in the form of
lyrical ballads.

ACTOR, SOLDIER, STUDENT Petőfi's father was
a butcher and café owner named Petrovics,
and his mother a servant. He was expelled
from school, after receiving a bad report, and
became an extra at the Hungarian National
Theater. After roaming the countries of the
Hungarian Empire as a volunteer soldier, he
became a traveling player and a student.

THE POET ACCLAIMED, THE MAN DESTROYED
In July 1849 General
Josef Bem made
Petőfi his aide-de-
camp. Austria,
then a world
power, was
unable to defeat
Hungary and
called upon
another great
power, Russia, to
help. The soldier-
poet was killed
during the Battle
of Segesvár, on
July 31.

'RISE UP HUNGARIANS!'
When they learned of
the Viennese uprising
in 1848, the leaders of
the youthful rebellion
met in the Café Pilvax
in Pest ● 58. On
March 15, Hungary,
too, rebelled.
Petőfi's *Nemzeti Dal*
('National Song') and
the proclamation of
the writer Mór Jókai
were circulated in the
universities and on
the streets of Pest.
Today Hungarians
still know
Petőfi's poem
by heart. The
twin parapets
of the steps of
the Hungarian
National
Museum (in the
gardens a few
hundred yards
from Petőfi's
statue) have
remained a
place of
national
remembrance.

INNER CITY PARISH CHURCH (Belvárosi plébániatemplom)

The Inner City Parish Church is a large composite building. Built in Romanesque style in the 12th century, it was refurbished in Gothic style (choir and north entrance) in the 14th century and in Renaissance style in the 16th century (the beautiful tabernacle in the chapel to the right of the choir dates from 1507). After being converted into a mosque by the Turks (as evidenced by the *mihrab* or prayer niche in the eastern wall, facing Mecca), it was partly destroyed by fire in 1723, then rebuilt in brilliant Austrian Baroque style (nave and façade) by the architect János György Paur in the late 18th century.

MÁRCIUS 15. TÉR

By continuing toward Elizabeth Bridge (Erzsébet híd) you come to Március 15 tér (March 15 Square), which commemorates the date of the 1848 uprising. To the east of the square lie the ruined 3rd-century Roman fortress of CONTRA-AQUINCUM and the INNER CITY PARISH CHURCH (Belvárosi plébániatemplom). The church is adjacent to Elizabeth Bridge, which until 1920 was

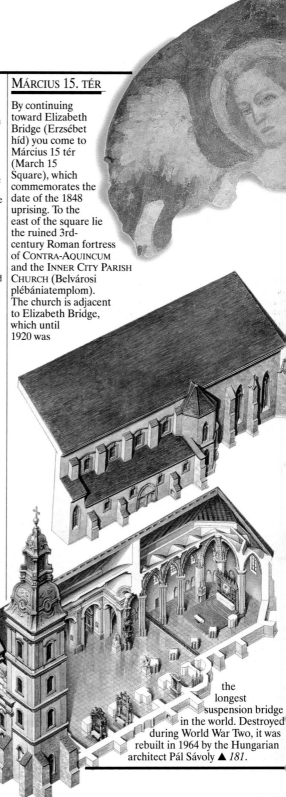

the longest suspension bridge in the world. Destroyed during World War Two, it was rebuilt in 1964 by the Hungarian architect Pál Sávoly ▲ *181*.

Fresco in the Inner City Parish Church.

VÁCI UTCA

A pedestrianized shopping and tourist street, Váci utca (which leads from Vörösmarty tér) is a fine example of the changes that have occurred since 1989. Nevertheless, the narrow streets that run across it are much more interesting, especially Régiposta utca, Kigyó utca and Párizsi utca. Here you can see the beautiful Baroque PÉTERFY MANSION (1755) at no. 2 Pesti Barnabás utca ● *70*, and the LORAND EÖTVÖS UNIVERSITY ARTS FACULTY at no. 1. By leaving the beaten tourist track and crossing Petőfi Sándor utca, you come to the attractive own-hall district that lies parallel to Váci utca. It is centered n KAMERMAYER KAROLY TÉR (named after the first mayor of he unified city) and SZERVITA TÉR.

ZERVITA TÉR The square is named after the Baroque ERVITE CHURCH (Szervita templom) built in 1732. Also of nterest is the former TURKISH BANK (Török Bankház) ● *81*, t no. 3, which has an Art Nouveau açade (1906) incorporating a huge nosaic of Hungaria, the symbolic epresentation of Hungary. The TOWN IALL (Polgármesteri Hivatal), an npressive and beautifully proportioned Baroque building located at nos. 9–11 Városház utca, was built in the early 18th entury by Anton Martinelli to house oldiers wounded in the war against the urks. SEMMELWEIS UTCA, which lies just ehind the town hall, was named after Dr gnác Semmelweis, who discovered the ure for puerperal fever (blood poisoning ontracted during childbirth). At no. 6, PEST COUNTY HALL (Pest Megyei Önkormányzati Hivatal) ● *75* is open to he public (the main entrance is at no. 7 Városház utca). It is a fine neoclassical ouilding, with two magnificent interior ourtyards. At the far end of Petőfi ándor utca is the JÓZSEF KATONA HEATER (Katona József Színház) ● *43*, vhich spearheaded avant-garde theater n the 1970s and is still one of the city's est theaters.

FRANCISCANS' SQUARE (Ferenciek tere) Just beyond the József Katona Theater lies the FERENCIEK TERE dominated by a beautiful building (1909) designed by Henrik Schmahl, in eclectic style ● *76*, as the Inner City Savings Bank. Its most interesting feature is the PARIZSI UDVAR, a shopping arcade based on the ones fashionable in early 20th-century Paris, which combines Moorish and Venetian architectural styles. The square is named after its 18th-century FRANCISCAN CHURCH (Franciskánus templom), in Italian Baroque style. In the center stands the NEREIDS FOUNTAIN (originally called he WELL OF THE NAIADS).

VÁCI UTCA PEDESTRIAN PRECINCT
With its fashionable boutiques, bookstores souvenir shops, and cafés, the Váci utca has a cosmopolitan atmosphere. The street also has a number of unusual architectural features, such as the original Art Nouveau interior of the PHILANTHIA FLORIST'S at no. 9, the Art Nouveau sculptural decorations and balcony of no. 8, and the THONET HOUSE (1889) at no. 11A, a masterpiece of Hungarian Secessionist architecture by Ödön Lechner ● *80*, ▲ *171*.

ARANY-EKSZER

THE FRANCISCAN CHURCH AND THE PARIZSI UDVAR
A relief on the wall of the church overlooking Kossuth Lajos utca recalls the Great Flood of 1838 ▲ *179*. It shows Baron Miklós Wesselényi using a boat to rescue people stranded by the flooding.

SERBIAN ORTHODOX CHURCH
The church (below), built b
the Serbs in th
17th century, has
beautiful iconostasi

THE KLOTILD PALACES These two buildings (nos. 5 and 6 Szabadsajtó út) were built in 1902, by Floris Korb and Kálmán Giergl, in eclectic style. Ferenciek tere and Kossuth Lajos utca represent a natural boundary within Belváros. O the other (southern) side lies part of the delightful university district. The multicolored dome of the UNIVERSITY LIBRARY (EGYETEMI KÖNYVTÁR), at no. 10 Ferenciek tere, provides a good starting point for this part of the walk.

EGYETEM TÉR

Strangely, this lively student quarter is not particularly popular with tourists. However, its cafés, theaters, university buildings and narrow streets make it one of the most attractive districts of Belváros.

THE UNIVERSITY CHURCH (Egyetemi templom)
As you turn down the Károlyi Mihály utca, you come to the Egyetemi tér (University Square). In 1785 the university moved from Buda to Pest. Today it is popularly known as ELTE (Lóránd Eötvös University) and its various departments are scattered throughout the city. As well as the Law Faculty, the square also has the city's most beautiful Baroque church: the University Church, built in 1725 and 1742. Its treasures include a copy of the *Black Madonna* of Czestochowa, a richly decorated pulpit and a beautiful portal carved by the Pauline monks.

PETŐFI MUSEUM OF LITERATURE The Petőfi Irodalmi Múzeum ◆ *264*, at no. 16 Károlyi Mihály utca, houses a collection of objects that once belonged to Hungarian poets and writers (Sándor Petőfi ▲ *119*, Endre Ady and Attila József ● *103*) and an archive center used by researchers. Kecskeméti utca (which leads to Kálvin tér) is a pleasant university street, with cafés and restaurants.

SERBIAN ORTHODOX CHURCH (Szerb orthodox templom)
As you turn southward, you come

SÓS
ANTIKVÁRIUM

RÉGI KÖNYVEK
KÖNYVTÁRAK
TÉRKÉPEK
METSZETEK
LEVELEZŐLAPOK
VÉTELE ÉS ELADÁSA

1056 BUDAPEST, VÁCI UTCA 73.
TELEFON: 337-6228 · 266-3204
sbence@mail.matav.hu

'ANTIKVÁRUM'
Budapest's many *antikvárum* are well worth a visit. These secondhand bookstores are popular with specialists and students, and some are truly amazing. KŐZPONTI ANTIKVÁRUM, at no. 15 Múzeum körút (opposite the National Museum), is full of treasures – both old books and old maps and prints. Next door, at no. 17, ZENEI ANTIKVÁRUM is a music lover's paradise: it is entirely devoted to old scores, books about music and rare recordings.

V. KER.
SZERB
UTCA
2 ⟵ ⟶ 4

> We are now in Pest, the eastern half of the city, which is younger and less beautiful than Buda. Even so, it was the dynamism of Pest that made the reputation of Budapest, and in 1900 it housed 83 percent of the city's inhabitants.'
>
> John Lukacs

to a quiet, shady district. At the intersection of Szerb utca and Veres Pálné utca stands the Serbian Orthodox Church. A little further on, the remains of Pest's old medieval wall (1¼ miles long) can still be seen at the corner of Bástya utca and Veres Pálné utca.

KISKÖRÚT

The Kiskörút (Little Boulevard) describes an arc between Deák Ferenc tér and Freedom Bridge (Szabadság híd ▲ 180). This main thoroughfare, which consists of three roads – Károly körút, Múzeum körút and Vámház körút – in succession, follows the line of the old walls of the medieval city. At the end of the 19th century an outer ring road, the Nagykörút (Great Boulevard) ▲ 164, was built running parallel to it.

DEÁK FERENC TÉR This square is the departure point and terminus for most of the city's bus and subway lines. Its name is often shortened to Deák tér. Its subway (*metro*) station includes the amazing UNDERGROUND RAILWAY MUSEUM (FÖLDALATTI VASUT MÚZEUM). To the south of the square is a neoclassical early 19th-century LUTHERAN CHURCH ● 75. The presbytery (at nos. 4–5 Deák Ferenc tér) – now the National Lutheran Museum – was formerly a school, which was attended by the young Sándor Petőfi ▲ 119.

HOTEL ASTORIA Built between 1912 and 1914, according to plans by Emil Ágoston and Arthur Hikisch, the Hotel Astoria ◆ 274 stands at the intersection of Károly körút and Kossuth Lajos utca. The hotel's beautiful entrance hall has the charm of an early-20th-century mansion, while the adjoining tearooms offer comfortable surrounding in which to meet people or enjoy a quiet read.

HUNGARIAN NATIONAL MUSEUM (Magyar Nemzeti Múzeum) ▲ 124 A little further along Károly körút is the Hungarian National Museum . Enjoy a walk in the museum gardens before continuing along Múzeum utca, bordered by beautiful private residences.

KÁLVIN TÉR. The square is dominated by a large CALVINIST CHURCH (Református templom), founded between 1816 and 1830 by József Hofrichter. The porch was designed by József Hild.

CENTRAL MARKET HALL (Központi Vásárcsarnok). From Kálvin tér, take the Vámház körút toward Freedom Bridge (Szabadság Híd). On the left, next to the BUDAPEST UNIVERSITY OF ECONOMICS ▲ 180, is the Central Market Hall . This vast brick-and-steel covered market, designed in 1896 by Samu Pecz, was restored in 1996.

Ferenc Deák (1803–1876), the 'nation's sage'.

The Hungarian National Museum ● 74 , ▲ 124, ◆ 265 This large neoclassical building was designed by Mihály Pollack (1837–47). Its construction marked an important step toward Hungary's national renaissance. Today it offers a number of thematic and chronological displays devoted to Hungarian history, from its origins to recent times. Exhibits include the Hungarian Crown Jewels.

Central Market Hall (main entrance).

In 1786 Count Ferenc Széchenyi, a rich and erudite art lover, began to build up his library and his collection of prints, maps, manuscripts, coats of arms, coins and archeology, to such an extent that he created a rich source of reference relating to the nation's history. In 1802, with the approval of Francis II (king of Hungary 1792–1830), he donated some 20,000 pieces to serve as the basis of the Hungarian National Museum (Magyar Nemzeti Múzeum), which was initially housed in the former Pauline Convent. The imposing neoclassical building designed by Mihály Pollack ● 74 has housed the museum since 1847.

HEAD OF HYGEIA (2nd century AD) This small marble head is a copy of a Hellenistic original. It was found in the Danube, in front of the Parliament building, in the late 19th century.

THE MUSEUM'S DEPARTMENTS The museum has departments devoted to archeology, the Middle Ages, modern history, medals and historical paintings, plus an archeological library and archives that contain documentation relating to excavations carried out in Hungary and photographic records of items in the museum's collections.

CYLINDRICAL-STEMMED VASE (first half of 3rd millennium BC) The archeological collection is divided into three sections, covering the prehistoric and Roman periods and the 'great invasions'. The characteristic shape of this vase was developed by the peoples living on the banks of the Tisza. Vases of this kind were often decorated with engraved or etched motifs.

CROWN OF CONSTANTINE IX MONOMACHUS (1042–55)

This gold diadem, composed of seven sections, is a masterpiece of Byzantine *cloisonné* enamel. The Byzantine Emperor Constantine IX, his wife Zoë and sister-in-law Theodora are represented on the three central sections.

SCYTHIAN DEER

Gold *repoussé* deer (6th century BC) from Zöldhalompuszta. The remains of a pale-blue *pâte-de-verre* inlay were found in the eye socket and the ear. Beneath the ear is the head of a bird of prey.

DEER WITH CORAL ANTLERS

(table decoration) The goldsmith Sebestyén Hann (1644–1713) worked mainly in Transylvania. This is one of several pieces by him in the museum.

CROWN OF THE HUNGARIAN KINGS (12th century)

The gold crown is divided into two parts. The lower part is known as the 'Greek crown' because it bears images of the saints inscribed with Greek characters, while the upper part, or 'Latin crown', has images of the Evangelists with Latin inscriptions.

FIFTY-DUCAT PIECE

(bearing the image of the Transylvanian prince Mihály Apafi, 1677) During the reign of Leopold I the gold forint began to be known as the ducat. The coin shown here was a royal gift and had no commercial value.

PARLIAMENT (Országház)
The Parliament building stretches for more 290 yards along the banks of the Danube. The tip of the dome is over 300 feet from the ground.

KOSSUTH LAJOS TÉR
Known as the 'standard bearer of independence', Lajos Kossuth (1802–94) was one of the principal instigators of the 1848 uprising. His statue (right) stands on the north side of the square.

Lipótváros (the 'town of Leopold'), named after Leopold II (1747–99), one of he Habsburg kings of Hungary and son of Maria Theresa, lies between the Danube and the Kiskörút (Little Boulevard). It is a district of offices, banks, ministries and large apartment blocks; a number of publications and political parties are based here. Lipótváros is very busy during the day – especially at lunch time, when the restaurants in Mérleg utca (next to Gresham Palace ▲ *138*) are packed – but in the evening it is extremely quiet and almost deserted.

KOSSUTH LAJOS TÉR

Situated between the Parliament building and the Ethnographical Museum ▲ *134*, Kossuth Lajos tér provides an ideal setting for the seat of the Hungarian government. The statues of Hungary's great historical and political figures dotted around the square add a touch of majesty to this broad esplanade, the venue for public demonstrations such as the 1956 uprising and its anniversaries, and the declaration of the Hungarian Republic on October 23, 1989.

Notable statues include LAJOS KOSSUTH on the north side of the square, FERENC RÁKÓCZI (the prince of Transylvania who in 1704–11 opposed the Habsburg presence in Hungary after the Turkish withdrawal; at the south end of the square); MIHÁLY KÁROLY (president of the short-lived Republic founded after World War One; to the north of the Parliament building); and IMRE NAGY (prime minister and martyr of the 1956 uprising ● *30*, ▲ *150*, in the southeast corner.)

KINGS AND SAINTS
The dome presents a summary of Hungarian history. Its sixteen marble pillars support statues of Hungarian kings and saints since the time of Árpád, flanked by statues of pages.

These statues represent (in a clockwise direction): Árpád, Stephen I (Saint Stephen), László I (Saint László), Kálmán the Possessor of Books, András II, Béla IV, Louis the Great, János Hunyadi, Matthias Corvinus, István Báthory, István Bocskay, Gábor Bethlen, György I Rákóczi, Charles III, Maria Theresa and Leopold II.

The Parliament
(Országház)

The Parliament building (Országház) is both the seat of Hungary's principal political institutions and the symbol of national independence. Its 691 rooms include the presidency of the Hungarian Republic, the apartments of the president and the leader of the Chamber of Deputies, the National Assembly, the prime minister's office, and the UN-designated Library of Parliament with its collection of over 400,000 books on history, law and political science.

IMRE STEINDL (1839–1902)
Steindl studied at the Viennese School of Fine Arts, under Friedrich Schmidt, and was particularly interested in Gothic architecture. In 1883 he won the competition for the best design for the Hungarian Parliament building. Out of the nineteen competing architects, he was the only one to choose the neo-Gothic style, inspired by the British Houses of Parliament. Work began in 1885, and the interior was completed in 1904.

AN IMPOSING BUT FRAGILE BUILDING
The extremely porous limestone used in the construction of the Parliament has been badly affected by pollution, and since 1925 the building has had to be repeatedly restored.

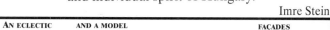

'In a building designed [to last] for centuries,
I could not use ephemeral details...which is why
I have made every effort to express the national
and individual spirit of Hungary.'

Imre Stein

AN ECLECTIC MASTERPIECE...

The Parliament is a fine example of eclectic architecture. The overall style is neo-Gothic, while the dome and general layout are neo-Renaissance, and the design of the various wings reflects the Baroque influence.

AND A MODEL OF SYMMETRY

The building observes the characteristic symmetry of Renaissance architecture. In the center a huge dome rises above the central hall. On either side of the dome, two identical wings contain the Chamber of Deputies (south wing) and the chamber of the former Upper House (north wing), which is now a conference hall. There are eighteen interior courtyards of varying sizes.

FAÇADES

The pediments of the façades have niches decorated with sculptures. The pediment of the main façade (right) overlooking the Danube, is decorated with arcades and surmounted by a balcony. The coats of arms of historic Hungarian towns are represented below the cornice.

Equestrian statue of Ferenc Rákóczi (János Pásztor, 1927).

ORIGINAL CEILINGS
The corridors of the various floors
(a total of 12½ miles) have an unusual
characteristic: the groined vaults of
their ceilings are supported by
triangular consoles.

▲ THE PARLIAMENT
(Országház)

The main halls and chambers are on the ground and first floors. The splendor of the interior decor (which combines Gothic, Renaissance and Byzantine styles), with its profusion of frescos, stained glass, sculptures and oak, mahogany and walnut ceilings, contributes to the solemnity of the building.

THE CHAMBER OF DEPUTIES It is in the form of a horseshoe. Like the conference hall, the various ante rooms rooms and reception room richly decorated neo-Byzantine Left: detail of the ceiling

PAINTINGS IN THE PARLIAMENT BUILDING
Among the numerous art treasures in the Parliament building are a mural by Körösfői-Kriesch depicting Attila and Buda hunting bison (in the Hall of the Hunt) and a monumental fresco of the conquest of Árpád (in the Munkácsy Hall). The audience chamber contains oil paintings by Lotz.

A METICULOUSLY DESIGNED CHAMBER
The various levels of the Chamber of Deputies are punctuated by a series of boxes and balconies to improve the acoustics. The chamber is lit by twelve huge chandeliers.

SYMBOLIC IMAGERY
The decoration of the Parliament building glorifies the virtues and victories of Hungary. It has a wealth of allegorical sculptures and historical paintings by Vajda, Körösfői-Kriesch, Lotz, Duditis and Munkácsy.

One of the pillars supporting the dome.

The main façade is decorated with statues of various Hungarian kings (from the conquest by the seven tribes to 1848), Transylvanian princes and distinguished military commanders.

Detail of the central gable of the main entrance. In the center are the crown and coat of arms of Stephen I.

1. Kossuth Lajos tér
2. Delegates' room
3. Debating room
4. Main staircase
5. Central hall
6. Parlor of the Chamber of Deputies
7. Chamber of Deputies
8. Munkácsy Hall
9. Hall of Tapestries
10. Function room
11. Conference Hall
12. Dining Hall
13. Nándorfehérvár Hall

Memorial to the victims of 1956 (Kossuth Lajos tér).

THE LION ENTRANCE
The Parliament building has a total of 27 entrances. The main entrance (Lion Entrance) is situated on Kossuth Lajos tér, at the top of a flight of steps flanked by two lions designed by Béla Markup. It opens onto the grand staircase, leading to the central hall beneath the dome.

> 'By its perfect beauty and its elegant lines, this remarkable medieval style creates a bridge between the material and spiritual world...'
>
> Imre Steindl, Architect of the Parliament building

THE DOME

The main staircase leads to the central hall beneath the star-shaped dome that forms the impressively proportioned heart of the Hungarian Parliament (almost 90 feet high and 65 feet in diameter). Its double framework is decorated with marble from Hungary and other countries. There are no figurative paintings: the sculptures and structural outline are highlighted with gold leaf and form a single, unified decor. The ribs of the vault are decorated with a variety of reliefs and the coats of arms of the kings of Hungary.

THE CONFERENCE HALL

While the layout of the conference hall, in the north wing, like that of the Chamber of Deputies, its decor is slightly different. The arches of the boxes are crowned with ornamental foliage. Behind the chairperson's seat are the coats of arms of the Houses of Anjou, Hunyadi, Jagiellon, Szapolyai and Habsburg.

On either side of it are paintings by Jantyik: on the right, András II announcing the Golden Bull of 1222; and on the left, the three estates offering their support to Maria Theresa at Pozsony in 1741. At second-floor level are sculptures symbolizing Glory, Wisdom, Unity, Rhetoric, War and Peace.

THE MAIN STAIRCASE

The staircase combines Baroque, Gothic and Byzantine styles. Its polychrome marble, the reddish-brown Swedish granite of its columns, the gold leaf of the Gothic arches and the multi-colored stained-glass windows by Miksa Róth all contribute to its lavish splendor. The grandiose frescos by Károly Lotz depict Hungaria, the symbolic representation of Hungary.

THE ETHNOGRAPHICAL MUSEUM ★
The huge central hall, designed in neo-Renaissance style by Károly Lotz.

Below: part of the Hungarian television building.

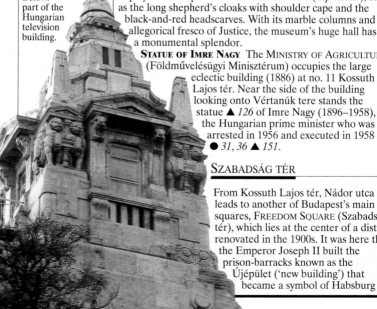

ETHNOGRAPHICAL MUSEUM (Néprajzi Múzeum) Opposite the Hungarian Parliament, at no. 12 Kossuth Lajos tér, the Ethnographical Museum occupies the former Palace of Justice designed by Alajos Hauszmann. In best thnographica tradition, the museum houses major collections of costumes, model peasant houses, and objects associated with weaving, pottery and embroidery. The items representing rural life (such as the gaily painted peasant furniture) are fine exampl of a fascinating form of decorative art, while the collections weaving illustrate the different regional variations. Also on display are examples of traditional costume (*nép viselet*), suc as the long shepherd's cloaks with shoulder cape and the black-and-red headscarves. With its marble columns and allegorical fresco of Justice, the museum's huge hall has a monumental splendor.

STATUE OF IMRE NAGY The MINISTRY OF AGRICULTURE (Földművelésügyi Minisztérum) occupies the large eclectic building (1886) at no. 11 Kossuth Lajos tér. Near the side of the building looking onto Vértanúk tere stands the statue ▲ *126* of Imre Nagy (1896–1958), the Hungarian prime minister who was arrested in 1956 and executed in 1958 ● *31, 36* ▲ *151*.

SZABADSÁG TÉR

From Kossuth Lajos tér, Nádor utca leads to another of Budapest's main squares, FREEDOM SQUARE (Szabadsá tér), which lies at the center of a distri renovated in the 1900s. It was here tha the Emperor Joseph II built the prison-barracks known as the Újépület ('new building') that became a symbol of Habsburg

> '...a mixture of giantism and exuberance, which corresponds to the hybrid alliance between the Hungarian capital and the Hapsburg eagle, and is also betrayed by the eclectic quality of the architecture.' Claudio Magris

Ethnographical Museum (central hall).

pression in Hungary. The square was subsequently named Freedom Square in an attempt to break with its pressive past. On one side of the square stands the S EMBASSY, where Cardinal József indszenty (1892–1975) sought refuge after e 1956 uprising and remained in 'internal ile' until 1971. Bishop of Veszprém, then rchbishop of Esztergom (1945–73) and, such, Hungary's Catholic Primate, indszenty became a cardinal in 1946. aving refused to secularize Roman atholic schools when the Communist gime was established in Hungary, he was rested (1948), tortured and condemned to rd labor for life. He was freed in 1955 and ayed a key role in the 1956 uprising, posing Soviet intervention in the same ay he had opposed the Kádár regime. He ft the US Embassy in 1971 and he went to ienna, from where he continued to criticize the regime. ehind Freedom Square (on the corner of Báthory utca and ulich utca) another square, the tiny BÁTHORY TÉR, also holds vignant memories. A small bronze oil lamp honors the emory of Count Lajos Batthyány (1806–49) ▲ *207*, head the first Hungarian national government during the 1848 prising, who was executed on October 6, 1849, in front of e barracks that have now disappeared.

Relief on the National Bank of Hungary.

Detail of the Bedő building, at no. 3 Honvéd utca.

MAGYAR NEMZETI BANK AND MAGYAR TELEVÍZÍO Two famous uildings, the National Bank of Hungary and what is now the eadquarters of Hungarian Television, stand opposite each her at nos. 8 and 9 Szabadság tér. Both were built at the art of the 20th century by Ignác Alpár (who also built ajdahunyad Castle ▲ *161*). The National Bank (1901) flects a strong Art Nouveau influence, while the Hungarian levision building is a fine example of the Secessionist style at originated in Vienna.

135

A MASTERPIECE BY ÖDÖN LECHNER
Pest's Post Office Savings Bank was built by Ödön Lechner in 1901, before Otto Wagner built its Viennese counterpart. It is characterized by an exuberant Art Nouveau style. This is reflected in its faience decorations and magnificent multicolored roof tiles, with plant and flower motifs, from the Vilmos Zsolnay porcelain manufactory ● 66, ▲ 147 at Pécs. The main hall is well worth a visit.

FORMER POST OFFICE SAVINGS BANK (Országos Postatakarékpénztár) ★ Head northward along Bank utca and turn down Hold utca. Here, at no. 4, you can admire Ödön Lechner's Post Office Savings Bank ● 80, 112, now part of the National Bank of Hungary.

SZENT ISTVÁN TÉR

On the south side of Szabadság tér, Hercegprímás utca takes you to Szent István tér (ST STEPHEN'S SQUARE) and Szent István Bazilika (ST STEPHEN'S BASILICA) ● 76. In spite of its name, the church does not have the traditional layout of a basilica. In fact it would be more accurate to refer to it as a cathedral, since the Archbishop of Esztergom ▲ 238 today bears the double title of

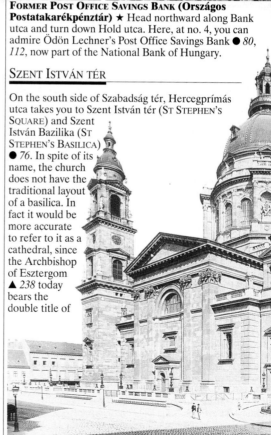

SZENT ISTVAN BAZILIKA
Built in the striking neo-Renaissance style favored by Miklós Ybl, St Stephen's Basilica is notable for its impressive proportions. It is 95 yards long and 60 yards wide; the tip of the dome is 315 feet from the ground.

'The greatest architect of this period was Miklós Ybl, the grand master of neo-Renaissance, whose works – the Customs House, the dome of St Stephen's Basilica and especially the Opera House – will be just as valid in the future as they are now.'

Hungary's Faces, 1938

rchbishop of Esztergom and Budapest. Inside is a statue Saint Elizabeth (1207–31), daughter of András II and fe of the Count of Thuringia. Widowed at the age of twenty, e joined the Franciscan Third Order and devoted her life the poor. There is also a reliquary containing the hand of int Stephen. A narrow staircase leads to the dome, which fers a magnificent view of the city – an absolute must for urists, who are often disappointed by the somewhat soulless gantism of the church's architecture. Behind the basilica, e buildings at no. 19 Bajcsy-Zsilinsky út are a fine example 1930s architecture.

ENTRAL EUROPEAN UNIVERSITY (Közép Európai Egyetem) om the basilica, Zrínyi utca leads southward to the river, ossing Október 6 utca and Nádor utca. At no. 9 is the rmer Festetics building, designed by Mihály Pollack (1826), hich is now the seat of the Central European University . ounded after the dismantling of the Berlin Wall, with a ew to forming a new Central European academic elite, e center is largely funded by the Hungarian-American illionaire George Soros. This neoclassical building also ouses the University's extensive English-language library. he entrance hall is decorated with allegorical statues.

OOSEVELT TÉR Situated at one end of Chain Bridge zéchenyi Lánchíd ● *74*, ▲ *183*), Roosevelt tér opens nto a promenade that runs ongside the quays of the anube, offering a magnificent ew of Buda. Overlooking e square is the HUNGARIAN CADEMY OF SCIENCES Magyar Tudományos Akadémia), onceived in 1825 by Count tván Széchenyi and built uring the 1860s, in neo-enaissance style, to plans by the Berlin architect Friedrich ugust Stüler and the Hungarian Miklós Ybl ● *76*, ▲ *140*. 1827 Széchenyi ● *35* – who made history by speaking ungarian, instead of Latin, at the Diet of Pressburg now Bratislava) in 1825 – donated the huge sum of 60,000 forints for the construction of the academy, with a view to helping the Magyar cause and developing the Hungarian language. Today it still has an important scientific library.

HUNGARIAN ACADEMY OF SCIENCES
The second floor is decorated with statues of great European scholars, among them Descartes, Galileo, Leibnitz, Lomonosov, Newton and the Hungarian linguist Miklós Révai.

V. kerület, Lipótváros
Roosevelt tér
6 ← → 5

'District V, Lipótváros, Roosevelt tér'

CONSTRUCTED IN THREE STAGES
The vast – it can hold 8,500 people – St Stephen's Basilica (Szent István Bazilika) has had a turbulent history. József Hild drew up the first plans in 1851, but died shortly afterward. He was succeeded by Miklós Ybl, whose dome unfortunately collapsed in 1868. Ybl died in 1891, and the church was finally completed fifteen years later by József Kauser.

GRESHAM PALACE ★
The façade of this palatial Art Nouveau building, designed by Zsigmond Quittner, is particularly impressive. It is decorated with mosaic friezes that catch the last rays of the setting sun.

GRESHAM PALACE ● *80, 81* (no. 5 Roosevelt tér) owes its name to the British insurance company that commissioned this grandiose building in 1907.

JÓZSEF NÁDOR TÉR As you leave Gresham Palace and cross József Attila utca, you come to József nádor tér, from where you can return to Belváros ▲ *116*. The square is named after Palatine Archduke (*nádor*) Joseph of Habsburg ● *34*, ▲ *199* (one of the sons of Leopold II), the first Hungarian magnate (1796) and one of the leading 'architects' of Pest's development. Today this elegant, shady square provides a pleasant setting for several large companies. The POSTAL BANK (Postabank) at no. 1 has a beautiful interior courtyard.

ÚJLIPÓTVÁROS

The Újlipótváros district (the name means 'new town of Leopold') is bounded by Váci utca ▲ *121* and Szent István körút (St Stephen's Boulevard) ▲ *164*. Many of its buildings date from the 1930s. Before World War Two it was a wealthy middle-class residential district and, along with the VIIth district, Pest's largest Jewish quarter. Today this part of the city is much sought after for its tranquillity and the elegance of its streets, especially near the quays and Szent István Park. Jászai Mari tér, at the end of Margaret Bridge (Margit híd), is a convenient place to begin this walk.

JÁSZAI MARI TÉR On the north side of the square is the extremely elegant late-19th-century PALATINUS APARTMENT BLOCK. To the south, at no. 19 Széchenyi rakpart (quay), is the dull, gray modern building that Hungarians jokingly call the WHITE HOUSE (Fehérház) ▲ *187*. It is the former Communist Party headquarters, where János Kádár, the Secretary General of the Party, had his offices until 1988. Statues of Marx and Engels have been relocated in Statue Park ▲ *110*. The building, which now houses various Party offices, is not open to the public.

POZSONYI ÚT This particularly beautiful street lies behind Jázai Mari tér (Pozsony is the Hungarian name for Bratislava, now capital of Slovakia). It has a number of buildings, with large interior courtyards, that offer a fine example of 1930s architecture.

RAOUL WALLENBERG UTCA On the way to Szent István Park, you cross Raoul Wallenberg utca. In July 1944 Raoul

György Konrád wrote about life in Újlipótváros in his autobiographical novel, *Ghosts from the Past*. In particular he describes Pozsonyi út, where he lived in hiding during World War Two until the Soviet troops arrived.

Wallenberg, a young Swedish diplomat, was sent to Budapest under the aegis of US, Swedish and Jewish refugee organizations to save Hungarian Jews threatened with deportation. Between October 1944 and the winter of 1945 he saved thousands of lives by delivering visas ('Wallenberg passports') to Jewish families all over the city, or by hiding them in 'protected houses' flying the flags of Sweden and other neutral countries. He was reported missing at the end of the war, but was captured – and may to be a spy for the United States. The street was named after him to commemorate his courageous actions.

SZENT ISTVAN PARK This delightful little park is one of the most sought-after residential areas in the capital. Its Bauhaus-style buildings (● 85), with balconies offering a splendid view of Margaret Island and the Buda Hills, are truly exceptional. Children play around the STATUE OF GYÖRGY LUKACS, who played a key role in Béla Kun's short-lived Hungarian Communist regime and, after the latter's exile to Moscow, served as Minister for Culture in Imre Nagy's government in 1956.

LEHEL MARKET (Lehel Vásárcsarnok) From the park, Victor Hugo utca (bordered by public housing units and other unprepossessing buildings from the Communist era) leads to Lehel tér. One of Budapest's most picturesque markets, the inexpensive and extremely popular LEHEL VASARCSARNOK, is held in this square. It offers an ideal opportunity to sample *lángos* – a savoury kind of pastry made with butter, resembling pizza base, and sometimes topped with vegetables. The square is dominated by the huge ST MARGARET'S CHURCH (Szent Margit templom), a 1930s copy of the (now ruined) 13th-century Romanesque Collegiate Church of Zsámbék, 25 miles from Budapest. The VISEGRADI UTCA – a working-class street crowded with small shops and *söröző* (beer bar), and teeming with life – brings you back to Szent István körút and the Nagykörút (Great Boulevard) ▲ 164).

GRESHAM PALACE, 'PEACOCK' GATE (left) Beyond the entrance passageway, with its beautiful wrought-iron "peacock" gate, is a huge glass-roofed arcade. Today the building is occupied by a casino.

ART NOUVEAU DETAIL (below) The Art Nouveau building at no. 152 Dózsa György út ▲ 149 (which lies to the north of Újlipótváros) was built in 1911 by the architects Lajos Schodits and Béla Eberling.

GYÖRGY LUKACS (1885–1971, left) In his *Geschichte und Klassenbewußtsein* (History and Class Consciousness, 1923), György (Georg) Lukács stressed the importance of the role played by the revolutionary intelligentsia in awakening the class consciousness of the working classes. He greatly influenced the mainstream of European Communist thought and regarded literature as a vehicle for the artistic representation of reality. In the 1960s the Budapest school of Marxist thought (also known as the Lukács school) became oriented toward 'critical Marxism'.

139

VI. kerület, Terézváros
Andrássy út
25 ←→ 25

1. POSTAL MUSEUM
2. OPERA HOUSE
3. HUNGARIAN BALLET INSTITUTE

ANDRÁSSY ÚT

Budapest's most elegant avenue bears the stamp of wealthy 19th-century imperialism. Designed by Miklós Ybl ● *76*, ▲ *137* and built between 1872 and 1885, Andrássy út links the city center with Heroes' Square (Hősök tere) ▲ *150*, a distance of almost 2 miles. A number of villas reflect the late-19th-century taste for neo-Renaissance, Romantic and eclectic architecture. The sometimes faded charm of these villas and mansions is a source of pleasant nostalgia for Budapesters strolling along this avenue. Originally named Sugárút (Radial Avenue), then Andrássy út, Sztálin út and Népköztársaság útja (Avenue of the People's Republic), today this testimony to imperial

GYULA ANDRÁSSY
(1823–1890) ● *30*

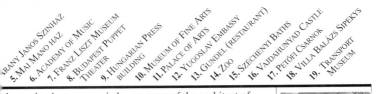

RANY JÁNOS SZÍNHÁZ
5. MAI MANÓ HÁZ
6. ACADEMY OF MUSIC
7. FRANZ LISZT MUSEUM
8. BUDAPEST PUPPET THEATER
9. HUNGARIAN PRESS BUILDING
10. MUSEUM OF FINE ARTS
11. PALACE OF ARTS
12. YUGOSLAV EMBASSY
13. GUNDEL (RESTAURANT)
14. ZOO
15. SZÉCHENYI BATHS
16. VAJDAHUNYAD CASTLE
17. PETŐFI CSARNOK
18. VILLA BALÁZS SIPEKYS
19. TRANSPORT MUSEUM

rban splendor once again bears name of the architect of
ne Austro-Hungarian Compromise of 1867 ● 29. If you
are feeling weary, you can always use the subway (metro)
▲ 117, which has stations dotted at regular intervals
along the entire length of the avenue. Andrássy út
is busy and crowded as far as the Oktogon metro
station, after which it becomes more
sophisticated and more residential.

**FROM BAJCSY-ZSILINZSKY ÚT TO THE
OPERA HOUSE** This part of the avenue
is a busy shopping street with Rococo
façades that conceal beautiful interior
courtyards and other unexpected features.
The extremely well-preserved early-20th-century
apartment block at no. 3 now houses the POSTAL
MUSEUM (Postamúzeum). It is also notable for its
entrance, decorated with frescos by Károly Lotz. The
museum traces the history of Hungary's postal services
and also of the telephone, including a section on
Tivadar Puskás, a colleague of Thomas Edison
at the time the telephone was invented.
The walls of the stairwell are decorated
with splendid frescos. Other courtyards
(nos. 43, 47, 79 and 83–5) are well worth
a visit. The HUNGARIAN STATE OPERA
HOUSE (Magyar Állami Operaház ● 76,
▲ 142), a majestic edifice built between 1873
and 1884, was designed in Italian Renaissance
style by Miklós Ybl, who was strongly influenced
by the Vienna Opera House. The façade has a
triple-arched portico flanked by huge statues of
Franz Liszt and Ferenc Erkel, the first director
of the Opera House ● 49. The first-floor
niches house the muses Terpsichore
(dance), Erato (love poetry),
Thalia (comedy) and Melpomene
(tragedy). At second-floor
level there are statues of
sixteen great European
composers.

THE OPERA
'The grand and
somewhat overly
prestigious Italian-
style Opera House
on Andrássy út
continues to reopen
each season with a
ritual performance
of Erkel's other
masterpiece *Bánk
Bán* (1861).... For
Erkel, torn between
the desire to put an
end to his country's
cultural isolation
and to remain faithful
to a classic national
style, the problem
lay in trying to
reconcile specifically
Hungarian themes,
rhythms and even
instruments with
European operatic
forms.'
Dominique
Fernandez

THE HUNGARIAN STATE OPERA
(Magyar Állami Operaház)

Score by Liszt ● *48*, ▲ *145* for the Hungarian State Opera.

Since the Hungarian State Opera House (Magyar Állami Operaház) opened on September 27, 1884 with a performance of *Bánk Bán* (1861) by Ferenc Erkel, it has been the home of both the Hungarian State Opera and the Hungarian Ballet Institute. A balanced program presents works by Erkel, Bartók and Kodály, as well as Mozart, Verdi and modern opera. Similarly the repertoire of the Ballet Institute includes classics such as Tchaikovsky's *The Nutcracker,* and contemporary ballet.

THE AUDITORIUM
The horseshoe-shaped auditorium, bedecked in gold and purple and crowned by a magnificent ceiling painted by Károly Lotz, can hold 1,285 people. Its excellent acoustics offer some consolation to members of the audience sitting in the third-floor gallery.

THE 'BÜFÉ'
In the interval you can enjoy coffee or champagne in the Büfé (bar), and at the same time meet opera lovers of all ages and from all walks of life. The decor has Bacchanalian imagery: the ceiling is decorated with three scenes by György Vastagh from the life of Dionysus, and there are eight paintings by Árpád Feszty on the walls.

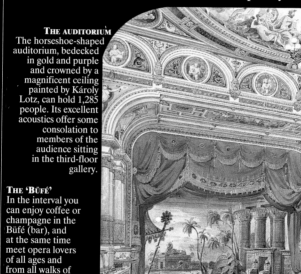

THE ORCHESTRA
The Opera is proud to have one of the oldest orchestras in Hungary. Most of its members belong to the Philharmonic Society, founded in 1853 by Ferenc Erkel ● *49* and Ferenc Doppler. It is also a symphony orchestra in its own right and gives performances with well-known soloists.

TWO COMPETITIONS AND A FESTIVAL
For several years the Budapest Opera House has regularly hosted two prestigious international (dance and operatic) competitions. In August it provides the setting for the city's summer opera festival, *Budafest*.

OPERATIC MEMORIES
A small first-floor museum, situated around the great marble stairway, traces the history of the Opera House through temporary exhibitions based on specific themes – posters, tickets, invitations, private and official letters, manuscripts, autographs, scores, costumes, etc.

Scene from Béla Bartók's *Duke Bluebeard's Castle* (1911) ● 51.

FAMOUS DIRECTORS AND CONDUCTORS
The Hungarian State Opera has had an impressive list of directors, including Ferenc Erkel, Gustav Mahler (right) and Arthur Nikisch. Its list of conductors is no less impressive – among them, Gustav Mahler, Arthur Nikisch, Egisto Tango, Sergio Failoni, Otto Klemperer and János Ferencsik ◆ 282. Each of these marked the golden age of the State Opera House with the stamp of his own individuality.

The ceiling of the auditorium.

FROM THE OPERA HOUSE TO THE ACADEMY OF MUSIC

Opposite the Hungarian State Opera House, at
no. 29 Andrássy út, are the best tearooms in Terézváros.
The CAFÉ MŰVÉSZ ◆ 277 – which translates as 'Café of the
Artists' – is an ideal place to enjoy a drink before an evening
at the opera, or tea and cakes to relieve the monotony of a
wet Sunday afternoon. There are a number of interesting
buildings on this side of the avenue. At no. 25 the DRECHSLER
HOUSE ● 5, designed by Ödön Lechner (1882), is named
after the café that once occupied the ground floor. Today
it is the home of the HUNGARIAN BALLET INSTITUTE ● 54.
You don't have to book in advance to look at the beautiful
entrance hall or watch student rehearsals on the upper floors.
Behind the Ballet Institute, at no. 35 Paulay Ede utca, is
the János Arany Theater (ARANY
JÁNOS SZÍNHÁZ), also known as
the New Theater (ÚJ SZÍNHÁZ)
János Arany (1817–1882,
▲ 187) was one of Hungary's
greatest poets and a friend
of Sándor Petőfi. Back
on Andrássy út, at no. 39,
is the DIVATCSARNOK
department store: its
Secessionist architecture and
the first-floor frescos by Károly
Lotz are a reminder that, when it
was opened in 1911, this was a luxury
store combined with a casino.

NAGYMEZŐ UTCA This street joins Andrássy út at right
angles just above the State Opera House. It is bordered
by theaters – among them, the Microscope
Theater(MIKROSZKÓP SZÍNPAD) and THALIA SZÍNHÁZ –
and a number of cabarets and nightclubs. For this reason
Budapesters refer to it as 'Broadway', but it is a pale
reflection of its New York namesake. It is also the home
of the FŐVÁROSI OPERETTSZÍNHÁZ l 44, where
Hungarians can indulge their passion for
operetta and comic opera.
At no. 20 the beautiful façade of
the HUNGARIAN AUTOMOBILE
CLUB (Magyar Autóklub) is
decorated with sculptures and
glass panels. The building also
houses the Mai Manó ház
photography gallery ● 61.
Above, detail from the façade
of the building.

**ARANY JÁNOS
SZÍNHÁZ**
(Új Színház ● 84)
The theater's
astonishing
Secessionist façade
is decorated with
mosaics, geometric
figures, globes and
statues of monkeys.

The Writers'
Bookshop (Írók
Boltja), at no. 45
Andrássy út
(below).

144

> 'The Liszt Academy is housed in a magnificent building [...].
> The training I received there was difficult and at times harsh, but
> those who survived the experience emerged as real musicians.'
>
> Sir Georg Solti, *Memoirs*

Back on Andrássy út, the glass-fronted WRITERS'
BOOKSHOP (Írók Boltja) at no. 45 occupies the premises of
the former Café Japan, at one time a favorite meeting place
for Budapest's literary set. Inside, everything is designed for
the readers' comfort: armchairs, low tables and a huge tea
urn. Public lectures are held here regularly. As you continue
along this narrow pedestrianized street, where a number of
student cafés have recently opened, you come to a quiet
neighborhood that is pleasant to stroll round.

ACADEMY OF MUSIC (Zeneakadémia) ★ When you reach
Liszt Ferenc tér, you cannot fail to be impressed by the
strains of music drifting from the open windows of the
ACADEMY OF MUSIC – which doubles as concert hall
and conservatory ▲ *146* – and by the architecture of
the building itself. The academy was built between
1904 and 1907 to plans by Flóris Korb and Kálmán
Giergl, and was greatly influenced by the designs of
Ödön Lechner ● *80*. Its eclectic style – a brilliant
combination of neo-Baroque inspiration, neoclassical
nostalgia and seductive Orientalism – is reflected in
the luxurious entrance hall, decorated with frescos
and ceramics from the Zsolnay manufactory ● *69*,
172. On the outside is a huge bronze statue of
Franz Liszt; above it are statues of Gounod and Bizet.
Next to the academy (at the intersection of Nagymező utca
and Király utca) there is an attractive pedestrianized square,
dominated by the Baroque ST ANNE'S CHURCH (Szent Anna
templom).

FROM OKTOGON TÉR TO HŐSÖK TERE Beyond Oktogon
tér ▲ *166*, Andrássy út widens out into an elegant and
sophisticated boulevard, with tree-lined side roads bordered
with villas, mansions and flowers. Near the intersection,
on the left as you walk up the avenue, a plaque at no. 60
recalls that the building was the secret-police headquarters
during the Horthy era ▲ *174* and later under Rákosi's
Stalinist regime. A little further on, you can glimpse
something of Budapest's musical past by visiting the
FRANZ LISZT MUSEUM (Liszt Ferenc Emlékmúzeum) – which
is off to the right, at no. 35 Vörösmarty utca. The pianist
and composer occupied the first floor of this building from
1879 until his death in 1886. As well as personal items
belonging to Liszt (pianos, harmoniums, desks,
portraits, etc.), the museum houses
a small concert hall used by the
students of the Academy of
Music. Nearby, at no. 69, is the
former ACADEMY OF FINE ARTS
(Képzőmüvészeti Főiskola),
built in Italian neo-Renaissance
style by Adolf Láng in 1877, and
the STATE PUPPET THEATER
(Állami Bábszínház). The
theater presents puppet shows
for audiences of all ages and is well
worth a visit. Until recently the LUKACS
KÁVÉHAZ (no. 70) – with its 1930s ground
floor and the Baroque decor of its first floor (a favorite
place for discreet meetings) – was one of the city's most
renowned coffee houses.

**LISZT'S
BÖSENDORFER PIANO**
'I play with my whole
body. Liszt was the
first [pianist] to do
this, and played with
his arms, shoulders
and back. He was the
first to break with the
tradition that limited
movement to the
fingers, which was
the legacy of
the harpsichord.
Ultimately little is

known about his
manner of playing.
Even my music
teacher, who was
himself a pupil of
Liszt, said very little
about it.'
Claudio Arrau

'Unlike Beethoven,
who ignored the
limitations of
physiology and
imposed his
tyrannical will on the
[pianist's] fingers,
Liszt accepted them
and used them for
what they were...'
Camille Saint-Saëns

Metro sign. *Földalatti*
literally means 'under
the earth'.

145

▲ THE ACADEMY OF MUSIC
(Zeneakadémia)

The Hungarian Academy of Music opened on November 14, 1875, at no. 4 Hal tér. Then in the fall of 1879 the academy and its president, Franz Liszt, moved to a new building, on what was then Sugár út (now Andrássy út), where Liszt lived and taught until his death in 1886. That building now houses the Franz Liszt Museum. The present academy building was opened on May 12, 1907; at the same time, the institution was renamed the Franz Liszt Academy of Music (Liszt Ferenc Zeneakadémia) in his honor.

ROTH'S FOUNTAIN
With its gleaming bronze backdrop the mosaic fountain (right) by Miksa Róth is a reminder that the academy was built between 1903 and 1907 (during the reign of the Emperor Franz Joseph) and designed by Flóris Korb and Kálmán Giergl.

'THE FOUNTAIN OF ART'
The entrance hall has a delightfully eclectic decor. In 1901 Aladár Körösfői-Kriesch, who studied under Bertalan Székely and Károly Lotz, went to live in Gödöllő ▲ 240, where, together with Sándor Nagy, he founded the 'Gödöllő School'. His wall painting *The Fountain of Art* (1907), on the first floor of the academy, reflects the influence of the English Pre-Raphaelites and is the product of a technique that sought to revive medieval artistic methods.

THE MAIN AUDITORIUM
This magnificent Secessionist masterpiece combines elegant lines and fineness of detail. Its acoustics make it the best concert hall in Hungary.

lthough remarkable
every respect, the
ecor of this temple
music has one

particularly
outstanding feature:
the greenish-blue and
yellow eosin glaze,

tinged with gold,
from the Zsolnay
manufactory ● 69,
▲ 172 at Pécs.

THE HUBAY QUARTET
[Left to right:
Szerémi, Popper
(cello), Hubay (first
violin), Kemény.]
Between 1886 and
1936 Jenő Hubay
taught the violin at
the Academy of
Music to some of
Hungary's greatest
musicians, among
them József Szigeti,
Stefi Geyer and Jelly
Arányi. He was
director of the
academy from 1919
until his death. Hubay
founded a famous
quartet, and wrote
operas, ballets, and
symphonies inspired
by Hungarian folk
music. In the 1930s
his school produced
such world-class
violinists as Zoltán
Székely, Ede
Zathurecky, Dénes
Koromzay and
Sándor Végh.

Miklós Perényi ◆ 282,
the 'Hungarian
Rostropovich'
(below).

THE TEACHING 'DYNASTY'
The music teaching was placed under
the aegis of great masters: Ferenc
Liszt ● 48 ▲ 145 (piano), Károly
Huber and his son Jenő Hubay
(violin), Hans Koessler (composition
and organ) and David Popper (cello).
They were assisted by István Thomán
and Béla Bartók ● 50 (piano), Zoltán
Kodály ● 50, ▲ 148 (composition and
musical notation), Leó Weiner
(chamber music) and Ernő Dohnányi
(piano), who at that time were less
well known. Their pupils in turn
became teachers at the academy.

KODÁLY CIRCUS (Kodály Körönd) A little further on, Kodály Circus is a masterpiece of architectural symmetry. Four large neo-Renaissance buildings, with beautifully structured balconies and windows, describe a circle around its edge. The rather ponderous statuary of the Circus does not detract from its elegance. The statues represent Miklós Zríny

DETAIL OF KODÁLY KÖRÖND

and György Szondy (heroes of the wars against the Turks), Vak Bottyán (one of the generals of Prince Rákóczi II ● 29, 47) and Bálint Balassi (the great 16th-century lyric poet ● 38). One of the houses (no. 89 Andrássy út) belonged to the composer Zoltán Kodály ● 50, ▲ 218, ◆ 283. The circus is situated in a district of elegant private residences, embassies, political-party headquarters and government ministries.

MANSIONS AND VILLAS It is worth taking a stroll along the smaller streets running parallel and at right angles, on either side of Andrássy út: Lendvay utca (Villa Groedel at no. 29), Délibáb utca, Bajza utca (LEDERER MANSION and SONNENBERG MANSION at nos. 42 and 23) and especially the quiet and elegant Benczúr utca, which is one of the most sought-after residential streets in the capital. Throughout the district, time seems to stand still. At no. 98 Andrássy út the former PALLAVICINI PALACE is a reminder of the dominance of the neo-Renaissance style in 19th-century Pest. In striking contrast is the beautiful Art Nouveau villa (1900) at no. 101 Andrássy út (on the corner of Bajza utca), known as the HUNGARIAN PRESS BUILDING.

THE PALACE OF ARTS (Műcsarnok)
Erected in 1896, the Műcsarnok was designed by Fülöp Herzog and Albert Schickedanz ● 95 in the style of a Greek temple. The pediment is adorned with a colored Byzantine-style fresco depicting Saint Stephen (Szent István) ● 38, ▲ 203 flanked by Saints Gerard (Gellért) ▲ 215 and Margaret (Margit) ▲ 188.

FERENC HOPP MUSEUM OF EAST ASIAN ART (Hopp Ferenc Kelet-Ázsiai Művészeti Múzeum)
As you return to Andrássy út, don't miss this museum at no. 103. The fascinating collections bequeathed to the state by Ferenc Hopp in 1919 include Indonesian puppets, Indian

statues and Tibetan *tanka* (painted banners). The Chinese
and Japanese collections are housed in the nearby RÁTH
GYÖRGY MÚZEUM, which occupies a splendid Art Nouveau
villa at no. 12 VÁROSLIGETI FASOR (formerly Gorky utca), one
of the prettiest streets in the district.

HEROES' SQUARE (Hősök tere) ▲ *150* Andrássy út comes
to an end at the impressive Hősök tere, with its famous
MILLENARY MONUMENT ● *76* built in 1896 to commemorate
the thousandth anniversary of the Magyar conquest of the
Carpathian Basin (*honfoglalás*, the word used by the
Hungarians is slightly ambiguous, meaning 'installation'
or 'conquest'). In the center of the square – which to some
extent symbolizes the triumph of Pest over Buda and of
Hungarian history over the Habsburg influence – stands a
column surmounted by a statue of the Archangel Gabriel.
Around its base are equestrian statues of Árpád and the
other six conquering Magyar chiefs ● *27*. In front of the
column is the Heroes' Monument ▲ *150*, and behind it a
colonnade surmounted by allegorical figures representing
Work and Wealth (on the left), Knowledge and Glory (on
the right), and War and Peace (in the center). The city's
two largest museums – the MUSEUM OF FINE ARTS
(Szépművészeti Múzeum) ★ ▲ *152* and the PALACE OF
ARTS (Műcsarnok) – face each other across the square. The
first, a fine neoclassical building, has a façade decorated with
copies of the sculptures on the Temple of Zeus at Olympia (in
the center is Apollo flanked by the Lapiths and Centaurs).
DÓZSA GYÖRGY ÚT. During the Communist era, Dózsa György
út – the broad avenue that runs along one side of the square –
was the official venue for the May Day celebrations and
military parades. The huge statue of Stalin that stood on the
avenue was pulled down during the 1956 uprising. The
Yugoslav Embassy stands on the corner of Andrássy út
and Dózsa György út, and ironically it was in
this beautiful Art Nouveau
villa that Imre Nagy and
György Lukács sought
refuge during the last
days of the 1956 uprising,
before being handed over to
Soviet troops and secretly
deported to Romania.

**THE MUSEUM OF
FINE ARTS ▲ *152***
The Museum of Fine
Arts was founded in
1896 to commemorate
the thousandth
anniversary of the
foundation of the
Hungarian state.
Designed by Albert
Schickedanz ● *95* and
Fülöp Herzog, it was
completed in
1906.

Villa Egger, 24
Városligeti fasor
(Emil Vidor, 1902).

FOURTEEN HEROES
Statues of fourteen
Hungarian rulers and
princes form a curved
double colonnade in
Heroes' Square:
Stephen I, László I,
Kálmán the Possessor
of Books, András II,
Béla IV, Charles
Robert, Louis the
Great, regent János
Hunyadi, Matthias
Corvinus ● *32*, princes
István Bocskay, Gábor
Bethlen, Imre
Thököly and Ferenc
Rákóczi II, and
regent Lajos Kossuth.

149

▲ Hősök tere : Heroes' Square

Budapest's largest square was designed by Albert Schickedanz ● 95 and György Zala.

Hősök tere is one of the largest and certainly the most symbolic squares in Budapest. It lies at the end of Andrássy út and contains the nation's two most important commemorative monuments: the Millenary Monument and the Heroes' Monument (originally the Tomb of the Unknown Soldier). Since 1896 successive governments have held parades and announced changes here; and it has also been a focus for protest marches, popular demonstrations (May Day) and gatherings, and official ceremonies. But above all, Heroes' Square is a place that reflects the nation's history.

SYMBOL OF A THOUSAND-YEAR-OLD NATION

In the center of the square stands the Millenary Monument, erected in 1896 to commemorate the thousandth anniversary of the foundation of the Hungarian state. Around its base are equestrian statues of Árpád and the other six conquering Magyar chiefs ● 27.

The statues of the seven chiefs surround a monumental column surmounted by the winged figure of the Archangel Gabriel, clutching an Apostolic cross in one hand and, with the other, holding the Hungarian crown above the chiefs. According to tradition, the chiefs chose

Árpád as their leader and his descendants became the first kings of Hungary. In the 1920s the Tomb of the Unknown Soldier was installed at the foot of the statue of Árpád.

SYMBOLS OF A NATION'S HISTORY

Today the square is very different from the one designed by Albert Schickedanz. The fountains and flowers have been replaced by paving decorated with geometric motifs, and the People's Democratic Government replaced the last five statues of the colonnade (five Hungarian kings) with the statues that stand there today.

After World War Two the statues of the Habsburgs were replaced by those of the heroes of Hungarian independence: Rákóczi, Thököly and Kossuth. In the 1950s Habsburg statues were melted down so that monuments could be erected to Stalin and Mátyás Rákosi (although not in Heroes' Square). In October 1956 the crowd overturned the huge statue of Stalin ● *36*.

MAY DAY 1919

The Habsburg statues on the colonnade of the Millenary Monument were removed during Béla Kun's short-lived Council Republic. For May Day of 1919 the colonnade, the statues of the Magyar chiefs and the column were draped in red. The sole decoration on the two great expanses of red was the famous Marxist slogan urging the working classes of Europe to unite.

EUCHARISTIC CONGRESS

The great Roman Catholic demonstrations organized during the interwar years reflected the close association between Catholic and Nationalist ideals.

During the International Eucharistic Congress held in 1938, the colonnade of the Millenary Monument served as a pedestal for the high altar.

NATIONAL FUNERAL

On June 16, 1989 a national funeral service was held on the square in memory of Imre Nagy and other victims of 1956. On August 20, 1991 some 200,000 people heard Pope John Paul II say mass here.

THE MILLENNIAL CELEBRATIONS

Although work began on the square in 1894, it was not opened until 1929. The celebrations, in 1896, to mark the thousandth anniversary of the foundation of the Hungarian state were held in City Park.

The collections of the Museum of Fine Arts are derived from th
Hungarian National Museum's collection of historical portraits,
which became the National Art Gallery and was housed in the
Academy of Sciences. Its nucleus was formed by Count Miklós
Esterházy's private gallery, which he sold to the state in 1870.
The National Gallery was further enriched by donations and
purchases, resulting in the establishment of the Old Masters
Gallery and the Prints and Drawings Room that today form
the core of the Museum of Fine Arts. The Ancient Greek and
Roman collection, extended since 1935, includes works from
the Greek, Etruscan, Roman and Carthaginian civilizations.

The museum's
collection of prints
and drawings includes
some 10,000 drawings
and 100,000 prints.
Many of the
Renaissance and
Baroque works are
from the Esterházy
collection. The works
bequeathed by the
artist István Delhaes
are mainly 18th-
century German and
Austrian prints and
drawings. The
watercolors and
drawings by French
artists (Delacroix,
Manet, Degas) were
bought in Paris by the
ministerial adviser
Pál Majovszky, who
donated them to the
museum in
1934.

**HEAD OF A
WARRIOR**
(Leonardo
da Vinci)

NIOBID
(Greek and Roman collection)The massacre of the Niobids by Apollo and Artemis, and the grief of their mother Niobe, the legendary queen of Phrygia, provided the inspiration for a celebrated sculptural group.

'HORSEMAN'
(Leonardo da Vinci, 1516–19)
This small bronze equestrian statue is the most famous item of sculpture in the museum. It was acquired in Rome around 1820 by the sculptor István Ferenczy and is thought to represent Francis I (king of France 1515–47), Leonardo's last patron.

GREEK CALYX WITH RED FIGURES
(6th century BC)

PORTRAIT OF A MAN
(Egypt, New Kingdom, 19th Dynasty, c. 1200 BC)In 1996 the museum opened the lower-ground-floor rooms devoted to its Egyptian collection. The collection, which includes statues, funerary steles, decorated sarcophagi, statuettes of servants, amulets, scarabs, jewelry and fragments of papyri, reflects many aspects of the Ancient Egyptian civilization.

153

The Danube School flourished during the first thirty years of the German Renaissance (1500–30). Notable artists included Albrecht Altdorfer and Lucas Cranach the Elder, one of the school's founders.

The museum has an impressive Italian collection, which represents all the major schools from the 13th–18th centuries. The German Renaissance (Albrecht Dürer, Hans Baldung Grien) and the 'Danube School' are also represented.

THE 'ESTERHÁZY MADONNA'
(Raphaël, 1508)
Although unfinished, this painting, right, reflects the beauty and harmony achieved at the height of the Italian Renaissance. This was one of the 637 paintings in the Esterházy collection.

PORTRAIT OF A MAN
(Sebastiano del Piombo)
This portrait, below, was painted in Rome c. 1515. The enigmatic expression and the idyllic landscape in the background are reminiscent of the artist's apprenticeship in Vienna, while the sitter's stately bearing attests to the influence of Raphaël.

'ADAM' AND 'EVE'
(Hans Baldung
Grien, 1484–1545)

'PORTRAIT OF A MAN'
(Albrecht Dürer,
1471–1528) (right)

**'THE BETROTHAL OF
SAINT CATHERINE'**
(Lucas Cranach the
Elder, 1516–18)
Saints Catherine,
Margaret, Barbara
and Dorothy are
dressed as ladies
at the court of the
Elector Frederick
the Wise of Saxony,
where Cranach was
employed as court
painter. This painting
was one of a
collection sent in
1770 from the
imperial collection in
Vienna to decorate
the royal apartments
in Bratislava. From
there, it was
transferred to the
Royal Palace in Buda,
where it was
'nationalized' in 1848.

Most of the justifiably renowned Spanish collection was purchased from Lord Edmund Bourke in London between 1818 and 1821 by Pál Esterházy, on behalf of his father Count Miklós Esterházy. The museum's Old Masters Gallery also has a number of 17th-century Dutch landscapes and genre paintings that are acknowledged masterpieces.

'MARY MAGDELENE IN PENITENCE'

(El Greco, 1580) The permanent collection has seven paintings by El Greco. Here the exaggerated proportions and almost unreal colors foreshadow the Mannerism that characterized the mature works of this 'most Spanish' of artists.

'ESTHER AND MORDECAI'
(Aert de Gelder, 1685)

'PEASANTS' REPAST'
(below left)
(Diego Velázquez, 1617–18)
In 1908, two years after the museum was opened, the gallery acquired this youthful work by Velázquez. The simplicity of the gestures, the richly painted contrasts of light and shade, the still life on the table, and the eloquent expressions of the three people sitting round it make this a masterpiece of Spanish genre painting.

'SAINT JOSEPH'S DREAM'
(above)
(Rembrandt van Rijn)

'WOMAN READING A LETTER'
(Pieter de Hooch, 1664)
The artist has depicted the familiar atmosphere of this Dutch middle-class interior with moving realism.

THE MUSEUM OF FINE ARTS

COLLECTIONS OF 19TH-CENTURY AND 20TH-CENTURY ART

The oldest paintings in the museum's modern collections are those by the Austrian artists of the Biedermeier period (1820–40). From 1910, the collections were complemented by a number of French Impressionist paintings and other important works.

'MARY MAGDELENE'
(Pierre Puvis de Chavannes, 1897)

'LADY WITH A FAN'
(Édouard Manet, 1871
The lady in question is Jeanne Duval, mistress of the poet Charles Baudelaire. The painting was acquired by one of the museum's directors, Elek Petrovics, who made a number of equally discerning acquisitions.

'MOTHER AND CHILD'
(Pablo Picasso, c. 1905)
his watercolor belongs to Picasso's 'Rose Period' (1904–6). The artist used pink to express moral and physical deprivation, and blue for his portraits of traveling performers.

'VERONICA'
(Oskar Kokoschka, 1911)
The artist based this expressionist work on medieval iconography showing the saint holding a veil on which the image of Christ's face had miraculously appeared.

French painters from the Romantic to the Post-Impressionist period are well represented in the museum's collection of modern art – among them, Delacroix, Corot, Courbet, Daubigny, Troyon, Manet, Pissarro, Puvis de Chavannes, Cézanne, Monet, Gauguin and Toulouse-Lautrec. Sculptors include Carpeaux, Despiau, Maillol and Rodin.

'BLACK PIGS'
(Paul Gauguin, 1891)
This was one of Gauguin's earliest Tahitian paintings. The museum also has one of his Impressionist works, *Jardin sous la Neige* (1879).

'SIDEBOARD'
(Paul Cézanne)

'CES DAMES'
(Henri de Toulouse-Lautrec, 1894)
This painting was acquired in 1913, at the same time as Gauguin's *Black Pigs*, at an exhibition held at the Ernst Museum in Budapest.

'BLUE VILLAGE'
(Marc Chagall, 1968)

CITY PARK

Like the park on Margaret Island ▲ 187, City Park
(Városliget ■ 22) is one of the city's most popular green
spaces (the two others are Szabadság-hegý and Gellert-Hegý
▲ 215). Designed in the late 19th century as a 'filter' for
the dust from the Central Plain, this haven of peace and
quiet is particularly beautiful in the fall. It is an ideal
place for a Sunday walk and a great favorite with children.
Conveniently situated on the edge of the city, it offers a
number of recreational facilities, including a lake that serves
as a boating lake in summer and an ice rink in winter.
On the shores of the lake, a Rococo building
houses a bar-restaurant that provides changing
facilities for skaters.

ÁLLATKERTI KÖRÚT Situated behind the
Museum of Fine Arts ▲ 149, 152, at no. 3
Állatkerti körút, GUNDEL is one of the
city's best restaurants. Nearby is the
entrance to BUDAPEST ZOO (Állatkert);
and a little further on, the MUNICIPAL
CIRCUS (Fővárosi Nagycirkusz) and
FUN FAIR (Vidám Park). Because of
their relative age (the roller coasters
are made of wood), they are reminiscent of the delightfully
old-fashioned amusement parks of New York's Coney Island.

SZÉCHENYI BATHS (Széchenyi Gyógyfürdő) ★ Still on the
Állatkerti körút, the majestic Széchenyi Baths ● 63 are an
ideal place to relax for an hour or two after a long walk
along Andrássy út. They are easily recognized by their
huge neo-Baroque dome, flanked by equestrian
statues. If you take the
'yellow metro' ▲ 117,
you can get off at the
Széchenyi fürdő
subway
station

ÁLLATKERTI KÖRÚT
This boulevard, built
in 1865 and renovated
in 1907, has some
delightful examples
of Art Nouveau
architecture – such as
the Elephant House
of Budapest Zoo,
which is decorated
with ceramic elephant
heads. Above: the
entrance to the
Elephant House.

n City Park), right in front
f the baths. The south wing, which
ouses the 'medicinal baths', was
uilt in the early 20th century and
as a richly decorated interior
f Art Nouveau mosaics.
he north wing was built
1 1927, in a more modern
eo-Baroque style. This
uge baths complex has
wimming pools, baths
nd saunas. A small flight
f steps leads from the
door to the outdoor pools.

AJDAHUNYAD CASTLE (Vajdahunyad

ára) The castle stands on a little island almost at the
enter of City Park. It was one of the buildings designed
y Ignác Alpár for the thousandth anniversary of the
oundation of the Hungarian state ● *30*, ▲ *150* in 1896.
n the main courtyard, the Romanesque Chapel of Ják is
copy of the 13th-century church at Ják (near Szombathely)
n western Hungary, while the Gothic tower on the right
as inspired by the castle at Segesvár (now Sighisoara) in
ransylvania. Also on the right is the Baroque façade of
e MUSEUM OF AGRICULTURE (Mezőgazdasági Múzeum),
eminiscent of the façade of the castle of the Esterházy
amily near Sopron. The museum's exhibits include some
plendid wine presses. Opposite the entrance is the famous
tatue of 'ANONYMUS' by Miklós Ligeti (1903). An important
gure in Hungarian history, the 'unknown chronicler' of
he Magyars ● *38* may have been a royal clerk at the court
of Béla III in the 12th century – hence the statue's
inscription, which reads *Gloriosissimi Belae Regis
Notarius* ('Clerk of most glorious King Béla').

161

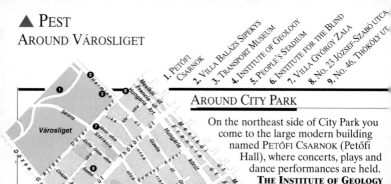

AROUND CITY PARK

On the northeast side of City Park you come to the large modern building named PETŐFI CSARNOK (Petőfi Hall), where concerts, plays and dance performances are held.

THE INSTITUTE OF GEOLOGY (Magyar Földtani Intézet)

★ As you leave the park and turn down Stefánia út, you come to the magnificent Institute of Geology at no. 14. Like the other buildings designed by Ödön Lechner ● *80*, the façade of this masterpiece of Hungarian Secessionist architecture (1897–9) combines Oriental inspiration with the Hungarian ceramic tradition. The symbol of the Institute is the globe supported by three statues that crown its pyramidal roof (opposite page, bottom right). A statue of János Böckh (1840–1909), one of the institute's directors, stands on the corner of Stefánia út and Szabó Jószef utca.

VILLA BALÁZS SIPEKYS ★ This splendid Art Nouveau villa, also designed by Ödön Lechner (1905), lies slightly to the north of the Institute of Geology, at no. 47 Hermina út. Today it houses the Institute for the Blind. The beautiful pink façade has a particularly striking domed verandah.

THE PEOPLE'S STADIUM (Népstadion) ★ Those interested in the 1950s and/or the history of sport during the Communist era can reach the People's Stadium via Dózsa György út. The stadium was built between 1948 and 1953, with a capacity of 100,000. It evokes the golden age of Hungarian football, when the national team (led by the famous no. 11, Ferenc Puskás) twice reached the final of the World Cup. Through Honvéd (the leading army team, based in the working-class district of Kispest ▲ *175*) and Ferencváros (Budapest's other great working-class club ▲ *174*), football served as the 'sports laboratory' of the Communist regime. The 1956 uprising put an end to this golden era: the Honvéd team found itself on the other side of the Iron Curtain when it came to European Cup matches, and many of Hungary's best players left the country. Today the district around the stadium is more or less deserted, especially along Kerepesi út, which lies between the Eastern Railway Station and Kerepesi Cemetery ▲ *170*.

THE PEOPLE'S STADIUM

Fifty years ago the Communist regime built Hungary's largest sporting facility. In the bid to 'bring sport to the people', the army formed its own football team: Honvéd.

In the 1950s, seventy thousand spectators would crowd into the rows of seats to watch Hungary play. It is a long time since the stands echoed to the exploits of Hungarian football.'

Benoît Hopquin, 1998

ART NOUVEAU IN BUDAPEST ● *80, 82*

THE INSTITUTE FOR THE BLIND ★ at no. 39 Ajtósi Dürer sor (bottom left) is one of the most beautiful buildings in District XIV. The work of architects Sándor Baumgarten and Zsigmond Herczegh, it was built in 1907.

1. MARGARET ISLAND
2. HOUSE OF LIGHT
3. VÍG THEATER
4. WESTERN RAILWAY STATION
5. STROZZI PALACE
6. THE GREAT SYNAGOGUE
7. ORTHODOX SYNAGOGUE
8. ROYAL HOTEL
9. MADACH THEATER
10. NEW YORK PAL

The Nagykörút (Great Boulevard) describes a huge semicircle between Margaret Bridge (Margit híd) ▲ *187* and Petőfi Bridge (Petőfi híd) ▲ *174*. It lies to the north of the Kiskörút (Little Boulevard) ▲ *123* and runs parallel to it for almost 2½ miles, like a symbol of the city's late-19th-century expansion. Reminiscent of the Ring in Vienna and the Grand Boulevards of Paris, the Nagykörút was opened in 1896 to commemorate the thousandth anniversary of the foundation of the Hungarian state ▲ *150*. It was a major project that involved the demolition of a great many buildings and the rehabilitation of the run-down districts in the vicinity of Margaret Bridge. The urban planning project gave an overall sense of structure and unity to this part of the city, linking districts that are socially very distinct. The Great Boulevard has five different names: (from north to south) Szent István körút, Teréz körút, Erzsébet körút, József körút and Ferenc körút. Much of the city's night life (theaters ● *42*, cinemas ▲ *168*, cafés ● *56*) is concentrated here .

SZENT ISTVAN KÖRUT Some of the city's best *antikvárium* ▲ *122* are to be found on Szent István körút (the one at no. 3 is famous for its prints and cards). Across the boulevard, on the right, are the antique shops of the Falk Miksa utca.

SZENT ISTVAN KÖRUT

MARGARET BRIDGE (Margit híd) Built by the French architect Ernest Gouin (1872–6), Margit híd marks the beginning of Szent István körút. Below JÁSZAI MARI TÉR the façades of the buildings bordering the boulevard have some interesting architectural features, both eclectic (atlantes and reliefs) and Art Nouveau (the former HOUSE OF LIGHT, at nos. 10–12). The VÍGSZÍNHÁZ (Víg Theater or Comedy Theater) ● *42*, at no. 14, built by the Viennese company Fellner & Helmer and opened in 1896, was for a long time the 'temple' of operetta ● *44* and comedy. Since its renovation in 1996 it has been offering a more international program, with Viennese operettas being largely replaced by (predominantly American) musicals.

NYUGATI TÉR The WESTERN RAILWAY STATION (Nyugati Pályaudvar) ★ stands on Nyugati tér. The square is also bordered by the SKÁLA METRO department stores, which introduced the consumer society to Budapest in the 1970s and 1980s. Today this is a fairly ordinary shopping district.

The Western Railway Station (Nyugati Pályaudvar) was built on the site of Pest's earliest railway station, from where the first train left for Vác on July 15, 1846. It stands on Nyugati tér and, in spite of its name, links the capital to north and east Hungary. It is, above all, renowned for its steel, brick and glass architecture. Although it has been extensively renovated, the splendid iron framework of the central concourse has been retained.

BUILT BY EIFFEL
This magnificent station was built in 1874–7 under the direction of Auguste de Serres on behalf of Gustave Eiffel's company.

THE AGE OF THE RAILWAY
Between 1890 and 1914, under the Austro-Hungarian Empire, Hungary experienced a transport revolution: some 6,850 miles of railroad track (almost half the national network) were laid. The development of the railway network and shipping on the Danube were the result of the policies of Gábor Baross, minister for public works and communications (1886–9), whose name can be seen on streets and squares throughout Hungary.

'VIRIBUS UNITIS'
This inscription, engraved on a marble lintel in the main concourse, marks the entrance to the former royal waiting room (now bricked up).

FAST FOOD, HIGH STYLE
In the 1990s a fast-food restaurant was opened in the former railway buffet, to the right of the main entrance. It has retained the original decor – the stuccowork, frescos, old lamp fittings and huge bay windows have all been left intact.

**'PESTI MÜSOR' AND
'PESTI EST'**
▲ 253, 257
These two
publications, which
come out every
Wednesday, provide
information about
Budapest's artistic
and cultural events.
Cinema and concert
programs appear
under the headings
Mozi and *Zene*
respectively.

**INTERIOR OF THE
GREAT SYNAGOGUE**
(holy ark)
The old Jewish
quarter evokes
a world that has
almost disappeared:
70 percent of the
city's Jewish
community perished
in the 1940s, and
only twenty of the
110 synagogues
that existed before
World War Two
have survived.
Today Hungary's
Jewish community
(almost 300,000) is
still the largest in
Central Europe.

TERÉZ KÖRÚT

Beyond
the railway
station, Teréz
körút (the
section of
Nagykörút
named after
Maria
Theresa) takes
you past the JÁTÉKSZÍN
THEATER, at no. 48, and
a fine neo-Renaissance
mansion (Alajos
Hauszmann, 1884),
modeled on the Palazzo
Strozzi in Florence, at no. 67.
The building at no. 33 has a
magnificent interior courtyard.
OKTOGON TÉR Oktogon tér, with its
fast-food restaurants, banks, newspaper kiosks and florists'
stands, lies at the intersection of Nagykörút and Andrássy út
▲ 145. Below the square, the boulevard becomes Erzsébet
körút.

ERZSÉBET KÖRÚT AND THE ZSIDO NEGYED

This section of the boulevard (Erzsébet körút) is named after
Queen Elizabeth ● 30, ▲ 182, 240, the wife of Emperor
Franz Joseph. It passes through Erzsébetváros ('Elizabeth
town'), one of the city's most densely populated districts. It is
also one of the busiest, with its cinemas ▲ 168, cafés and
small shops, both in the courtyards and on the upper floors of
the buildings. To the south of the boulevard is the old Jewish
quarter (Zsidó negyed) whose beauty and melancholy make it
one of the capital's most attractive districts.

THE GREAT SYNAGOGUE (zsinagóga)★
Europe's largest synagogue ● 78, at
nos. 2–8 Dohány utca, can hold up to
3,000 people. After a long period of
work, it has now been completely
restored. The three-story edifice,
designed by the Viennese architect
Ludwig Förster, was built between
1854 and 1859. It is characterized by
a mixture of Byzantine and Moorish
architectural elements, including two
spectacular onion-shaped domes. Its
huge capacity was justified by the size
of the Jewish community, which before
World War Two represented 25 percent
of the city's population. Beyond the
synagogue stands the HEROES' TEMPLE
(Hősök temploma), designed by Ferenc
Faragó and László Vágó (1929–31), a
memorial to Hungary's Jewish soldiers
killed in World War One.

Outside, a commemorative plaque indicates that Theodor Herzl (1860–1904), the founder of modern Zionism and author of *The Jewish State* (1896), was born in a house adjoining the synagogue. In the outer courtyard is a large HOLOCAUST MEMORIAL (Imre Varga, 1991), bearing the names of thousands of holocaust victims.

KIRÁLY UTCA The streets adjacent to the Great Synagogue (Király utca, Dob utca and Wesselényi utca) form the heart of the old Jewish quarter and conceal some of Budapest's most enchanting secrets: terraced courtyards planted with acacias, balconies with decorative ironwork, marvelous archways, and some truly delightful public squares. There are splendid courtyards at nos. 20, 25, 26, 27 and 28 Király utca; and no. 20 Dohány utca has an extremely elaborate courtyard and stairwell. The district also has some of the city's most intriguing passageways. For example, the GOZSDU COURTYARD – which runs between no. 16 Király utca and no. 11 Dob utca – consists of a series of interconnected courtyards and internal galleries, enlivened by fascinating craft workshops. At no. 29 Kazinczy utca are the ORTHODOX SYNAGOGUE and the strictly kosher HANNAH restaurant (entrance at no. 35 Dob utca). Another synagogue (1872), with Moorish-style architecture, stands at no. 11 Rumbach Sebestyén utca. On the corner of Dob utca and Rumbach Sebestyén utca is a striking Secessionist mansion, designed by László and József Vágó, with colored-ceramic wall panels. KLAUZÁL TÉR, a haven of quiet in the busy city center, is a good place to pause for a rest – and to visit one of the old kosher patisseries (for example, the one at no. 22 Dob utca).

ÁRKÁD BAZÁR (Dohány utca 22–24) Designed by László and József Vágó, this department store was built in 1908–9 in a mixture of the Secessionist and Modern styles. The nuts and bolts that, at first glance, appear to be holding together the white ceramic tiles of the east façades are in fact decorative bosses.

ERZSÉBET KÖRUT

Erzsébet körút is bordered by many of the city's theaters and cinemas. Among the most popular cinemas are the HORIZONT (no. 13) and the HUNNIA (no. 26). The MADÁCH SZÍNHÁZ, at nos. 31–3, is a theater with a reputation for presenting successful musicals and reviews ● *42*.

NEW YORK PALACE A little further on (on the left, at nos. 9–11) stands the New York Palace (1891–5) ● *77*, built as the offices of an American insurance company by architect Alajos Hauszmann, in eclectic style with a neo-Renaissance façade. On the ground floor is the legendary CAFÉ NEW YORK, a popular meeting place among the early-20th-century left-wing intelligentsia who produced *Nyugat* ('The West') ● *57*. The journalists of the literary review *2000* also held their editorial meetings here. The magnificent interior, with its twisted Rococo columns, velvet hangings and Art Deco chandeliers, occupies two floors. Today the café is a major tourist attraction, with the inevitable gypsy music and insistent waiters, etc. All that remains of its glorious past is the array of caricatures depicting the left-wing intellectuals who once met at the café.

THE NATIONAL JEWISH MUSEUM (Országos Zsidó Múzeum) The museum is on Wesselényi utca, just behind the Great Synagogue. Exhibits include items from Jewish religious history and photographs of the 1944 ghetto ● *30*. It has a section dedicated to the victims of the Holocaust.

▲ BUDAPEST, CAPITAL OF THE HUNGARIAN CINEMA

Peter Lorre in *Remorse*, by Josef von Sternberg.

Paradoxically, Hungarian cinema gained recognition through the Hungarian exiles who made a name for themselves in Hollywood, such as directors Alexander Korda and Michael Curtiz, actors Peter Lorre and Béla Lugosi. However, although among the most talented in Europe, Hungarian cinema was not fully appreciated until the 1960s. Having enjoyed its golden age in the 1960s and 1970s, Hungary – like so many other countries in Eastern Europe – is now finding it difficult to adjust to the antidotes to austerity imposed since 1989 which has meant few films produced and few international successes. However, the close relationship between Budapest and its cinemas has survived the changes. In addition, these splendid buildings continue to serve as places for a sociable or solitary drink or for a quiet read.

ÖRÖKMOZGÓ FILMMÚZEUM

Many of Budapest's cinemas have a bookstore or café, or both. The Örökmozgó, linked to the Hungarian Film Institute, is a favorite with the city's film buffs. It presents carefully selected top-quality films and organizes numerous foreign-film festivals. In the evening you can go there to buy a magazine, or to enjoy a drink or read the daily papers in its studious yet relaxed atmosphere.

CORVIN CINEMA

When it was opened in 1923, with a seating capacity of 1,200 the Corvin ▲ *174* was the city's largest cinema. Today it has been completely renovated and is a multi-screen complex. As well as its six cinemas, it has a very pleasant café and a gallery; and you can buy videos there. The Corvin was the first of a new generation of cinemas in Budapest.

Left: publicity for Robert Capa's *Monsieur Verdoux* (1947) – 'Charlie Chaplin's latest film'.

Below: a scene from Miklós Jancsó's *The Round-Up* (1965).

Left: a scene from István Szabó's *Colonel Redl* (1985). Right: Béla Lugosi in *Dracula* (1927).

A MASTERPIECE OF HUNGARIAN CINEMA

The Béla Balázs Studio was founded in 1958 to provide a means of expression for a new generation of Hungarian film directors: Judit Elek, István Gaal, Pál Gábor and István Szabó. Szabó's *Mephisto* (1980) was internationally acclaimed and received an Oscar for the best foreign film.

AN OPPRESSIVE DESTINY

Miklós Jancsó's *The Round-Up* (1965) portrays rebels crushed by the oppressive machinery of power. Károly Makk's *Love* (1971) tells the poignant story of a woman and her dying mother-in-law, who are gradually destroyed as they wait for the man they love to be released from prison. Its pessimistic yet lyrical treatment of 'destiny' is typical of Hungarian cinema.

Below: Márta Mészáros *Intimate Journal* (1982), also known as *Diary for my Children.*

THE POST-COMMUNIST ERA

Sweet Emma, Dear Böbe (István Szabó, 1992)
Bolshe Vita (Ibolya Fekete, 1998)

These two films set out to express the problems of the post-Communist era. István Szabó's chosen theme was the awkward metamorphosis of teachers of Russian, who 'recycled' themselves as teachers of English in an attempt to adapt to the new situation. His intimate chronicle of everyday life provides a disillusioned and deeply moving account of life in Budapest. Ibolya Fekete's *Bolshe Vita* (above) adopts a more cheerful but nonetheless realistic approach to the difficult integration of Russian immigrants marooned in the city, ostensibly waiting for visas to the West.

WORLDS APART
József körút bisects Józsefváros ('Joseph town') – the district named after Emperor Joseph II – both geographically and socially. While the Hungarian National Museum and Kálvin tér ▲ *123* are situated in a quiet middle-class neighborhood to the west of the boulevard, Rákóczi tér (to the east) lies in a working-class 'red-light' district, poignantly described by Giorgio and Nicolà Pressburger in their Homage to the Eighth District. The streets, some of which have dilapidated façades, provided the setting for a number of clashes during the 1956 uprising.

BLAHA LUJZA TÉR This busy, noisy square is one of the city's major intersections. It is dominated by huge concrete apartment blocks built in the 1970s. The subway station below the square has become a makeshift market, with unlicensed street vendors, Peruvian musicians, and Transylvanian peasants peddling their wares.

ERKEL THEATER (Erkel Színház) As you turn down Rákóczi út toward the Eastern Railway Station, you come to the Erkel Theater at no. 30 Köztársaság tér (Square of the Republic). The former Communist Party Headquarters, at no. 26, was the scene of bloody clashes during the 1956 uprising ● *36*.

THE EASTERN RAILWAY STATION (Keleti Pályaudvar) The Keleti Pályaudar (1884) – on the north side of the square – is the terminus for all trains traveling to Budapest from the West. Since 1989 it has witnessed the arrival of large numbers of immigrants from Eastern Europe in search of a new life.

KEREPESI CEMETERY (Kerepesi Temető) The Kerepesi Temető, to the south

This photograph showing the Madách Színház and the New York Palace ▲ *167* was taken from József körút.

1. ...RKEL THEATER
2. FORMER COMMUNIST PARTY HEADQUARTERS
3. EASTERN RAILWAY STN
4. KEREPESI CEMETERY
5. COVERED MARKET
6. JÓZSEFVÁROS PARISH CHURCH
7. SZABÓ ERVIN LIBRARY
8. CORVIN CINEMA
9. TRAFÓ
10. MUSEUM OF APPLIED ARTS

f the station, can be reached by tram (no. 23 or 24) along e Fiumei út. Its shady paths and carefully tended lawns ake it a pleasant place in which to walk. As well as being e official burial place for such national heroes as Lajos ossuth ● *35*, Ferenc Deák ▲ *123*, Lajos Batthyány ▲ *207*, ndre Ady and Lujza Blaha, many of the martyrs of the 956 uprising are buried in the northwestern part of the emetery (Division 21). Not far from the Pantheon of the Vorking Class Movement is the tomb of János Kádár ● *37*, e former premier of Hungary and First Secretary of the ungarian Communist Party, whose epitaph reads: 'I lived or Communism and the people'. The Art Nouveau tombs f the Jewish Cemetery (at the eastern end of Kerepesi emető, entrance in Salgótarjáni utca) may be more odest, but they are certainly more beautiful. As you ave the cemetery, retrace your steps to Fiumei út and ake your way across Józsefváros toward the Danube nd the western end of Nagykörút. This will take you to more prosperous and well-cared-for neighborhood.

ÁKÓCZI TÉR The district to the north of ákóczi tér is typical of the working-class istricts of old Budapest, with their large ypsy population. This is the preserve of angsters and prostitutes. It is worth king a walk down the charming old reets that run at right angles to the éri Miksa utca, and discovering VÁSÁR SARNOK, the picturesque covered market behind ákóczi tér. The market, built in 1897, has been enovated recently, after being destroyed by fire. he dilapidated interior courtyards, the old orozó wine bars and the paved streets of this istrict give the impression that you have stepped ack into the past.

ORVATH MIHALY TÉR The square, which lies off ózsef körút on Baross utca, is dominated by the ÓZSEFVÁROS PARISH CHURCH (1797–1814), a fine xample of triumphant Baroque architecture. n front of the church stands the statue of Péter ázmány (1570–1637), the Archbishop of Esztergom who ed the country's Counter-Reformation.

UTENBERG TÉR To the west of Rákóczi tér is the beautiful utenberg tér. There is a splendid Art Nouveau building t no. 4, and the surrounding streets are delightful.

IKSZATH KALMAN TÉR Another tiny square, this is e home of the legendary TILOS AZ-A BAR. During the 990s it presented performances by the cream of the ungarian avant-garde and alternative movements. lthough closed at the time of writing, it is due to be eopened. Meanwhile, there are always the student bars nd the friendly atmosphere of the nearby Krúdy utca. urther west is the more aristocratic neighborhood, with nposing residences, that surrounds the Hungarian lational Museum (Magyar Nemzeti Múzeum) ▲ *124*.

ZABO ERVIN LIBRARY (Szabó Ervin Könyvtár) Though less than pristine condition, the Szabó Ervin Könyvtár at no. 1 Szabó Ervin tér) is well worth a visit. Built in 1887, has a magnificent reading room with remarkable uccowork and mosaics and huge chandeliers.

THE MUSEUM OF APPLIED ARTS ★ (Iparművészeti Múzeum) ▲ *172* This fairy-tale building, near the intersection between Ferenc körút and Üllői út, was one of the first works (1896) of the master of Hungarian Secessionism, Ödön Lechner ● *80*. As you approach it, you are

immediately struck by the dazzling colored roof-tiles and decorated ceramics from the Zsolnay manufactory ● *66*, ▲ *172*. With their traditional and exotic motifs, they reflect the artists' desire to rediscover the Asiatic roots of the Magyar people and create a specifically Hungarian decorative style (*magyaros*) ● *80, 82*.

▲ THE MUSEUM OF APPLIED ARTS
(Iparművészeti Múzeum)

The Museum of Applied Arts was founded in 1872. Its principal promoter was the chief conservator, Jenö Radisics, who instigated the construction of the present building. The building was opened by the Emperor Franz Joseph on October 25, 1896, as part of the celebrations to commemorate the thousandth anniversary of the foundation of the Hungarian state. The museum has five departments: metalwork (including gold and silver), furniture, textiles, ceramics and glassware, and minor collections.

SIDEBOARD
(Endre Thék cabinet makers, Budapest, 1900–6) Among the many items of furniture on display, the Hungarian and French Art Nouveau collections deserve a special mention.

VASE
(Zsolnay manufactory, Pécs, 1899) The Zsolnay manufactory was a family firm founded in 1853 by Vilmos Zsolnay. It became extremely successful in the early 20th century due to the collaboration of numerous artists who created its 3,000 decorations and 4,000 designs ▲ *147*.

VASES ● *66*
(Zsolnay manufactory, Pécs, 1899–1900)

PENDANT (Oszkár Tarján, 1904)
For this silver-and-enamel pendant, the artist drew his inspiration from Japanese art, which was very much in vogue at the time. However, his work also reflects the influence of René Lalique.

'SHIP OF LOVE' PENDANT
(17th century)
The museum has all sorts of metalwork, in gold and silver and other metals. The Esterházy collection includes some extremely valuable pieces, both from Hungary and other countries (especially Germany).

TAPESTRY
(Cassandra, Aladár Körösfői-Kriesch, 1908)
This tapestry, which can be seen in the textiles department, was influenced by the Pre-Raphaelite movement.

COMPOSITION IN GLASS
(Zoltán Bohus, Budapest, 1980)
The department of ceramics and glassware has a wide range of works, from classical and medieval times to contemporary artists, including a remarkable international collection of Art nouveau glassware.

PETŐFI BRIDGE
An earlier bridge, built between 1933 and 1937, was designed by Pál Algyai and named after Miklós Horthy (1868–1957), Hungary's authoritarian regent from 1920 to 1944. The present Petőfi híd, named after the 19th-century poet ▲ *119*, spans the river (some 560 yards) between the southern end of the Nagykörút (Great Boulevard) and the Lágymányos district – once marshland, then the site of a small lake after embankments were built. In 1995 Lágymányos híd, the capital's most recent bridge, was opened to the south of the district. Lágymányos was hoping to host the 1996 World Fair, but the bid failed. However, a new campus for the University's Faculty of Sciences is now being built on the site.

FERENC KÖRUT AND FERENCVÁROS

To the south of Üllői út, the Ferenc Körút runs through the district of Ferencváros ('Francis town'), named after Emperor Francis II, who came to the throne in 1792. The district around Boráros tér and Angyal utca is an extension of the working-class district of Józsefváros ▲ *170*. In the 1950s Ferencváros had the city's most popular football team ▲ *162* – which symbolized the hopes of the city's working classes, especially the Vasas steelworkers. The club still exists today: its stadium is at no. 129 Üllői út.

CORVIN KÖZ This small street, near the intersection of Ferenc Körút and Üllői út, is dominated by the neo-Baroque façade of the Corvin Cinema ▲ *168*, one of Budapest's best-known cinemas.

Another aspect of the district's new cultural dimension is the TRAFÓ (below) ● *43*, recently opened in a former power station at the intersection of Tüzoltó utca and Liliom utca – an echo of the regeneration of disused industrial sites in other parts of Europe. This contemporary arts center, devoted to live performances (both theater and dance), also has a large exhibition hall and a huge basement café run by the former management of the FIATAL MŰVÉSZEK KLUBJA ('Young Performers' Club'), or FMK, which inspired the avant-garde artistic movement of the 1980s.

THE MUSEUM OF APPLIED ARTS (Iparművészeti Múzeum) ★ Back on Üllöi út, the Museum of Applied Arts ▲ *172* is at nos. 33–7, near the intersection with Ferenc körút.

The working-class districts of Újpest, Rákospalota, Kispest, Pesterzsébet, Csepel, Óbuda and Budafok became part of Budapest when the city was being rebuilt in the 1950s. Since then the administratively unified capital has consisted of twenty-three districts (kerület), twelve of which form the outer suburbs. Although areas such as Csepel Island *14, 20* used to be heavily industrial, there are some pleasant surprises – for example, Kőbánya (literally, 'stone quarry') in District X and Kispest in District XIX.

KŐBÁNYA

Actively worked from the 17th to the 19th century, to extract stone for building the city's houses, Kőbánya's underground quarrying galleries are now used for producing mushrooms and beer.

NEW MUNICIPAL CEMETERY (Új Köztemető) The no. 95 bus (from Baross tér) or the no. 28 tram (from Blaha Lujza tér) will take you to the Új Köztemető. This is where Imre Nagy ● *36, 37*, prime minister at the time of the 1956 uprising, was buried anonymously with a number of his colleagues (plots 300 and 301). After the national funeral service ● *31*, ▲ *151* held in June 1989, a memorial was erected to the martyrs of 1956. In the northeastern section of the cemetery is the JEWISH CEMETERY, which has many extremely beautiful, though neglected, tombs. It can be reached, via Kozma utca, from the no. 37 tram terminus.

> 'He [Ödön Lechner] used new materials, such as pyrogranite, glass, steel and ceramics, and made extensive use of the most unusual decorations.'
>
> Dominique Fernandez

KISPEST

FLEA MARKET (Ecseri Piac) The city's main flea market (Ecseri Piac), at no. 154 Nagykőrösi út, is well worth a visit (catch a no. 54 bus from Boráros tér). It is one of the largest flea markets in Central Europe and, although less picturesque than the one at Pécs, has a wide variety of stalls. You will find absolutely everything, including beautiful Transylvanian vases and, with luck, paintings on glass (the Central European equivalent of religious icons, but with more restrained and sometimes naïve designs). In winter you can buy hot wine flavored with cinnamon, which helps produce a very friendly atmosphere.

THE WEKERLE HOUSING ESTATE (Wekerletelep) ★ ▲ *176* To reach this remarkable housing estate, situated near the flea market, take the metro to the 'Határ út' subway station and from there turn down Pannonia utca to Kós Károly tér. Conceived from the outset as a major garden-city project, the Wekerletelep was instigated by and named after Sándor Wekerle (prime minister 1892–95 and 1917–18).

ENTRANCE TO THE SCHMIDL TOMB The crypt of the Schmidl family (near the cemetery gates on Kozma utca) is decorated with Art Nouveau ceramics and mosaics (1903), the result of a collaboration between Ödön Lechner ● *80* and Béla Lajta ● *82, 83*.

▲ THE WEKERLE HOUSING ESTATE
(Wekerletelep)

This garden city was built by architect Károly Kós in the village of Kispest, mainly between 1909 and 1929, in order to house some 20,000 manual workers and administrative employees. Today it is still a self-contained entity, despite becoming part of Budapest when the outer suburbs were officially incorporated into the capital in 1949. At first glance, the distinctive geometric layout of the Wekerletelep looks rather like a tapestry design. In spite of the simplicity of the urban planning, the architecture – the work of fifteen architects selected by means of a competition – is extremely interesting.

KÁROLY KÓS (1883–1977)

Károly Kós was born in the Bánát region (now in Romania) and was one of the first

became the tireless promoter of the 'Transylvanian School' of architecture,

architects to develop a modern style of architecture based on Hungarian history, legends and folklore. When the Treaty of Trianon (1920) gave Transylvania to Romania, Kós left for the Transylvanian capital of Kobozsvár, now called Cluj in Romanian, where he

which sought to emphasize the region's multiculturalism. At the same time, he devoted himself to recording the cultural heritage of Transylvania (Hungarian, Romanian and Saxon village life, costume, and peasant customs and traditions),

arguing that 'We should ensure that our souls are deeply rooted in the soil on which we wish to build.'

A VILLAGE WITHIN A CITY
Four Transylvanian-style porchways give access to a central square. The estate was designed to house those who had come to work in the city, and provide all the services they required for their everyday lives. The tenants were all given their own individual gardens, arranged around the apartment buildings. Today the estate still conveys the impression of a small self-contained, self-sufficient village, in a peaceful setting of trim, domesticated greenery. This theme is reflected by the statue, depicting Károly Kós taming a monster, that stands in the central square.

THE DANUBE,
BANKS AND BRIDGES
Miklós Mátyássy

The Zero Kilometer Stone
on Clark Ádám tér
▲ 183, 206.

Budapest's first stone bridge was built by the Romans to lir
the town of Aquincum with the fort of Trans-Aquincum ▲ 22'
It stood some 300 yards north of the present Árpád Bridg

After flowing past Szentendre Island, the Danube flows through Budapest for a distance of 17 miles, during which its width varies between 400 and 600 yards. Since Roman times the river has been a main communications route, and Budapest is often regarded as its principal city. This is probably because the Danube has always dominated and molded the site of the city and, directly or indirectly, affected the lives of its inhabitants. Indeed, the collapse of the Communist regime began with protests against the series of hydroelectric dams known as the 'Dunosaur', part of which was due to be built at Nagymaros, just under 40 miles upstream from Budapest.

CROSSING THE DANUBE
Before Chain Bridge (Lánchíd) was opened in 1849, the river crossing had to be made by rowing boat, ferry or pontoon; or, in winter, across the river's frozen surface. This was how the Mongols reached Transdanubia in 1241, and how Matthias Corvinus ● 32 crossed the river for his coronation. From 1891, crossing the ice was prohibited.

> 'Budapest feels like a capital – it has the majestic and imposing air of a city playing a key role in history.'
>
> Claudio Magris

REGULATING THE DANUBE

The construction of bridges made hazardous crossings unnecessary. The disastrous floods of March 1838 highlighted the need to regulate the course of the river as it flowed through the city. To prevent ice from forming, several of the islands were linked to the banks and to Margaret Island; in order to contain the river, quays were built on either side; and its width was standardized. The engineer Pál Vásárhelyi was a prominent patriot and a tireless advocate of regulation. His colleague Ferenc Reitter suggested converting the backwater on the Pest side into a navigable Venetian-style canal. However, his suggestion was ignored, and in 1871 the Nagykörút (Great Boulevard) was built instead.

THE EBB AND FLOW OF FORTUNE

When World War Two reached Budapest, in 1944, the Danube provided the setting for a number of atrocities. Jews were shot right into the river; hotels and apartment blocks were bombed; and bridges (including Chain Bridge, above) destroyed by the retreating German army. The Danube and its banks were gradually rebuilt and eventually restored to their former glory. They are now classified as a UNESCO World Heritage Site.

BATHING, BANKS AND BRIDGES

The building work on the bridges, apartment blocks and hotels of Pest did not prevent postwar Budapesters bathing in the famous Danube Baths (Duna fürdő), a section of the river enclosed by huge nets. The banks were given paved quaysides and steps (greatly appreciated by fishermen and schoolchildren playing truant), which become submerged at high water. Finally, the two sides of the river were linked by new bridges.

Left: Chain Bridge and Margaret Bridge (Margit Híd).

179

▲ FREEDOM BRIDGE TO ELIZABETH BRIDGE

1. PETŐFI BRIDGE
2. FREEDOM BRIDGE
3. ELIZABETH BRIDGE
4. CHAIN BRIDGE
5. MARGARET BRIDGE
6. ÁRPÁD BRIDGE

THE 'TURULS' ON THE TOWERS
Freedom Bridge (Szabadság híd), with its elaborate decorations, and four towers, reflects the spirit of 1896, the thousandth anniversary of the founding of the Hungarian state ▲ 150. This is why each tower is surmounted by a *Turul*, the mythical bird said to have guided Árpád ● 27 across the Carpathian Mountains.

HOTEL GELLÉRT AND GELLÉRT BATHS

FREEDOM BRIDGE

BUDAPEST UNIVERSITY OF ECONOMICS (Fővám tér) This 185-yard-long building, designed by Miklós Ybl ● 76, ▼ 136 in neo-Renaissance style, was built in 1871-4, is graced by colonnaded porticos, statues of Greek gods, and allegorical images of the virtues and trades. In 1948 the former Customs Office became the Karl Marx University, and that name was retained until 1990. The university still has a large statue of Karl Marx in the entrance hall.

FREEDOM BRIDGE (Szabadság híd)

This bridge was built between 1894 and 1896 by János Feketeházy and Aurél Czekelius. The decorative details were the work of Virgil Nagy, a lecturer at the nearby Technical University; his enameled blazon (below) of the kingdom of Hungary (the combined arms of Hungary and its various territories) is surmounted by the Hungarian crown. The bridge was opened on the Pest side of the Danube in the presence of the Emperor Franz Joseph. Originally known as the Franz Joseph Bridge, it retained that name for the next fifty years. Destroyed by the Germans in 1945, it was rebuilt in 1946 and renamed Freedom Bridge.

his unpretentious
onastery, built in
32, was designed by
ároly Weichinger,
mbining Modern
d Hungarian neo-
omanesque styles.
ogether with the
ave Church ▲ 216,
djacent to it, it
elongs to the
auline monks.
plaque in the

Polish Chapel honors the memory of the Polish refugees who sheltered there in the 1940s. In 1951 the church was boarded up and the Pauline Order (the only Hungarian order) proscribed. In 1990 the Paulines reopened the church and monastery.

The Rudas Baths (Rudas Gyógyfürdő és Uszoda), which have existed since the 15th century, enjoyed their golden age under Hungary's Turkish rulers. The magnificent octagonal Turkish bath house (*hammam*), with columns supporting

the central dome, was built between 1560 and 1570 by Pasha Mustapha Sokoli. The complex also has a covered swimming pool and steam baths. Today the baths are a popular meeting place and have a drinks stand and newspaper kiosk in the entrance hall.

LIBERATION MONUMENT

CITADEL

GELLÉRT HILL

RUDAS BATHS

ELIZABETH BRIDGE

STATUE OF SAINT GELLÉRT

STATUE OF THE EMPRESS ELIZ.

BELVÁROS

INNER CITY PARISH CHURCH

Joseph Bridge (now Freedom Bridge). Its span (over 300 yards) made it the largest chain bridge in the world until 1926.

The first Elizabeth Bridge (above) was built between 1897 and 1903 by the architect and one of the engineers who built the Franz

ELIZABETH BRIDGE (Erzsébet híd)
The present suspension bridge, designed by Pál Sávoly, was opened in 1964. All that remains of the original Erzsébet híd, which was destroyed in 1945, are its name (commemorating the Empress Elizabeth ▲ 182, 240, the great protectress of the Hungarian people), its two piers and its elegance.

ELIZABETH, QUEEN OF HUNGARY

The statue of the Empress Elizabeth (1837–98) ● 30, ▲ 240 by sculptor György Zala (1937) originally stood in Pest. It managed to survive World War Two, but was removed in 1947. Forty years later it reappeared in Buda, where it stands today (on tiny Döbrentei tér), surrounded by the access roads to Elizabeth Bridge.

THE VÁRKERT KIOSZK AND BAZÁR

The neo-Renaissance Várkert (Castle Garden) Kioszk and Bazár were designed by architect Miklós Ybl ● 76, whose statue stands in the palace gardens on Ybl Miklós tér. The Kiosk was built between 1874 and 1879 to house the pumping station for the palace water supply. It has since been restored (right) and is now a casino and restaurant. An arcade (the Várkert Bazár) and stairway lead to the palace gardens, laid out between 1875 and 1882 with pavilions, terraces, columns and statues. The gardens are bounded by arcades and an apartment block.

STATUE OF THE EMPRESS ELIZABETH — DÖBRENTEI TÉR — TABÁN PARISH CHURCH — CASINO

INNER CITY PARISH CHURCH — MÁRCIUS 15 TÉR — STATUE OF SÁNDOR PETŐFI — ORTHODOX CHURCH — MARRIOTT HOTEL

DANUBE CORSO ▼ 118

Today the Duna korzó is bordered by the Marriott, Forum and Atrium Hyatt hotels, which stand on the site of their legendary predecessors – the Hungária, Bristol, Carlton and Ritz – built in the early 20th century. These vanished symbols of luxury, with their unique view of the Danube and the Royal Palace, were a favorite meeting place with the city's young smart set. The Bristol, the only one of these great luxury hotels to survive the bombing of World War Two, was demolished in the 1970s to make way for the Marriott.

Right: detail of the Pest Vigadó ● 79, ▼ 118.

ADAM CLARK

Chain Bridge (Széchenyi lánchíd) ● 74, ▲ 184 is the oldest of Budapest's bridges. Designed by English engineer William Tierney Clark, it was built between 1839 and 1849 under the direction of the Scottish engineer Adam Clark (right), who was brought to Hungary by Count István Széchenyi ● 35, ▲ 185.

ENTRANCE TO PALACE GARDENS

ROYAL PALACE

NATIONAL GALLERY

BUDA CASTLE FUNICULAR

TURUL BIRD

PEST VIGADÓ

FORUM HOTEL

ATRIUM-HYATT HOTEL

ROOSEVELT TÉR

CHAIN BRIDGE

THE GUARDIANS OF CHAIN BRIDGE ● 74

A pair of lions stand guard at either end of Chain Bridge. It is often claimed that the sculptor, János Marschalkó, depicted these fearsome creatures without tongues. In fact their tongues can only be seen from the front (which in no way detracts from their monumental quality). In 1867 the Emperor Franz Joseph took a solemn oath at the foot of the bridge in Pest, before crossing into Buda to be crowned King of Hungary in the Castle District.

Chain Bridge was nearly never completed. In spring 1849, as the imperial troops retreated before the advancing Hungarian army, the Austrian commander General Hentzi would have blown it up if Adam Clark had not flooded the chambers containing the explosives. During World War Two the bridge was less fortunate: it was destroyed in 1945. Rebuilt, it reopened in 1949, a hundred years after the original inauguration.

CASTLE HILL TUNNEL ● *35*, ▲ *206*. The neo-classical entrance of the Castle Hill Tunnel (Alagút), built by Adam Clark, adds the finishing touch to this harmonious complex.

'DRAWING THE DANUBE'

On the quayside, in front of a neo-Renaissance building designed by Miklós Yb (soon to be renovated), an unusual object catches the eye. Behind the window of a cast iron casing, a needle traces a line on paper with a scale marked on it. It is in fact a recording instrument, which monitors the water level of the Danube. Each week in the early 1990s the film director and conceptual artist Gábor Császári replaced the paper with the work of a different artist, on which the needle 'drew the Danube'.

CHAIN BRIDGE · SÁNDOR PALACE · CASTLE THEATER · BATTHYÁNY PALACE · BEM RAKPART · FRENCH INSTITUTE · FISHERMEN'S BASTION · MATHIAS CHUR

GRESHAM PALACE · ST STEPHEN'S BASILICA · ARANY JÁNOS UTCA · SZÉCHENYI RAKPART · SZÉCHENYI UTCA · IMRE UTCA

GRESHAM PALACE ● *80, 82*, ▲ *138* AND **CHAIN BRIDGE** (Lánchíd)

THE PRESENCE OF THE RIVER
The Danube is very much in evidence throughout Budapest, and the names of certain districts are associated with water. For example, one of the most picturesque districts in Buda – called Víziváros (Watertown) ▲ 206, while Vizafogó ('víza catcher') – to the north of the Újlipótváros district ▲ 138, in Pest – is named after an impressive fish from the Black Sea, which before the regulation of the Danube was the delight of Budapest's fishermen.

HILTON HOTEL

CALVINIST CHURCH

LUTHERAN CHURCH

NATIONAL ARCHIVES

ST ANNE'S CHURCH

BATTHYÁNY SQUARE

I. KER.
BATTHYÁNY
TÉR

ZOLTÁN UTCA

GARIBALDI UTCA

PARLIAMENT

COUNT ISTVÁN SZÉCHENYI
(1791–1860) ● 35 ▼ 136, 213
'Széchenyi, whose many philanthropic works included Chain Bridge, the first bridge across the Danube, shot himself in the head when the clinic for nervous illnesses, where he frantically wrote his various manifestos, threatened to send him to a lunatic asylum.'
Renaud Camus

RIVER TRAFFIC
The Danube still carries a great deal of river traffic – including tugs, ice-breakers, *vízbusz* ('water buses'), and the Budapest–Vienna hover link. Ukrainian and Russian river steamers dock in the city center, while seagoing vessels put in at the free port of Csepel, to the south of the city.

MARGARET BRIDGE (Margit híd)
The two sections of Margaret Bridge span the two branches of the Danube and meet at the southern tip of Margaret Island. Like the Western Railway Station ▲ 165, the bridge was a French project.

MARGARET BRIDGE AND THE TWIN TOWERS OF ST ANNE'S CHURCH
● 70, ▲ 207 The bridge was built between 1872 and 1876 by the engineer Ernest Gouin and a French construction company.

CHURCH OF THE ST ELIZABETH NUNS — IMRE NAGY TÉR — MILITARY TRIBUNAL — KIRÁLY BAT...

MINISTRY OF AGRICULTURE — PARLIAMENT — ETHNOGRAPHICAL MUSEUM — STATUE OF MIHÁLY KÁROLYI — SZÉCHENYI RAKPART

'Pest'
I was born in Pest on the banks of our beautiful river./ I have the rich, fresh colors of the map before me./ Its sky is broken by the clouds and hills,/ Beyond them, the sun sinks below the horizon.
János Arany

MARGARET BRIDGE: A VICTIM OF HISTORY
An attempt to blow up the bridge during World War Two tragically echoed the *inauguration of the Bridge*, one of the *balladd* of the poet János Arany (1817–82), in which he described a series of suicides. The bridge had been mined by the Germans and the charges were accidentally detonated during the rush hour in November 1944, with the loss of six hundred lives. The bridge was finally destroyed by the Germans in 1945, and rebuilt after the war. Eleven years later the student protest march in October 1956 ● 36 crossed Margaret Bridge on its way from the statue of General Bem ▼ 119 to Parliament.

he Romans built
ortifications and
llas on Margaret
sland. In the Middle
ges the Franciscans,
ominicans and
remonstratensians
uilt churches and
onvents, while the
rchbishop of
sztergom and the
nights of the Order
f St John built
ortified castles at the
north and south ends
of the island. After
the 13th-century
Mongol invasion
Margit, the nine-year-
old daughter of Béla
IV and the Byzantine
princess Maria
Lascaris, was sent to
the island that now
bears her name to be
brought up as a nun.
She died there twenty
years later. During
the Turkish
occupation the
churches and
convents were
destroyed. The island
then remained
deserted until 1796,
when the Palatine
Archduke Joseph of
Habsburg ● 34 chose
the island as the site
for a villa, surrounded
by a vast English-style
garden.

The sirens that
decorate the piers of
Margaret Bridge are
the work of the
French sculptor
Thabart.

FLÓRIÁN CHAPEL

BEM RAKPART

STATUE OF GENERAL BEM

PRZEMYSL MEMORIAL

MARGARET BRIDGE

THE 'WHITE HOUSE'

JÁSZAI MARI TÉR

▲ A HEALTH RESORT

In 1867 a mineral
spring was discovered
with medicinal
properties that made
it possible to build a
spa complex on the
island. The water was
bottled as Margaret
Island mineral water
(Margitszigeti
Ásványvíz) and
became a feature of
Hungarian dinner
tables. In 1900 the
island was linked to
Margaret Bridge,
which made it
accessible to
pedestrians and
motor vehicles; and
its popularity as a
public park has
increased since 1950,
when the Árpád
Bridge was opened at
the north end of the
island. With its
Olympic-size
swimming pool,
boathouses, tennis
courts and Palatinus
Baths ▲ 188, it is also
the capital's most
popular sports center.

▲ A LITERARY RETREAT

During the second
half of the 19th
century Margaret
Island was a
favorite haunt of
the poet János
Arany (left),
who dedicated
several poems
to its ancient
oak trees. Other
writers – Gyula
Krúdy, Ferenc
Molnár, Sándor
Bródy and Ernő
Szép – also used the
island as a literary
retreat.

▲ MARGARET ISLAND
(Margit-sziget)

In medieval times, under the Arpadian dynasty, Margaret Island was a royal hunting reserve and was known as the Island of Rabbits. At various points in its history it has also been called the Island of Our Lady, the Island of Our Lord, Danube Island and Palatine Island. Today it is one of the city's most popular green spaces. Regular open-air concerts are held there.

THE DOMINICAN CHURCH AND CONVENT were built between 1246 and 1255 by Béla IV. The king had promised that if Hungary emerged victorious from the Mongol invasion he would build a convent and have his daughter Margit (above) brought up as a nun. Margit was sent to the island at the age of nine and, having refused to marry the king of Bohemia, died in the convent in 1271 – a year after Béla, who died there in 1270. Béla was buried on the island, as were Margit and her brother Stephen V. With the arrival of the Turks in 1541, the nuns left for Pozsony (now Bratislava), taking the remains of Saint Margit with them. The ruins of the church were excavated in 1838.

PALATINUS BATHS Fed by the island's thermal springs, the Palatinus Baths have a number of pools and lawns. Budapesters regard them as a beach and often spend the day there. In front of the baths is a nude statue (below) by the French sculptor Émile Guillaume.

The island's features include the Centenary Monument, a sculptural group by István Kiss erected in 1973 to commemorate the thousandth anniversary of the unification of Buda, Pest and Óbuda; the Alfréd Hajós Swimming Baths, or National Sports Pool, with its exposed concrete structure and red-brick exterior; the Ramada Hotel (Miklós Ybl, 1872); and the Thermal Hotel (1979), which has a large hydrotherapy unit.

THE WATER TOWER Built between 1909 and 1911, this reinforced-concrete tower, which houses the Office of Weights and Measures, doubles as an exhibition center and monument; 170 feet high, it offers an interesting view of the capital.

Buda

Péter Buza

▲ BUDA
CASTLE HILL
(VÁRHEGY)

Castle Hill *(Várhegy)* is bounded by the Danube to the east, and the green Buda Hills to the north, west and south. Its unique setting explains why human settlements developed here much earlier (from prehistoric times) than on the opposite bank of the river. Buda remained the preferred site until the 19th century, when Pest's extensive areas of virgin land were claimed by industrial expansion. Castle Hill – less than a mile long and no more than a third of a mile wide – is a limestone-and-marl hill that rises to just under 1,600 feet and slopes steeply in places. Like a great land-locked galleon, it seems to drift with the river, its prow turning into the current.

The first town, built in the 10th century on the southern slopes of the hill, was destroyed during the Mongol invasions (1241–2). After these invasions, it was decided to move the population to better protected sites. As a result, the populations of Víziváros and Pest were moved

RAVEN, EMBLEM OF MATTHIAS CORVINUS (Royal Palace, gate) Castle Hill is like an open-air museum. Plaques bearing the word *műemlék* identify monuments of historic and artistic interest.

to the refortified town of Buda. The first urban center of any importance dates from the 13th century, when Béla IV built a castle on the hill, but it was not until the reign of Sigismund of Luxembourg (1387–1437) that Buda became the site of a permanent royal residence.

THE ROYAL PALACE

HISTORY OF THE PALACE ● 70   Built at the southern end of the hilltop, the first Royal Palace *(Királyi palota)* was the residence of Louis the Great. Today nothing remains of this Gothic edifice – which was continually modified for three hundred years,

Ingreſſus tartaroᵹ in hungaria tempõribus regis Bele quarti

The Mongols invading Hungary.

VIEW OF PEST AND CHAIN BRIDGE
There are three ways for visitors to climb Castle Hill. You can take one of the many flights of steps (*lépcső*), from Hunyadi János út (to the east) or behind Vérmező Park (to the west); or walk up Várfok utca and through the Vienna Gate (*Bécsi kapu*), to the north.

before being totally destroyed by the Christian armies when they drove the Turks out of Buda in 1686. A veritable legion of Dutch, Italian and French masters worked on the Royal Palace during the reigns of Sigismund of Luxembourg (king of Hungary and Holy Roman Emperor) ● *28* and Matthias Corvinus ● *32*, who made it a European cultural center. On the pretext of protecting the interests of János Sigismund, son of János Szapolyai (1526–40), against the pretender Ferdinand of Habsburg, the Turkish army occupied the castle and sacked the palace of King Matthias. Following the reconquest of 1686, a smaller Baroque palace was begun in 1715. But by the end of the 19th century it had almost doubled in size. Miklós Ybl and Alajos Hauszmann were the last great architects to work on the palace, which was completed in neo-Baroque style in 1904. On the point of losing World War One, the occupying German army withdrew to the palace, which became a target for the Russian artillery. Disregarding the opinion of experts who maintained that it was beyond restoration, new architects set to work on the ruined palace. They cared little for the eclecticism ● *76* of Ybl and Hauszmann, and rebuilt the Royal Palace without reference to the previous structure. Those who, at first glance, see only 'a monstrous palace next to an ancient but recently restored church' (Le Corbusier, in *Voyage d'Orient*, 1911) can take heart from the fact that the palace contains some marvelous treasures in its library and museums, which include the Castle Museum ▲ *192* (part of Budapest History Museum) and the Hungarian National Gallery ▲ *194*. Finally, archaeologists have excavated the entire fortification system surrounding the hill.

191

The main sections of the Budapest History Museum are the Castle Museum and the Kiscell ▲ *224* and Aquincum ▲ *228* museums. The various floors of the Castle Museum present the history of the Royal Palace, together with the more general history of the city, from the Hungarian conquest to the present day. Since 1968 it has occupied Building E of the former Royal Palace.

HOODED PROPHET (OR APOSTLE)
(15th century)

GLASS GOBLET
(15th century)
The goblet is decorated with the arms of Queen Beatrice, the wife of Matthias Corvinus ● *32*.

HOODED KNIGHT
(15th century)
This beautiful white-limestone head came from the Friss Mansion. Its style reflects the influence of southern-German statuary.

DRAGON
(14th century)

This stove-tile fragment came from the wing of the palace built in the 14th century. By then the royal ceramic workshop had evidently achieved a high level of technical skill.

DETAIL FROM A FRESCO
(late 14th or early 15th century)
This fresco, showing a pair of dancers and a fool, was discovered in a house in Táncsics Mihály utca.

SAINT PAUL THE HERMIT
(15th century)
Keystone decoration showing Saint Paul, the first hermit, who lived in the Lower Thebaid in the 3rd century. On one of the trees is a raven, holding a piece of bread in its beak; the other is growing in a rocky landscape.

APOSTLE
(15th century)

WOMEN'S HEADS
(15th century) Glazed stove tile.

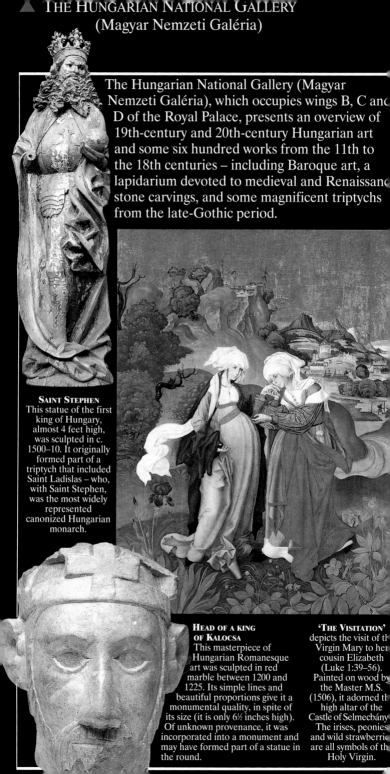

THE HUNGARIAN NATIONAL GALLERY
(Magyar Nemzeti Galéria)

The Hungarian National Gallery (Magyar Nemzeti Galéria), which occupies wings B, C and D of the Royal Palace, presents an overview of 19th-century and 20th-century Hungarian art and some six hundred works from the 11th to the 18th centuries – including Baroque art, a lapidarium devoted to medieval and Renaissance stone carvings, and some magnificent triptychs from the late-Gothic period.

SAINT STEPHEN
This statue of the first king of Hungary, almost 4 feet high, was sculpted in c. 1500–10. It originally formed part of a triptych that included Saint Ladislas – who, with Saint Stephen, was the most widely represented canonized Hungarian monarch.

HEAD OF A KING OF KALOCSA
This masterpiece of Hungarian Romanesque art was sculpted in red marble between 1200 and 1225. Its simple lines and beautiful proportions give it a monumental quality, in spite of its size (it is only 6½ inches high). Of unknown provenance, it was incorporated into a monument and may have formed part of a statue in the round.

'THE VISITATION'
depicts the visit of the Virgin Mary to her cousin Elizabeth (Luke 1:39–56). Painted on wood by the Master M.S. (1506), it adorned the high altar of the Castle of Selmecbánya. The irises, peonies and wild strawberries are all symbols of the Holy Virgin.

'THE CRUCIFIXION'
This panel (c. 1480–90) decorated the high
altar of the Church of St Nicholas at Jánosrét.
The scene, set against a hazy landscape,
suggests a slightly Flemish influence.

THE SIBIU ANGELUS
This triptych (1510–20) combines
Renaissance motifs and Gothic decoration.

**'SAINT DOROTHY
OF BARKA'**
(c. 1410–20)
One of the finest
examples of the
Hungarian
'tender style'.

The Hungarian National Gallery has a large collection of 19th-century art, ranging from neoclassical and Romantic works to academic paintings and *plein-air* landscapes. In particular, it includes the works of Mihály Munkácsy and László Paál, to whom several rooms are devoted. The 20th-century collection reflects the major European trends between 1900 and 1945, including Art Nouveau, Cubism and avant-garde art.

'DÉJEUNER SUR L'HERBE' (1873) Pál Szinyei Merse (1845–1920) was one of the first Hungarian Impressionists. He broke with academic tradition when he painted this extremely natural and vividly colored scene.

'PORTRAIT OF A WOMAN' (1910) István Zádor (1882–1963) studied in France, and French influences are apparent in the composition and pastel tones of this portrait of his wife.

'OCTOBER' (1903)
Károly Ferenczy (1862–1917) was a master of *plein-air* painting – as can be seen from this view of the garden of his family home in Erdély, Transylvania, suffused by the bright sunlight bathing the countryside.

'WOMAN WITH BIRDCAGE' (1892)
This major work by József Rippl-Rónai
(1861–1927) ● *96* was painted during the
artist's 'black period', when he was living and
working in Paris. The subject is treated
extremely economically.

'WOMAN IN WHITE-
SPOTTED DRESS' (1889)
When József Rippl-
Rónai painted this
elegant Parisienne,
he was beginning to
abandon the techniques
of his master, Mihály
Munkácsy, and opening
up to the influences of
Art Nouveau, Japanese
prints and French
painting.

'SELF-PORTRAIT'
(1896–1902)
Tivadar Csontváry
(1853–1919) was a
passionate man who
became an artist late
in life. This self-
portrait, painted at
the beginning of his
career, reflects the
influence of the
Munich School.

▲ BUDA
CASTLE HILL (Várhegy)

MATTHIAS FOUNTAIN
It is said that visitors
who throw a coin into
the fountain will
return to Budapest.

THE GUARDIANS OF THE PALACE The four lion statues
guarding the entrance to the Lion Court (Oroszlános
udvar) are the work of János Fadrusz (1904). The first
two are depicted as snarling menacingly, the other two
as roaring.

**EQUESTRIAN STATUE OF PRINCE
EUGENE OF SAVOY** A little over
three hundred years ago Buda was
liberated from the Turkish
occupation by an alliance of
European Christian armies that
practically destroyed the city. One
of the military commanders involved
in the siege was Eugène de Savoie-
Carignan (1663–1736), better known
as Prince Eugene of Savoy. The
great-nephew of Cardinal Mazarin,
Eugene had joined the army of the
Emperor Leopold I after Louis XIV
had refused to give him command
of a regiment. He liberated Buda
in 1686, defeated the Turks at Zenta
in 1697, and captured Belgrade from
them in 1717. The equestrian statue
of the prince – who was a man of
culture, as is evident from the books
and works of art that this friend
of Leibnitz assembled in his Venetian mansion – stands in
front of the castle's main entrance. The statue was
commissioned by the town of Zenta, which was then unable
to pay the artist. At the suggestion of Alajos Hauszmann,
one of the architects in charge of restoring the palace, the
statue was bought by Franz Joseph and erected on a spot
that had been earmarked for a statue of the emperor – and
which offers one of the most spectacular views of Budapest.

**PRINCE EUGENE
OF SAVOY**
The bronze
equestrian statue of
Prince Eugene of
Savoy, by József
Róna (1900).

MATTHIAS FOUNTAIN (Mátyás kút) Behind the statue of
Prince Eugene of Savoy, a narrow passageway leads to the
northwest courtyard of the palace. On the right stands the
Matthias Fountain (Mátyás kút), a bronze masterpiece by
Alajos Stróbl (1904). The sculptural group, with its extremely
natural detail, was inspired by a ballad written by the
poet Mihály Vörösmarty ● *42*, ▲ *116*, which
tells of Matthias Corvinus' encounter, while
out hunting, with Szép Ilonka (Ilonka the
Beautiful).

THE HABSBURG CRYPT (Nádor kripta) The medieval Chapel of St Sigismund was rebuilt during the reign of the Empress Maria Theresa and used as a fortified church before being almost completely destroyed for the second time. The wall of the choir backs onto the artificial rocks of the Matthias fountain. All that remains of the chapel is the Nádor kripta, the burial place of the Palatine Archduke Joseph, son of Leopold II, which was subsequently rebuilt and can be reached from the National Gallery. Under the Habsburgs the *nádor* (Palatine) was the imperial representative in Hungary, and Archduke Joseph was appointed Palatine in 1796. For the next fifty years, 'the most Hungarian of the Habsburgs' took an active part in the development of the dual city ● *34*, ■ *2*, ▲ *187*. In 1820 his daughter, who died in infancy, was buried in the crypt. Archduke Joseph, who died in 1847, is buried in a sarcophagus surmounted by a recumbent marble effigy sculpted by György Zala.

LUDWIG MUSEUM In 1991 this museum of contemporary art was established in the north wing of the palace (Building A). The works on display include the five hundred or so paintings donated to the city of Budapest by the German artists Peter and Irene Ludwig.

NATIONAL SZÉCHÉNYI LIBRARY (Országos Széchényi Könyvtár) The National Széchényi Library was founded in 1802 by Count Ferenc Széchényi, the father of István Széchenyi ● *35*, ▲ *185*. His private collection, which he left to the state, consisted of some fifteen thousand books and two thousand manuscripts. In 1895, after being housed in several temporary locations, the library was transferred to Building F in the Royal Palace, specially refurbished for the purpose. Its reading rooms are primarily used by students and

LOUIS THE GREAT (14th-century manuscript) The collections of the National Széchényi Library comprise some two million books and five million documents (posters, photographs, manuscripts, obituaries, maps, periodicals). It houses most of the publications written either in Hungarian or by Hungarians or about Hungary, known collectively as *Hungarica*.

THE ROYAL CHAPEL (Budapest History Museum ▲ *192*) Rediscovered in the 1960s, this small 14th-century Gothic chapel escaped the modifications and destruction suffered by the rest of the palace.

ÚRI UTCA
Neo-Baroque façade.

CASTLE THEATER
In 1784 Joseph II, who dissolved more than one religious order, made this Carmelite chapel part of the royal estates. Six years later he gave his permission for it to be converted into a theater. The building became the first permanent theater in the city, giving performances of Hungarian and German plays alternately and also staging concerts. On May 7, 1800 virtuoso pianist Ludwig van Beethoven and horn player Giovanni Punto performed in the theater.

researchers. Visitors may be disappointed by the functional nature of the building, as there is no trace of the former royal apartments. However, its windows offer an unrivaled view of Budapest.

THE CASTLE DISTRICT

ST GEORGE'S SQUARE (Szent György tér) This square, which lies between the Royal Palace to the south and Dísz tér to the north, is named after the church that stood here in the Middle Ages. Bounded on one side by the main palace gates (surmounted by a Turul, the mythical bird of prey that supposedly led Árpád ● 27 over the Carpathian Mountains), it gives access to the upper station of the BUDA CASTLE FUNICULAR (Budavári Sikló) ▲ 206.

SÁNDOR PALACE (Sándor palota) This is a neoclassical edifice by Mihály Pollack which was built in 1806 for the counts of Sándor. It is decorated with reliefs by the Bavarian master sculptor Anton Kirchmayer. Since the second half of the 19th century, it has been the seat of the presidency of the Council of Ministers.

CASTLE THEATER (Várszínház) The Sándor Palace used to be linked to the Castle Theater by a footbridge. The theater, built in 1736 in late-Baroque style, originally housed a Carmelite chapel. Destroyed in the 1940s, it was subsequently rebuilt and reopened in 1978. Today it is an annex of the Hungarian National Theater (Nemzeti Színház).

TÁRNOK UTCA AND ÚRI UTCA Tárnok utca begins on the north side of DÍSZ TÉR. Most of the two-story Gothic-style houses were destroyed during the confrontations between Christians and Turks in the early 18th century, and the entire district was rebuilt in Baroque style. During its reconstruction, 14th-century corbeled houses were discovered at nos. 14 and 16 Tárnok utca and no. 31 Úri utca. In places the galleries of a troglodyte settlement that run beneath these two ancient streets break through the 33-foot surface layer of Castle Hill. Used as wine cellars in peacetime, they offer shelter in time of war or unrest, since they have plenty of hiding places and their own wells. No. 9 Úri utca gives access to the caves under Castle

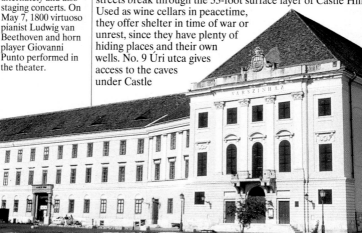

The said town of Buda is a goodly commercial
l kinds of merchandise. And it produces more
most, which are somewhat fiery.
Bertrandon de la Broco

THE HOLY TRINITY COLUMN (Szentháromság oszlop) ● 71
The Baroque Holy Trinity Column has stood in the center of Szentháromság tér since 1714. Often called the 'plague column', it was erected by Buda town council after an outbreak of plague that is evoked on one of its reliefs. Another relief depicts the construction of the column.

Hill. Today the caves are occupied by the BUDA CASTLE WAXWORKS (Budavári Labyrinthus), and historical figures are displayed in a small section of a 6-mile gallery.

SZENTHÁROMSÁG UTCA This road leads from Úri utca to the very center of Castle Hill. On the corner of the two streets stands a statue (György Vastagh, Junior, 1937) of András Hadik (1710–90), an ordinary hussar who became a military commander and favorite of Maria Theresa of Austria. His sword, which the artist used as a model, is now in the MILITARY HISTORY MUSEUM (Hadtörténeti Múzeum), at no. 40 Tóth Árpád sétány. During his time as military governor of Buda, Hadik lived at no. 58 Szentháromság utca, built in Baroque style around 1720.

BUDA'S FORMER TOWN HALL (Régi Budai Városháza)
Buda's Former Town Hall was built in the late 17th century b the Italian architect Venerio Ceresola on the ruins of Gothic buildings. The work was carried out in several stages and lasted almost seventy-five years. The elegantly proportioned building, with its beautiful interior staircase, ceased to function as a town hall in 1873, when Buda and Pest were united ● 29. Today it houses the Collegium Budapest (Academy of Sciences).

MATTHIAS CHURCH (Mátyás templom) ★ The Matthias Church ● 77 – the popular name for the Church of Our Lady (Budavári Nagyboldogasszony templom) – is one of Budapest's architectural gems. All that remains of the original 13th-century building, and of what is generally regarded as the medieval church, are the lower section of the south bell tower and the interior pillars of the MARY PORTAL on the south façade. Although it was used by the Turks as a place of worship, all traces of Turkish occupation were eradicated during its first reconstruction (one of the architects was János Hölbling ▲ 201). The church was almost

STATUE OF PALLAS ATHENE
Beneath the balcony of Buda's former town hall stands a statue of Pallas Athene (right). The original statue – presented to the city by the Italian stonemason Carlo Adami, who wanted to make a name for himself in Buda – has been replaced by a copy. The edifice that Athene was invoked to protect (in her capacity as goddess of wisdom, rather than of war) was Baroque Buda's first administrative building.

entirely rebuilt between 1873 and 1896 under the direction of [Fr]igyes Schulek, who drew his inspiration for the new building [fr]om the Gothic remains discovered on the site. The church's [C]OLLECTION OF SACRED ART is one of the richest in Budapest. [T]he ROYAL FUNERARY CHAPEL (next to the St Imre Chapel) [c]ontains the double sarcophagus of King Béla III and his queen, Anne of Châtillon; its three naves are decorated in Gothic style.

STATUE OF SAINT STEPHEN Alajos Stróbl sculpted this bronze equestrian statue of Saint Stephen

The arms of Hungary and King Matthias Corvinus (Matthias Church).

1906), [t]he first king of [H]ungary and founder of the [H]ungarian state, to suit the taste of [t]he period. One of the four reliefs that [d]ecorate the neo-Romanesque limestone plinth shows [Fr]igyes Schulek, who designed the plinth, [p]resenting a model of the Matthias Church [t]o the king.

HILTON HOTEL Designed by Béla Pintér, the [H]ilton Hotel (Hilton Szálló) was opened in [1]976. The statues of the monks Julianus and [G]éllert (1937) – not to be confused with [S]aint Géllert, whose statue is on Géllert Hill [—] which stand on the east side of Fishermen's [B]astion, serve as a reminder that the hotel [w]as built on the site of a Dominican [m]onastery. Today the tower of the former [D]ominican church houses the hotel's casino; [a]nd several of the stone pillars from the nave [h]ave been reused in the Dominican Courtyard, where [c]oncerts are held. The courtyard offers a marvelous view of [P]est, framed by a Gothic setting.

THE FISHERMEN'S BASTION (Halászbástya) ● 77 The [F]ishermen's Bastion was built by Frigyes Schulek in 1905, [i]n neo-Romanesque style, on a site once occupied by a fish [m]arket. It forms a balcony in front of the Matthias Church [a]nd offers a magnificent view of Pest. The bronze statue of [J]ános Hunyadi, the military commander who fought the Turks

MATTHIAS CHURCH, DETAIL OF THE MARY PORTAL
The Matthias Church witnessed the marriage, in 1476, of Matthias Corvinus ● 32 and Beatrice of Aragon ● 33, ▲ 192; the coronation, in

1876, of the Emperor Franz Joseph (for which Liszt composed his *Hungarian Coronation Mass*); and, in 1916, that of the last Habsburg emperor, Charles I (Károly IV) ● 96. It is the city's most beautiful church.

TANCSICS MIHALY UTCA
The ERDÖDY PALACE (below), at no. 7, and the ZICHY MANSION (built for Miklós Zichy) ▲ *226*, at no. 23, are well worth a visit.

ERDŐDY PALACE ● *71*
This magnificent Baroque building houses the MUSIC HISTORY MUSEUM (Zenetörténeti Múzeum), which includes an intriguing display of old musical instruments.

DETAIL OF THE FISHERMEN'S BASTION
The seven Hungarian tribes led by Árpád ● *27* are represented by seven turrets.

in the late 15th century, stands on Hunyadi János út, which runs below the bastion. A little further on is a replica of St George and the Dragon by Márton and György Kolozsvári (14th century).

ORSZÁGHÁZ UTCA (Parliament Street) Beyond the palace, Országház utca runs down the broader, northern slope of Castle Hill. In the 15th century it was referred to as 'the Italian street', after the Tuscan artists and craftsmen who lived there. The houses at nos. 18, 20 and 22, which date from the 14th and 15th centuries, are the district's only surviving medieval buildings. The street's present name is a reminder that in the 1790s the Diet (Parliament) of Buda met in the large building at no. 28, known as the EGYKORI BUDAI ORSZÁGHÁZ (Old Parliament Building). Not long after, in 1806, the Diet of Buda was dissolved, at the same time as the Holy Roman Empire. Together with no. 49 Úri utca, this building – which is notable for its *copf* style (a German and Central European variety of Rococo) ▲ *231* – formed part of the Cloister of the Poor Clares. Both were built in the 1780s, under the direction of Franz Anton Hillebrandt. From the late 18th to the early 19th century, no. 28 served as the seat of the Hungarian legislature and supreme court. Its great ceremonial hall (now used by the Hungarian Academy of Sciences) and main staircase attest to the building's former splendor. During the second half of the 19th century, grand balls were held there.

FORTUNA UTCA At one time this street, which runs parallel to Országház utca, was named after its German inhabitants; previously, in the Middle Ages it was named after the French courtiers of King Sigismund. The easternmost row of houses is reached via a gateway. The late-17th-century *copf*-style ▲ *231* building at no. 4 now houses the COMMERCE AND CATERING MUSEUM (Kereskedelmi és Vendéglátóipari

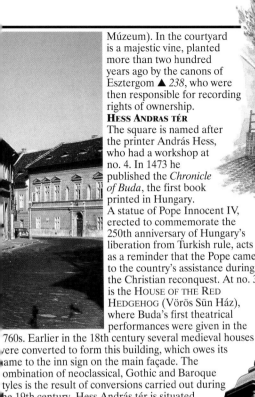

Múzeum). In the courtyard is a majestic vine, planted more than two hundred years ago by the canons of Esztergom ▲ *238*, who were then responsible for recording rights of ownership.

HESS ANDRÁS TÉR

The square is named after the printer András Hess, who had a workshop at no. 4. In 1473 he published the *Chronicle of Buda*, the first book printed in Hungary. A statue of Pope Innocent IV, erected to commemorate the 250th anniversary of Hungary's liberation from Turkish rule, acts as a reminder that the Pope came to the country's assistance during the Christian reconquest. At no. 3 is the HOUSE OF THE RED HEDGEHOG (Vörös Sün Ház), where Buda's first theatrical performances were given in the 1760s. Earlier in the 18th century several medieval houses were converted to form this building, which owes its name to the inn sign on the main façade. The combination of neoclassical, Gothic and Baroque styles is the result of conversions carried out during the 19th century. Hess András tér is situated in the heart of an old Jewish district and at the MEDIEVAL JEWISH PRAYER HOUSE (Középkori Zsidó Imaház), which is open to the public, you can see the remains of two synagogues. The first Jewish community was already settled around Dísz tér when, after the 13th-century Mongol invasions, Béla IV (1237–70) brought Jewish, German and Italian immigrants into the city. Subsequently Louis the Great (1342–82) drove the Jews out of Hungary – and then brought them back again. The new arrivals settled on the northern slopes of Castle Hill. Opposite the synagogue was the house of the Jewish prefect, a post created by Matthias Corvinus to provide an intermediary between himself and the Jewish community.

BÉCSI KAPU TÉR On the west side of the square there are four houses ● *71* that reflect the principal architectural styles of Castle Hill. The HUNGARIAN NATIONAL ARCHIVES (Magyar Országos Levéltár), built in 1923 according to plans by Samu Pecz, also stands on this side of the square.

STATUE OF ARTEMIS
A statue of the Greek goddess stands near to the southwest corner of the Mary Magdelene Tower.

THE MARY MAGDELENE TOWER (Mária Magdolna Torony)
The Mária Magdolna Torony (on the corner of Országház utca and Kapisztrán tér) is all that remains of a Franciscan church built between the 13th and the 15th centuries. During the Middle Ages, the church was the one where the local Hungarian population worshipped.

VÍZIVÁROS

THE BUDA CASTLE FUNICULAR (Budavári Sikló)
Today this hillside lift is mainly used by tourists.

CLARK ÁDÁM TÉR The district of Víziváros (Watertown) occupies the narrow strip of land – which widens out to the north – between the Danube and Castle Hill. During Roman times a road ran through the area, along the river. In the Middle Ages it was a district of craftsmen, fishermen and traders. There are several vestiges of the Turkish occupation, in particular the Király Baths ▲ *208*. The major development of Víziváros took place in the 19th century, following the construction of Chain Bridge, the first permanent bridge across the Danube ● *35*, ▲ *183*. The construction of the CASTLE HILL TUNNEL (Alagút) ▲ *184* made Clark Ádám tér a major intersection for roads from the north, south, east and west of the city. The BUDA CASTLE FUNICULAR (Budavári Sikló) was originally brought into service in 1870 for the employees of the Royal Palace. It was then operated by a steam engine. The cabins were attached to the strong metal cable of the winch, with the ascending cabin acting as a counterweight for the descending cabin. Today the funicular is run by electricity.

FŐ UTCA The main street of Víziváros runs parallel to the river. In the 1860s to 1870s the district's first mansions were built backing onto it, with their façades overlooking the Bem rakpart (Bem Quay). The side next to the river is bordered by ancient chestnut trees, and since the late 19th century Fő utca has been a very attractive street. The most interesting buildings are found near Corvin tér, where the late-18th-century houses at nos. 3, 4 and 5 are on a par with those around the Royal Palace. A little further on, at no. 20 Fő utca, the KAPISZTORY HOUSE dates from the same period, although its was originally medieval. The patisserie opened here in 1850 – and still existing today – became famous for its furnishings, commissioned by the then owner Ede Friedl. The French Institute (left) can be seen from the corner of Pala utca.

THE FRENCH INSTITUTE (Francia Intézet) The first French Institute was founded in Pest in 1940. The impressive post-Modern building which opened in 1992, at no. 17 Fő utca, looks a little out of place amid the eclecticism ● *76* of the buildings of Víziváros. The Institute has a library and café, and organizes a wide range of cultural events and activities designed to promote Franco-Hungarian relations in a cordial and convivial atmosphere. In front of the building stands the STATUE OF FRIENDSHIP by Pierre Székely Péter. The CALVINIST CHURCH ▲ *185* on Szilágyi Dezső tér was built in neo-Gothic style in the late 19th century.

THE FRENCH INSTITUTE
The plate-glass building that houses the French Institute looks like a huge ship floating in the heart of the city.

ᴮATTHYÁNY TÉR Fő utca runs northward to Batthyány tér (known in the 18th century as Upper Market Square), the historic center of Víziváros. Today it is an intersection for a number of public transport links: the no. 2 (red) line of the metro, the terminus for the HÉV suburban railway (its other terminus is at Szentendre ▲ *230*), and several bus routes ◆ *245*. The magnificent Baroque Sᴛ Aɴɴᴇ's ᴄʜᴜʀᴄʜ (Szent Anna templom, below) ★ ● *70*, ▲ *186* was begun in 1740, under the direction of Kristóf Hamon and Mátyás Nepauer. Inside is a group showing the Virgin Mary being presented in the Temple of Jerusalem, sculpted by Károly Bebó (1770–3); the pulpit (with the exception of the reliefs) is also the work of Bebó; and the Chapel of the Holy Sepulcher has an impressive wrought-iron screen that dates from the mid 18th century. At nos. 3 and 4 there are two magnificent old houses overlooking the river. The Hɪᴋɪsᴄʜ Hᴀ́ᴢ (1795), at no. 3, is named after the master builder ▲ *213* who lived there; the four reliefs above the ground floor are allegories of the seasons. Nearby is the delightful asymmetrical building of the Wʜɪᴛᴇ Cʀoss Iɴɴ (Fehér Kereszt Fogadó) ● *110*, formed by the amalgamation of two older houses in 1770. At the end of the 18th century this famous inn presented theatrical performances. Its distinguished guests included the Emperor Joseph II and (according to local legend) Casanova, after whom the night club on the ground floor is named. The square is bounded to the north by a former Franciscan monastery (18th–19th century), later the hospital of the Baroque Cʜᴜʀᴄʜ oꜰ ᴛʜᴇ Sᴛ Eʟɪᴢᴀʙᴇᴛʜ Nᴜɴs (mid 18th century). In front of the former monastery is a bronze statue of Ferenc Kölcsey (1790–1838), who wrote the Hungarian national anthem (Himnusz). At nos. 82 and 89 Fő utca are the Kɪʀᴀ́ʟʏ Bᴀᴛʜs ★ ▲ *208*, probably the most beautiful Turkish baths in Budapest.

Lᴀᴊᴏs Bᴀᴛᴛʜʏᴀ́ɴʏ (1806-1849) On March 17, 1848 the Emperor Ferdinand I made Count Lajos Batthyány head of the first independent Hungarian government. Batthyány was a member of the liberal opposition and supported the Austro-Hungarian Compromise. Realizing that it was doomed to failure, he resigned his post, though he remained a member of the Diet (Parliament). When Franz Joseph succeeded Ferdinand, Austrian troops invaded Hungary, and Batthyány was tried and executed. His successor, Lajos Kossuth ● *35*, was more fortunate and managed to escape.

Construction of the Király Baths (Király Gyógyfürdő) ● 62 probably commenced when Arslan, the Turkish governor of Buda from May 1565 to August 1566, started to build a wall around the city. Completed by Arslan's successor, Pasha Mustapha Sokoli, they survived the Christian reconquest of Hungary. The modernization and extensions begun in the 18th century mainly involved extending the baths and left the original Turkish structure intact.

ABOUT THE BATHS

After the Turkish withdrawal, Leopold l gave the baths to his personal physician, Frigyes Ferdinánd Illmer. They then changed hands several times before being sold to Leonhard Aigner, who undertook the first major structural alterations. In the 18th century they were variously known as the Balneum Civitatis Inferioris, Das Baad in der Wassersdadt, Spithal-Baad (after the nearby military hospital) and finally Königs Baad, after Ferenc König, their owner from 1796 (König being transposed into Hungarian as Király). The neoclassical extensions were completed by Mihály König.

THE FOOT BATH AND STEAM BATHS

THE NEOCLASSICAL WING ON Fő UTCA

In the late 19th century the level of Fő utca was raised. As a result, the first-floor balcony was lost. Major renovation work was carried out between 1954 and 1959, when the street level was lowered again.

The regularly spaced 'bottle bottoms' in the brickwork of the vaults create a soft, diffuse light.

THE WING ON GANZ UTCA

The interior of the neoclassical wing on Ganz utca forms a cloister around which the private baths are arranged. The square on the corner of Ganz utca and Fő utca was originally occupied by the right wing of the Baroque building, which was demolished to make room for this part of the building and its domes.

Oxidation from the copper covering the four domes seeps inside and contributes to the general tonality of the building.

THE COLD SHOWERS

1. Thermal spring
2. Main pool (97°F)
3. Small pool (79°F)
4. Small pool (104°F)
5. Steam bath (113°F)
6. Steam bath (131°F)
7. Steam bath (149°F)
8. Showers **9.** Main courtyard
10. Private bath cubicles
11. Pasha's private bath (including a large bath for four people and a sauna)
12. Resting room **13.** Massage room
14. Fő utca **15.** Entrance **16.** Ganz utca

GIRL WITH PITCHER
(Lukács Baths)

FELHÉVIZ

Budapest's many thermal springs have made it a leading spa city. Traditionally its waters are divided into two groups: the springs that rise to the north of the city center, and those which rise along the geographical fault line of the deep ravine that forms the bed of the Danube in the Budapest region. The northern springs are referred to as the Felhéviz (Upper Thermal Springs). This part of the city was built in the vicinity of what is now the Buda end of Margaret Bridge ▲ 186. In the 13th century the bath houses of the Order of the Knights Hospitallers stood here.

LUKÁCS BATHS The Lukács Gyógyfürdő baths complex, at nos. 25–9 Frankel Leó út, was built in the second half of the 1880s. People come from all over the world to take the waters here and, in particular, for the mud baths. Hence, on

'FATHER OF THE ROSES'
Gül Baba utca and the Gül Baba Türbe (at no. 14 Mecset utca).
If you walk northward along Frankel Leó út, cross Margit körút and turn left into Gül Baba utca, you will come to the türbe (shrine) and Rózsadomb (Rose Hill).

the cornerstones in the courtyard of the complex are a number of votive plaques ● *63*, in a variety of languages, donated by people cured of their ailments. The most elegant ones date from the late 19th and early 20th century. The Lukács Baths were extended and modernized in 1984.

THE EMPEROR'S BATHS (Komjádi Császár uszoda) Entirely rebuilt in 1840 in neoclassical style, the Komjádi Császár uszoda (at no. 8 Árpád fejedelem útja) quickly became a favorite venue for the city's well-to-do society. The new complex replaced the Baths of Bey Veli, built by the Turks in the 16th century. Ten springs feed the pools and treatment rooms with 3.3 million gallons of hard sulfurous water per day, at temperatures of between 63°F and 149°F. The waters are used to treat locomotive, nervous and muscular disorders, and as postoperative therapy for road-accident victims.

It was hard to imagine, during these explorations, the skyline – the clusters of domes, minarets and moving crescents – that Charles of Lorraine and his companions would have seen at the time of the reconquest....'

Patrick Leigh Fermor

RÓZSADOMB ★

GÜL BABA TÜRBE Situated in the south of District II, Rózsadomb (Rose Hill) is a wealthy residential district. The villas of its quiet streets are partially hidden by handsome trees. Some of these villas – nos. 14 and 16 Cserje utca, and several in Törökvész utca – are striking examples of 1930s architecture *84*. The first villas began to appear on these slopes (previously used for growing grapes) after the opening of Margaret Bridge in the 1870s. In the middle of the hill, near the Felhévíz baths and overlooking the Danube, stands a small domed octagonal building that dates from the 16th century. This is the Gül Baba Türbe, the funerary monument of a dervish who is still venerated by Muslims as a saint (legend has it that he planted a rose garden here – Gül Baba means 'Father of the Roses' in Turkish). The shrine was converted into a Christian chapel in the 17th century, but later restored to its original form.

Both the Szent Antal templom (above), at no. 137 Pasaréti út, and Lakóház (below), at no. 97, were designed by Gyula Rimanóczy and date from 1934.

PASARÉT

Less than a hundred years ago the fastest-flowing mountain stream in the Buda region tumbled down this valley (once known as 'the Devil's Ditch'). In the early 20th century the hillside was built on, with a dense network of streets which make this residential district in effect an extension of Rózsadomb. Pasarét (meaning 'the Pasha's pasture') is like something out of *The Arabian Nights*, as visitors who walk along the long Bimbó út will discover. In terms of architectural history, the most interesting houses such as Villa Zenta are found around Házman utca and on Napraforgó utca ★ ● *84*. Nevertheless, age apart, it is often difficult to distinguish them from the more recent houses on either side of Bimbó út – which, along with Pasaréti út, has become the district's main thoroughfare – or from those on Kapy utca, Gábor Áron utca, Orsó utca, Lepke utca and Hermann Ottó út.

VAROSMAJOR

THE PARK The district of Városmajor is situated in the northeast of District XII. The site of the present STADT MAYEROFF PARK was a hay meadow before the Turkish occupation; and again afterward, when it was used to supply the troops garrisoned in Buda Castle. In the 1780s it became a public park. The layout was conceived by a man named József Talherr, who set out to plant it with three thousand species of plants and trees. The elms that have survived from his original planting serve as a reminder of his efforts to beautify the area. In the late 18th century Városmajor became the favorite 'retreat' of the inhabitants of Buda, many of whom built villas here. The houses on Városmajor utca, which runs along the western edge of the park, are the most representative of the new residential district built in this narrow valley leading through the hills. At no. 44 is the villa of the Hungarian artist Miklós Barabás ● *92*, famous for his Romantic portraits and historical scenes.

TWO CHURCHES, A THEATER AND A RAILWAY The small Városmajor Parish Church (VAROSMAJORI PLÉBANIATEMPLOM) stands beside the park, at no. 5 Csaba utca. Designed in 1923 by Aladár Árkay, it combines traditional Transylvanian and Finnish Romantic styles. In 1936 Aladár Árkay and his son Bertalan built another, more modern, parish church (left) next to the earlier one. A little further on, to the northwest of the church, there is an OPEN-AIR THEATER that shows films and also stages musicals. The lower terminus of the COG RAILWAY (Fogaskerekű Vasút) is at no. 16 Szilágyi Erzsébet fasor, which runs along the northwest side of the park. The railway was opened to the public in 1874. Its upper terminus is on Széchenyi Hill (Széchenyi-hegy) ▲ *218*, just over 2 miles away and 1,030 feet higher up.

KRISZTINAVAROS

This district, which is a northern extension of Városmajor, used to feature on military maps as a hay meadow for the troops garrisoned in Buda Castle. It forms a narrow – and today intermittent – green belt that stretches between Pasarét and the Tabán; in other words, from the northeastern part of District XII to the center of District I.

VÉRMEZŐ In 1795 this park witnessed the execution of the leaders of the Hungarian Jacobins, who had been convicted of disseminating the revolutionary ideas of the Enlightenment and attempting to overthrow the monarchy. The site of the executions became known locally as Vérmező ('the field of blood'), and eventually the name was officially adopted. After World War Two it was converted into a park, and a memorial stone in memory of Ignác Martinovics and his colleagues was placed on the site of the scaffold. A little further on is the SOUTH STATION (Déli Pályaudvar), which is the terminus of the no. 2 (red) line of the *metró*.

KRISZTINA TÉR Built by Kristóf Hikisch, whose house can still be seen in Víziváros ▲ 207, Krisztinaváros Parish Church, or OUR LADY OF THE SNOWS (Havas Boldogasszony), was inaugurated in 1797. It replaced a wooden chapel that had become famous because of a holy icon (see right). As a result, it received a visit from the Empress Maria Theresa, who authorized Buda town council to name this outlying district – in those days mainly farms and vineyards – Krisztinaváros ('Christine town') after one of her daughters. Like the original chapel, the restaurant known as THE GREEN TREE became a cult center – although in a somewhat different vein, since it glorified earthly rather than heavenly pleasures. The new restaurant built on the site has little in common with its predecessor, except for its name. On February 4, 1836 the marriage of Count István Széchenyi ● 35, ▲ 137, 185 and Crescentia Seilern was celebrated in the church. By then the village had already achieved the proportions of a town, and even boasted a number of mansions. The church was renovated in eclectic style ● 76 in the late 19th century, and extended in the 1930s to 1940s. As a result, its furnishings are a combination of Baroque, Empire and Modern styles.

KRISZTINA KÖRUT At no. 57 is ÁLDÁSY HOUSE (Áldásy Ház), a bourgeois residence of palatial dimensions. Built in the early 19th century, it has since been renovated and today houses the Hungarian theater research institute. At the southeast corner of Krisztina tér lies HAYDN PARK (formerly Horváth Gardens), which has provided the venue for a summer theater season for several decades. The DÉRYNÉ patisserie on the corner of Krisztina körút and Roham utca is named after Madam Déry, a famous Hungarian actress and well-known gourmet.

TABÁN

This district is situated on the slopes of Gellért Hill (Gellért-hegy ▲ 215) and Sun Hill (Nap-hegy), which lie across the valley from Castle Hill. There is evidence to suggest that the site has been inhabited since prehistoric times. Later the Romans settled in the Tabán, and in the Middle Ages a town grew up around the chapel

KRISZTINAVÁROS IN THE MID 19TH CENTURY
In 1700 a chimney-sweep named Péter Pál Francin, who had survived the plague epidemic of 1649, made a pilgrimage to the town of Re, in northern Italy, in order to give thanks to the Virgin Mary. He returned with a copy of a painting of the Holy Virgin, and built a wooden chapel to house the icon. This chapel among the trees became the center of a small village. The painting brought back by Francin is now in Krisztinaváros Parish Church.

COUNT ISTVAN SZÉCHENYI (1791-1860) ● 35 ▲ 137, 185

TABÁN PARISH CHURCH IN THE SNOW
Church of St Catherine of Alexandria.

that stood where the Parish Church is now. Until the fire of 1810 the winding streets that ran along this charming valley, and the houses – many of them ancient – that clung to the northern slopes of Gellért Hill, were reminiscent of the Viennese suburb of Grinzing. With a hundred or so establishments selling wine by the bottle, the old Tabán must have been a busy district, full of temptations. This may well explain the white cross that once stood in what was then the central square and is today an area of grassy hillside. According to reliable historical sources the cross was in fact an infamous pillory, to which those judged guilty by the local court were tied.

TABÁN PARISH CHURCH (Tabáni plébániatemplom)
The Tabán Parish Church, also called the Church of St Catherine of Alexandria (on Szarvas tér, near to the Danube) was built in 1728–36, in Baroque style, by the Carinthian master builder Keresztély Obergruber. Its façade was renovated in 1880–1. In a niche below the organ the church has a copy of *The Tabán Christ* (the original is in Budapest History Museum ▲ *192*), a fragment from the carved Romanesque tympanum of the 12th-century chapel that stood here. On the same wall is a painting of the fire that destroyed much of the Tabán district in 1810. The Tabán Parish Church is one of the district's few historical remains (which can be counted on the fingers of one hand). Two of the others are worthy of mention.

STAG HOUSE The triangular building at no. 1 Szarvas tér (Stag Square) was built in the early 1700s. Originally it housed a restaurant, THE GOLDEN STAG (Arany Szarvas vendéglő). The building, which today houses a restaurant of the same name, is still graced by the splendid inn sign – a relief (opposite) of a golden stag, harassed by hounds.

SEMMELWEIS MUSEUM OF MEDICAL HISTORY (Semmelweis Orvostörténeti Múzeum) The second historical building of interest, at nos. 1–3 Apród utca, is the small but impressive manor house where the famous physician Ignác Semmelweis (1818–65) was born and is

A street in the Tabán, c. 1910.

buried. He is known as the 'savior of mothers', since his discovery of the cause of puerperal fever saved many women from dying in childbirth. A commemorative plaque honors the memory of József Antall, Hungary's first Prime Minister (1990–3) of the post-Soviet era, who was the museum's director. If you walk around the outside of the building, you will come to a delightful old-fashioned courtyard – a fine example of the district's former charm.

GELLÉRT HILL ★

Seen from Pest, Gellért-hegy – a dolomitic hill that rises to a height of 425 feet above the quays of the Danube – looks like a veritable mountain. Its rocky slopes fall steeply to the valley floor, leaving little room for the road that runs along the river. The half-hour climb to the top of Gellért Hill is a pleasant walk and offers some splendid views of the city through the trees.

THE CITADEL (Citadella) At the top of Gellért Hill stands a circular fortress known as the Citadel , built by the Austrian army after the 1848–9 uprising ● *29*, ▲ *119*. A few strategically placed cannons made this an ideal vantage point from which to keep an eye on the city and its population. In the late 19th century the army abandoned the fortress, and it became the property of the Hungarian government. Today the Citadel, which encircles the brow of the hill like a stone crown, provides a spectacular viewpoint ★, encompassing the whole of Budapest and its environs. There is a restaurant inside the walls.

THE LIBERATION MONUMENT
This symbol of the city's liberation from the Germans can be seen from all over Budapest. Now that the Communist star on the plinth has been removed, it is possible that the

monument will be regarded as an allegory of political and economic liberalization.

LIBERATION MONUMENT (Szabadság-Szobor) Today the Liberation Monument by Zsigmond Kisfaludi Stróbl simply consists of a 45-foot-high bronze statue. It was erected in 1947 to commemorate the liberation of the city from the Germans by Soviet troops. Many people believe that it was originally commissioned as a memorial to the son of Miklós Horthy ▲ 174. Originally a second statue, of a Soviet soldier armed with a machine gun, stood at the feet of the slender female figure holding the palm of victory. Liberty was well guarded!

THE CAVE CHURCH (Sziklakápolna) There are two ways of coming down the hill. If you climbed the steps that follow the castle walls, you might like to take the path that runs from the west wall of the Citadel (via Szirtes út, Kelenhegyi út, Rezeda utca and Verejték utca) to Szent Gellért tér, at the end of Freedom Bridge (Szabadság híd ▲ 180). It takes you through the residential district built on the southwestern slopes of the hill in the early 20th century. Among the painters and other artists that lived in the typically Hungarian houses was Gyula Kann Kosztolányi, a master of Art Nouveau, who designed a house and studio for himself at nos. 12–14 Kelenhegyi út (now unfortunately extremely run down). On Verejték utca you can visit the CAVE CHURCH (Sziklakápolna) or CHAPEL IN THE ROCK (Sziklatemplom), which occupies a natural cave in the hillside, known for centuries as St Stephen's Cave. The church is currently used by the Pauline monks – the only Hungarian monastic order ▲ 181 – and is a major place of pilgrimage, rather like Lourdes. The Paulines have been celebrating mass in the church since 1929. The monastery, a small building with a number of towers, is built against the hillside and stands on the bank of the river.

HOTEL GELLÉRT AND GELLÉRT BATHS (Gellért Szálló and Gellért Gyógyfürdő) ★
The square in front of the Cave Church offers a splendid view of the architectural complex of the Hotel Gellért ● 82, probably the most glamorous showcase of this spa city, and Gellért Baths ● 63, designed by Artúr Sebestyén, Ármin Hegedűs and Izidor Stark, and built between 1912 and 1918. Behind the hotel is an open-air 'wave pool'.

HOTEL GELLÉRT
The palatial Hotel Gellért is certainly one of the most elegant hotels in Budapest. Since the 1910s the hotel and its baths have welcomed many of the crowned heads of Europe. The waters (115°F) of the thermal springs above which the hotel is built were already being used to cure a variety of ailments in the Middle Ages.

> 'Budapest had its orchards, the green breasts
> of the Buda Hills and the fields and
> forests beyond, stretching to the high mountains
> on the edge of the city.'
>
> John Lukacs

THE BUDA HILLS

The Buda Hills constitute a relatively wild area to the west
of the city. It is not hard to imagine that its forests were once
the preserve of deer, wild boars and other creatures from
children's fairy tales. Today the hills are only half-an-hour
from the city center, and are an ideal place for a nature walk
or leisurely stroll.

SAS HILL (Sas-hegy) The bare summit of the
dolomitic Sas Hill rises like a bastion to the
west of Gellért Hill. The greater part of
the hill consists of a 75-acre nature
reserve – which can only be visited
with an authorized guide, who will
be able to point out the protected
plant and animal species. Some of
these species (such as the St Stephen's
pink, the Buda centaury and the
Pannonian lizard) are only found on
Sas Hill. The vines that grew on the south-
facing slopes from early medieval times to the
end of the 19th century produced a red wine that was
known and sold throughout the Austro-Hungarian
Empire – until the vines were destroyed by a parasitic
fungus (Peronosporales). In 1931 the school and institute
of OUR LADY OF ZION (now part of Budapest's educational
system) was built according to plans by Gustáv Reisch.
This monumental building, the only one on the hill, has
some remarkable architectural features.

THE PUBLIC CEMETERY (Farkasréti temető)
Between Sas Hill and Freedom Hill (Szabadság-hegy) is
a broad, flat saddle, which in 1894 was chosen as the site
for Buda's Public Cemetery (Farkasréti temető). It is the
second largest cemetery in Budapest and serves as a national
pantheon. This role was originally fulfilled by the Kerepesi
Cemetery ▲ *171* – but when, under the Communist regime,
religious burials were discouraged, those who wanted
such a burial were interred here. The most famous are
undoubtedly Zoltán Kodály and Béla Bartók ● *50*, ▲ *142*,

**GELLÉRT BATHS,
INTERIOR AND DOMES**
The decorative details
of the medicinal
baths, mud baths,
'champagne-bubble'
pools, and other
facilities are among
the most beautiful
examples of Art
Nouveau architecture.

**ST IMRE OF THE
CISTERCIANS**
(nos. 23–5 Villányi
út) The majestic
neoclassical façade
(1938) overlooks
the Feneketlen tó
(Feneketlen Lake,
or Bottomless Lake).
Once part of the
Tabán, this area
now belongs to the
Lágymányos district
▲ *174*, which was
developed in the
early 20th century.

146 and Georg Solti ● *53*, whose tombs can be found in the artists' section of the cemetery. Many of the funeral monuments are in themselves works of art – Kodály's is signed by Pál Pátzay, and Bartók's was sculpted by Miklós Borsos.

Svab Hill (Sváb-hegy) The hill can be reached by the Cog Railway, which leaves from Szilágyi Erzsébet fasor ▲ *212* In the early 19th century Sváb Hill, was a favorite place for excursions and holidays among Budapesters. In the 1850s private villas and chalets began to be built on the hill, for use during the summer months.

Gradually small communities were formed, with schools and local administration. The most charming area is probably the double valley basin that forms part of the hills of Zugliget, another residential and holiday district. Walkers will particularly appreciate the DISZNÓFŐ FORRÁS ('Pig's Head Spring'), which is said to have flowed across the hunting reserve of King Matthias Corvinus ● *32*. Today wild boars still inhabit the area – a fact that has not gone unnoticed by the local restaurant, which serves roast boar and boar stew.

HŰVÖSVÖLGY A little further north is Hűvösvölgy ('Cool Valley'), which lies at the end of another series of hills: the Hármashatár-hegy ('Three Frontiers Hill'). This has been a popular place to walk for almost two hundred years, but in the 19th century it also became a popular site for holiday villas. From here the CHILDREN'S RAILWAY (Gyermek Vasút) – formerly the Pioneers' Railway (Úttörők Vasút) ◆ *256* – runs to SZÉCHENYI HILL (Széchenyi-hegy), its stations marking many of the places for walks and excursions in the Buda Hills. Another way to enjoy the hills is to take the chairlift (left) that runs from the corner of Zugliget utca and Csiga utca to the top of JÁNOS HILL (János-hegy). The no. 190 bus also runs up János Hill, offering an opportunity to drink in the beauty of the Buda Hills, especially from Istenhegyi út and Eötvös utca.

JÁNOS HILL CHAIRLIFT
Sváb Hill is in fact a series of hills, the highest of which is János Hill at 1,730 feet. The last half-mile is covered by chairlift (*libegő*). The stone ERZSÉBET LOOKOUT TOWER (Erzsébet kilátó), which offers one of the best views of the Buda Hills, was designed by Frigyes Schulek ▲ *203*. Built in 1910, it was named after the Empress Elizabeth ● *30*, ▲ *182*, *240*, who liked and helped the Hungarian people (something that was fairly rare among the Habsburgs).

Old photograph of the Cog Railway (right).

ÓBUDA
József Vinkó

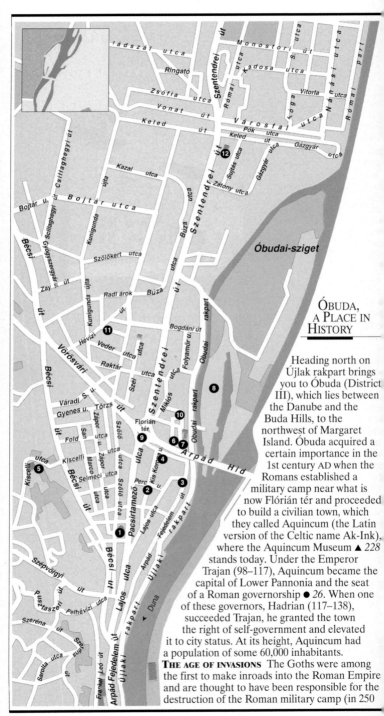

ÓBUDA, A PLACE IN HISTORY

Heading north on Újlak rakpart brings you to Óbuda (District III), which lies between the Danube and the Buda Hills, to the northwest of Margaret Island. Óbuda acquired a certain importance in the 1st century AD when the Romans established a military camp near what is now Flórián tér and proceeded to build a civilian town, which they called Aquincum (the Latin version of the Celtic name Ak-Ink), where the Aquincum Museum ▲ *228* stands today. Under the Emperor Trajan (98–117), Aquincum became the capital of Lower Pannonia and the seat of a Roman governorship ● *26*. When one of these governors, Hadrian (117–138), succeeded Trajan, he granted the town the right of self-government and elevated it to city status. At its height, Aquincum had a population of some 60,000 inhabitants.

THE AGE OF INVASIONS The Goths were among the first to make inroads into the Roman Empire and are thought to have been responsible for the destruction of the Roman military camp (in 250

nd 270) and the town of Aquincum (in 376). Then in the
arly 4th century the Huns conquered the Carpathian Basin.
he military exploits of their leader Attila are recounted in
he *Nibelungenlied* (Song of the Nibelungs), where he appears
nder the name Etzel. The suggestion that his castle,
tzelburg, was built on the ruins of the military camp of
quincum is supported by the chronicle of the Emperor
rederick Barbarossa (12th century), which talks about 'the
wn of Attila'. After Attila's death, in 453, his vast empire
isintegrated. The capture of the site by Hungarian tribes in
he 9th century is described by Anonymus ● 38, ▲ 161 in his
esta Hungarorum, which tells how they crossed the Danube
nd reached the town of Attila under the leadership of Árpád
 27, ▲ 150, 180. The dynasty founded by Árpád renamed
he town Buda (a common first name at that time). According
o legend Árpád, was buried there.

HE MIDDLE AGES In 1241 a powerful Mongol army led by
atu Khan, the grandson of Genghis Khan, defeated the
lungarians at the Battle of Muhi. But because of the death
f the Great Khan (Genghis' son, Ogedei), the conquering
rmy withdrew, despite having reached the gates of Vienna.
hat same year Bishop Rogerius presided over the Easter
estivities celebrated by Béla IV in the old town of Buda –
hich Rogerius described as the geographical and
dministrative center of the country, but which now lay in
uins. In view of its destruction, Béla IV decided to take up
esidence on a more secure hill. The new seat of the royal
ourt became known as Buda, and (as recorded in an official
ocument dating from 1261) the former seat of the royal
esidence was renamed Vetus Buda or Óbuda (Old Buda).

HE MODERN AGE After the division of the country into three
arts (1541), Buda and its environs (including Óbuda) were
nnexed by the Ottoman Empire for the next 145 years.
)buda lost all administrative importance, and many
lungarian peasants fled the occupied territory. A captain
rom Esztergom, Miklós Pálffy, decided to help the
lungarians leave Óbuda (they are said to have escaped in a
ingle night) and settle in Esztergom. For more than ten years
)buda was uninhabited, until the liberation of Buda in 1686.

'On the evening of my
arrival in the camp,
the Danube was a vast
roadway of red – then
blue – ice, furrowed
by currents that left
ruts as deep as
chariots tracks.'
                Marguerite
                Yourcenar,
          Memoirs of Hadrian

**MILITARY TOWN
AMPHITHEATER**
(2nd century AD)
The amphitheater
(its ruins can be seen
at the intersection
of Pacsirtamező utca
and Nagyszombat
utca) had a seating
capacity of fifteen
thousand. The French
writer Marguerite
Yourcenar describes
its atmosphere
through the eyes of
Hadrian: 'These
Danubian legions
functioned with the
precision of a freshly
oiled war machine;
they had nothing in
common with the
sleepy garrisons I
had encountered
in Spain... Along
these borders, where
skillful strategy would
have been, at least
temporarily, crucial
in winning the favor
of certain nomadic
chieftains, the soldier
completely eclipsed
the statesman...'
        Memoirs of Hadrian

In the 18th century Óbuda became a small Baroque town
under the aegis of the rich Zichy family ▲ 226. During the
19th century it enjoyed a certain level of industrial and
commercial development, due in particular to the Óbuda
shipyards (Óbudai Hajógyár) ▲ 226 and the Goldberger
printed-textiles factory. With the urban development of the
1970s, Óbuda lost much of its old character and acquired a
more modern appearance.

ÓBUDA THROUGH THE AGES

CLOISTER OF THE POOR CLARES The Cloister of the Poor
Clares was built in Óbuda in the 14th century, at the
intersection of what are today Kis Korona utca, Perc utca
and Mókus utca, near the Franciscan monastery. An earlier
cloister of the Poor Clares had been built at Nagyszombat in
1238. Some 215 feet long by 65 feet wide, the Óbuda cloister
became the mother house of the order's convents throughout
Hungary and a center of education for the daughters of the
nobility. Medieval documents attest to its remarkable beauty.
Its founder was Elizabeth of Poland, wife of Charles I
(1308–42) and mother of Louis the Great of Anjou (1342–82
● 28. The charter of foundation (1344) records that she had
the cloister, church, cemetery and storehouses built to
ensure her own and her parents' salvation. Elizabeth
also arranged that she would be buried here,
though her ashes were eventually taken to
Pozsony (now Bratislava), before the
region was devastated by the
Turks. The church and the load-
bearing walls of the wings have
been rebuilt, and can be seen at
no. 3 Mókus utca (next to the
primary school).
  A VANISHED WORLD Old Óbuda,
where Germans and Jews lived
and worked together in an atmosphere of mutual respect, no
longer exists. The houses of these thousands of industrious
craftsmen have long since disappeared, as have their trade
signs ▲ 224. Mókus utca is one of the few
streets that has preserved the
atmosphere of this past age –
including the delightful
Kéhli Mama

...beneath the plane trees of the baths, in the porch of the house opposite, by night in small stations, in a boat on the Danube, at Normafa and beneath the kiosks of Buda – he was still waiting for a woman...'

Gyula Krúdy

PORCH OF THE KISCELL MUSEUM
Kiscelli utca runs steeply up to the museum from Bécsi út. The museum ★ ▲ *224* occupies a former Trinitarian monastery (the church was completed in 1760, the cloister in 1784). The top of Kiscell Hill (Kiscelli-hegy) offers a view of the modern district – a concrete jungle of public housing units, built from the 1960s onward.

restaurant, where Gyula Krúdy (*see left*) used to have lunch. Krúdy's novels are imbued with the atmosphere, scents and colors of old Óbuda, and populated by the beautiful women who formed part of its intrinsic charm.
THE FORMER ÓBUDA SYNAGOGUE In the 18th century a Jewish community settled in Óbuda. This settlement was encouraged by the Zichy counts, since the community's commercial activity relaunched the city's trade, while the taxes collected greatly increased their income. The former Óbuda Synagogue (which was predated by other synagogues) stands at no. 163 Lajos utca. The large neoclassical building was built in the early 1820s by the architect András Landherer. After World War Two the diminished Jewish Community could not afford to rebuild the synagogue and it was taken over by the national-heritage

ÓBUDA PARISH CHURCH
The church was built in Baroque style (1744–9) by János György Paur. The carved Rococo pulpit and the statues of Saint Flórián and Saint John of Nepomuk (1753–4) that stand on the square in front of the church are the work of Károly Bebó. On the plinths of the statues are the coats of arms of Count Miklós Zichy ▲ *226* and his wife.

▲ THE KISCELL MUSEUM
(Kiscelli Múzeum)

The Kiscelli Múzeum houses the modern-history department of Budapest History Museum, and a museum of modern art. The church and cloister were originally occupied by the Trinitarian Order, then used as barracks and, later, as a military hospital. In 1912 Miksa Schmidt, an antique dealer and maker of Viennese furniture, bought the monastery buildings which he bequeathed to the city in 1935. They were converted into a museum, in accordance with his wishes.

AN UNUSUAL BALLOT BOX
(19th century)
This unusual object relates to the introduction, in 1765, of secret ballots for the election of members of the municipal council. Balls were placed in the brass dishes, and the results posted on plaques suspended between the columns.

INSTALLATION BY THE ARTIST RÓBERT SWIERKIEWITS (1994)

STATUES FROM THE HOLY TRINITY COLUMN
The museum has many relics from the past that bring the history of Buda and Pest to life. The Baroque statues of the Holy Trinity Column ● *71*, ▲ *202*, erected during an outbreak of plague in the city, are particularly intriguing.

SIGN OF A LOCKSMITH AND WROUGHT-IRON CRAFTSMAN
The museum's splendid collection of craftsmen's signs gives an idea of what a 19th-century street would have looked like when metal signs replaced painted wooden boards.

the hill on which the museum stands was named after a copy of the statue of the Virgin of Mariazell (in Austria) placed there in the 18th century. 'Klein Mariazell' became Kiscell. The cells of the former cloister have been converted into small exhibition rooms re-creating 18th-century interiors. The furniture of the Steindl studio is a marvelous example of the Hungarian Biedermeier style.

MODERN AND CONTEMPORARY ART

Budapest's Municipal Art Gallery was founded in 1933. Twenty years later, in 1953, its collections were transferred to the recently opened Hungarian National Gallery ▲ *194*, except for the paintings that remained the property of the municipality. These are now housed in the Kiscell Museum. In the 1960s a collection of contemporary art was opened, and in 1988 the former church hosted its first exhibition. Today it is a prime venue for Hungarian and international contemporary art. It is also an ideal venue for concerts and other performances. Reproduced here are *Encounter in a Cemetery* (above) by István Farkas; *At the Theater* (far left) by Pál C. Molnár; and *Girl Icon* (left) by Lajos Vajda ▲ *233*.

Fő tér
The Zichy Mansion (above left) is at no. 1 Fő tér, and the town hall of District III (above right) at no. 3.

department. Since 1986 it has been used as studios by Hungarian television. The tympanum above the portico is still crowned by the twin tablets of the Ten Commandments.

ZICHY MANSION The beautiful and imposing Zichy Mansion stands at no. 1 Fő tér. It was built for Miklós Zichy between 1746 and 1757 in a Rococo style derived from German Baroque ● *70* and was designed by a master stone mason from Buda, Henrik János Jäger. It was carefully restored after being damaged in World War Two and has a particularly beautiful carved staircase. Today the mansion and its outbuildings house four museums: the PINCE GALLERY, the KASSÁK MEMORIAL MUSEUM (devoted to the work of Lajos Kassák, a key figure in Hungarian Constructivism but also a writer, a poet, and activist), the ÓBUDA LOCAL-HISTORY MUSEUM and the VASARELY MUSEUM.

VICTOR VASARELY
Victor Vasarely was born Győző Vásárhelyi, in Pécs, in 1908. He served his apprenticeship in Budapest, where he was influenced by the Bauhaus tradition, and in 1931 went to live and work in Paris. He developed his artistic concepts and philosophy through a form of geometric abstraction that became known as kinetic art or Op Art. He donated hundreds of his works to Hungary.

ZSIGMOND KUN FOLK ART COLLECTION
This collection is housed on the top floor of an 18th-century apartment block, opposite the Zichy Mansion, on Fő tér. In 1976 Zsigmond Kun and his wife donated their collection to District III. This small museum of folk art has collections of Hungarian ceramics, textiles, sculpture and furniture.

ÓBUDA ISLAND (Óbudai-sziget) The Óbuda shipyards were developed at the southern end of Óbuda Island, from 1834 onward, on the narrow branch of the Danube. At the time they were the country's most important industrial complex. The huge shipyard founded around 1867 by an Austrian steam-navigation company covered an area of some 30 acres. Most of its installations were built on the Hajógyár peninsula (Hajógyári-sziget), to the west of the winter port, which is joined to Óbuda Island by a narrow strip of land. Today the island is a venue for rock concerts and other forms of musical entertainment, including the annual DIÁKSZIGET FESTIVAL, which attracts visitors from all over Europe. The island also has many public tennis courts and giant slides for children.

MILITARY TOWN BATHS The remains of the Thermae Majore (Military Town Baths) can be seen in the ROMAN BATHS MUSEUM (Fürdö Múzeum), located in the Flórián tér underpass. They were discovered in 1778 by workmen digging a lime pit. From then on they were excavated on a regular basis by István Schönvisner, professor of Latin at Pest University. The news of this archeological discovery caused a sensation in Vienna, and the Empress Maria Theresa financed the excavations. In 1849 workmen laying pipes

> 'Of all the districts in Budapest, [Óbuda] was the most provincial, to the point that you felt you were in an olden-day village on the Danube, with its single-story houses, winding streets and rural-Baroque churches.'

> John Lukacs

beneath Szentendrei út discovered a Roman inscription which confirmed Schönvisner's theory that the baths had been built for the permanent garrison (Legio II Adjutrix) of Aquincum. The excavations were finally completed in 1984. It has now been established that, like many Roman baths of this period, the Flórián tér complex had changing rooms, a tepid bath, a hot bath, a steam bath, a cold bath, a cool room and an open-air swimming pool. The water for the baths came from two main sources: aqueducts carried water from the thermal springs (still in use today) of Római Fürdő, while a system of pipes running beneath the Vörösvári Valley brought water from the hills to the west of the military town. The soldiers exercised in a huge gymnasium (260 feet by 100 feet). The nymphaeum, a large central room surrounded by altars dedicated to the health-giving powers of the nymphs, probably served as a place for meetings and public business.

IMRE VARGA GALLERY (Varga Imre Gyűteménye) The Varga Imre Gyűteménye, at no. 7 Laktanya utca, has a permanent exhibition of the works of the sculptor Imre Varga. His public commissions (depicting, among others, Miklós Radnóti, Zoltán Kodály, Béla Bartók, Mihály Károlyi, Attila József and Franz Liszt) can be seen throughout Hungary. His Prometheus in Chains – a piece of ruthless realism – hit the headlines in 1965. This contemporary visual artist (born in 1923) is one of the greatest and most prolific Hungarian sculptors of the 20th century.

HERCULES VILLA This Roman villa (2nd–3rd century AD) is situated at nos. 19–21 Meggyfa utca, on the northern edge of the Roman military town. Its name comes from the scenes depicted on its mosaic floors. These show Hercules shooting an arrow at the centaur Nessus, who is carrying off Deianeira ▲ 26; and Hercules drinking with the satyrs. In the garden of the villa are sarcophagi (3rd–4th century AD), the villa's baths, the watchman's quarters and the underfloor central heating system. More mosaics can be seen in the nearby buildings erected in the 1960s to protect the remains of the paving.

KASSAK MEMORIAL MUSEUM
(no. 1 Fö tér)
The museum presents the very varied artistic and literary works of Lajos Kassák (1916–67).

THE AQUINCUM MUSEUM ▲ *228*
The museum occupies a building (a copy of a Greek temple) erected in 1894 on the site of Roman Aquincum, which was systematically excavated in the late 19th century. It is surrounded by the excavated remains of the Roman civilian town.

▲ THE AQUINCUM MUSEUM
(Aquincumi Múzeum)

Hydra, (water organ).

The five rooms of the Aquincumi Múzeum house the religious, functional and decorative objects discovered during the excavation of the Roman civilian town. A sculpture of Mithras ● *26* killing the life-giving cosmic bull attests to the importance of his cult in Aquincum. The cult of this Persian god of light spread to the ports and garrisons of the Western Roman Empire, in particular along the banks of the Danube and Rhine, during the 2nd century AD.

Detail from a fresco.

NEMESIS (2nd century AD). The Greek goddess Nemesis was the personification of divine vengeance. She is depicted here with a torch in her right hand and a globe in her left. At her side is a griffin resting one of its paws on a wheel.

AN UNUSUAL MUSICAL INSTRUMENT
In 1930 a portable water organ (hydra) was discovered among the ruins of a building in the civilian town. An inscription on a small bronze plaque revealed that Gaius Julius Viatorinus presented this organ to the firefighters of Aquincum in 228. Visitors to the museum can see a working reconstruction (top of page).

Below: marble sculptural group.

AROUND
BUDAPEST
Miklós Mátyássy

Right: detail of a Roman tombstone (Lapidarium, Szentendre).

THE DANUBE BEND, FAMED FOR ITS NATURAL BEAUTY
The caves, gorges and broad-leaved forests make this mountainous section of the Danube one of the most visited beauty spots in Hungary. The region is also rich in game (wild boar, deer) and was one of the favorite hunting grounds of the kings of Hungary.

Between Esztergom and Budapest the Danube makes a sharp turn and flows between the Visegrád and Pilis Hills on the right bank and the Cserhát and Börzsöny Hills on the left, before entering the Great Plain. The Danube Bend (Dunakanyar) ■ *18*, ▲ *118*, ◆ *248* is one of the most beautiful and most visited regions in Hungary. Traversed by the Romans, Magyars, Turks, Serbs, Germans and Slovaks, it is particularly rich in history. The right bank is notable for the former royal seats of Esztergom ▲ *238* and Visegrád ▲ *235* and the 'Mediterranean' town of Szentendre, while the left bank has a series of picturesque villages, nestling at the foot of the Börzsöny Hills, and the Baroque episcopal town of Vác ▲ *234*. The primarily agricultural Szentendre Island is renowned for its strawberries.

SZENTENDRE

In contrast to Vác, which is steeped in Catholic tradition, Szentendre is characterized by its simplicity, intimacy and harmony. Unfortunately the hordes of tourists, cheap restaurants and stores selling souvenirs and knickknacks mar the overall effect. But you only have to wander away from the main square and stop in front of a window grille, doorway or flight of steps, or pause to enjoy a hilltop view of tiled roofs with the Danube and Szentendre Island in the background, to understand what attracted so many artists to the town.

HISTORY Illyrians, Celts, Romans (their camp was called Ulcisia Castra), Huns, Lombards and then the Magyars inhabited this site, which from 1146 was known as Sanct Andreas. The town's present-day appearance, so reminiscent of Mediterranean Balkan towns, is due to southern

'In the late afternoon, opposite the end of the island where I had spent the day, I reached Szentendre, a small rural Baroque town, with its pathways, paved streets, tiled roofs and onion-shaped domes.'

Patrick Leigh Fermor

lavonic influences. In 1690 some 40,000 Serbs, under the adership of their patriarch Arzenje Cernojevic, fled from ne Turks and sought refuge in Hungary. Around 6,000 of nese refugees settled in Szentendre, which had become epopulated during the Turkish occupation. In the space of nly a few decades the town was transformed into a thriving enter of Serbian culture, with seven Orthodox churches, a ishop's palace, a teachers' training college nd a high school. This period of prosperity ame to an end in the 19th century, when ne town suffered a series of fires, floods nd epidemics, plus an outbreak of hylloxera, which devastated the town's raditional red-wine production.

ő tér. In the center of the main square Fő tér) is a commemorative cross erected y the merchants' guild. The square has two nuseums and an art gallery, and a number f other interesting buildings. The NIKOLICS IOUSE (Nikolics Ház), built in 1800, is chly decorated in copf style (or Zopfstil), German and Central-European variation f Rococo characterized by the use of trapwork moldings. Other Rococo uildings include the former KORONA RESTAURANT (1770), adorned with stucco ine branches, and the BLAGOVEŠTENSKA CHURCH ▲ 232 or CHURCH OF THE ANNUNCIATION (on the corner of Görög utca, vhich leads down to the quayside). Built in 1752 by the Greek nerchants of Szentendre, who lived on Görög utca (Greek treet), it was designed by András Mayerhoffer ● 70, ▲ 240. Outside, on one of the side walls, are the tombstone of a Greek merchant and a fresco depicting Saint Helen and Saint Constantine (the Roman emperor Constantine the Great). The icons of the richly carved Rococo iconostasis, dedicated o the Annunciation, are the work of the artist Mihály Zsivkovics. On the corner of Bogdányi utca (which takes you o PREOBRAŽENSKA CHURCH) stands the delightfully named NOSTALGIA HOUSE, a Baroque building now devoted o tourism. From 1812 to 1816 the copf-style ▲ 231 uilding at no. 6 Fő tér was a Serbian teachers' raining college. Today it houses the Ferenczy

The narrow streets of Szentendre, its hills, houses, churches and Orthodox crosses give the feeling of a town on a human scale.

SZENTENDRE AND THE ARTS
In the late 19th century artists helped to put Szentendre (which now has sixteen museums) back on the map. To such an extent that by 1928 the local Society of Painters was able to attract well-known Post-Impressionist and Constructivist artists. A few years later Lajos Vajda founded the Szentendre School, which became increasingly oriented toward Surrealist and avant-garde art. The town's first 'artists' colony' was built in the 1930s, and a second colony was established in the 1970s. In the early 1980s a new generation of Hungarian avant-garde artists used to meet in the Vajda Lajos Stúdió.

Sign of the
Kovács Margit Múzeum.

ARCHITECTURE

Visitors to Szentendre tend to be impressed not so much by individual monuments (although some are remarkable in their own right) as by the overall impression of the town. Its Baroque and Rococo mansions and churches, and its simple houses have a balance and harmony reminiscent of certain Italian towns.

CROSS OF THE MERCHANTS' GUILD AND BLAGOVESTENSKA CHURCH
The Rococo cross, decorated with icons, was erected in 1763 by Serbian merchants to thank God for protecting the town against the plague.

Múzeum. Károly Ferenczy (1862–1917), the founding father of modern Hungarian painting and the Nagybánya colony of Impressionists, lived and worked in Szentendre during the early part of his career. The museum offers an excellent overview of Ferenczy's own paintings, together with the work of his wife, Olga Fialka, and their twin son and daughter – Béni, a sculptor, and Noémi, a tapestry designer – who were born in Szentendre in 1890.

MARGIT KOVÁCS MUSEUM The seemingly naïve colored figurines and reliefs for which the controversial sculptor and ceramist Margit Kovács (1902–77) is known were inspired by Romanesque and Hungarian folk art. A delightful collection of her work, donated to the town by the artist, is housed in an early-18th-century Baroque building (no. 1 Vastagh György utca, near Fő tér) that has at various times served as salt warehouse, post office, parish office and merchant's premises.

ČIPROVAČKA CHURCH Built between 1750 and 1794 by refugees from Čiprovač (a town in the Srem region of Eastern Slavonia), this church is the largest in Szentendre. It is dedicated to Saint Peter and Saint Paul and has been a Roman Catholic church since 1918.

BARCSAY MUSEUM The artist Jenő Barcsay (1900–88), who developed a highly individual Constructivist style, taught at the Academy of Fine Arts in Budapest. He donated the entire

> Szentendre is a sort of Danubian Montmartre, where the colors of the houses and the paintings exhibited in the streets blend with the colors of the river, and where those who have time to linger are enveloped by a light-hearted, fluid gaiety...'
>
> Claudio Magris

ontents of his studio (paintings, mosaics and various projects or mural compositions in Szentendre) to the town, where he ad lived and worked since 1929. The collection is housed in what was originally two buildings, one Baroque and the other eoclassical.

OWN HALL Although its façade had become the symbol of zentendre, it was renovated in its present neo-Baroque style n 1929. The rest of the building dates from the 18th century.

OPOVAČKA CHURCH The church was built by refugees from Opovac in 1746, in massively proportioned Baroque style. It was taken over by the Calvinists in 1913, and its iconostasis transferred to Hercegszántó in southern Hungary.

CATHOLIC PARISH CHURCH This church was built in the early 14th century, using the walls of an earlier 13th century church, and renovated in the 15th and 18th centuries. Its restoration in the 1950s revealed many Romanesque and Gothic elements, including a sundial on top of a buttress. The frescos in the choir date from the 1930s.

BÉLA CZOBEL MUSEUM Béla Czóbel (1883–1976) was a Hungarian Fauvist and representative of the Paris School. From 1945 until his death, he was president of the Szentendre Society of Painters. The museum (at no. 1 Templom tér) presents his own characteristically colorful work and that of his wife, Mária Mondok (1896–1971).

POŽEREVAČKA CHURCH Built by refugees from Pozerevac in 1759, this church is dedicated to the Archangel Michael. It stands on the site of an earlier wooden church (1690), from which it has retained the iconostasis (1740). The main entrance is of later construction, as is the church tower (1794).

LAJOS VAJDA MUSEUM A leading 20th-century Hungarian artist and a key figure in the second generation of Hungarian avant-garde art, Lajos Vajda (1908–41) ▲ 225, 231 spent much of his short life in the town. His drawings, collages and paintings are imbued with motifs both from Szentendre and from the rural architecture of the surrounding area – which he studied methodically, together with his friend and colleague Dezső Korniss, with a view to creating a new Central-European art form. Several works by Korniss can be seen at the museum.

RAB RABY TÉR RÁBY HÁZ (*see above right*) is situated in the old Catholic Dalmatian district and is one of a pair of houses that used to belong to a local winegrower. The date of their construction (1768) can be seen above the Baroque entrance, where the two façades meet.

CHURCH OF THE TRANSFIGURATION (Preobraženska Church) This church (at no. 40 Bogdányi út) was built between 1741 and 1746 by Serbian tanners from Bosnia. The decorative elements of the façade were added later. The raised iconostasis, with its gilt Corinthian columns, is reminiscent of Russian and Ukrainian iconostases and was the first of its kind in Hungary. On a hill not far from the church stands the BOSNIAN TANNERS' CROSS, erected by the tanners' guild in the

LITERARY HISTORY
The Ráby House is named after Mátyás Ráby, the steward of Joseph II who denounced the abuses and fraudulent practices of the town's municipal employees. He was thrown into prison and later exiled. Mátyás Ráby became the hero of Mór Jókai's novel *Rab Ráby*.

COMMEMORATIVE CROSSES
These crosses are an important feature of Szentendre. The Tsar Lázár Cross stands on the Danube embankment. In 1690 the remains of this Serbian prince, executed after the Battle of Kosovo (1389), were temporarily housed in a church in Szentendre before being taken back to Serbia. The Serbs erected a Corinthian column surmounted by a wrought-iron cross on the site of the church.

INTERIOR OF THE BELGRADE CHURCH
The icons of the richly carved iconostasis were painted by Vazul Osztojics, an artist from Újvidék (now Novi Sad, in Serbia).

CHURCHES AND CROSSES
When the Serbs arrived in Szentendre they settled in seven districts, according to their region of origin. Each community built its own wooden church, facing east in accordance with Orthodox tradition. In the 18th century these wooden churches were replaced by stone buildings in Baroque or Rococo style. The Catholic Dalmatians shared Szentendre's parish church with the Hungarians and Germans. As the Serb population gradually left the town during the 19th century, Catholics and Protestants took over some of the Serbian Orthodox churches.

18th century, in a peaceful little square that offers a splendid view of the Danube.

THE IMRE ÁMOS AND MARGIT ANNA MUSEUM The Surrealist painter Imre Ámos (1907–44) died a victim of hard labor in a prison camp. His was a dreamlike, mystical world in which even the simplest of objects assumed symbolic meaning, the world of a Humanist at odds with his age. His wife – Margit Anna (1913–77), cofounder of the postwar European School, which brought together the proponents of abstract and Surrealist art – derived inspiration for her work from primitive art.

THE SERBIAN ORTHODOX CATHEDRAL On entering the gardens of the USPENIJE CHURCH (CHURCH OF THE ASSUMPTION), surrounded by trees and bounded by tombstones, you are immediately aware of a sense of calm, intimacy and simplicity. This Serbian Orthodox Cathedral, built in Rococo style in 1756–64, is also known as the BELGRADE CHURCH, since it was erected by the descendants of refugees from Belgrade. The SERBIAN ORTHODOX MUSEUM situated in the grounds, near the bishop's palace, houses some outstanding treasures of Serbian and Hungarian church art.

VÁC

The geographical situation of Vác (below) was ideally suited to human settlement and was inhabited from the end of the Bronze Age. During the Middle Ages the town, whose name appears in official records for the first time in 1075, enjoyed a period of prosperity. It was one of the ten sees founded by Stephen I ● 27, ▲ 239, and during the reign of Matthias Corvinus ● 32 Bishop Miklós Báthory transformed it into a cultural center. Between 1544 and 1686 Vác changed hands several times, though it was mostly under Ottoman control, and entered a period of decline. In the 18th century the extensive building program carried out by bishops Althan, Esterházy and, in particular, Kristóf Migazzi gave the town its

'We heard as much German as Hungarian on the awakening quayside of Visegrád; it was spoken by the Swabians that Géza had told me about.'

Patrick Leigh Fermor

present blend of late-Baroque and neoclassical architecture.
RELIGIOUS BUILDINGS Between 1761 and 1777 the cathedral was built on what is now Konstantin tér (Constantine Square) under the aegis of Bishop Migazzi. The cathedral's French architect, Isidore Canevale, who resided in Vienna, was inspired by the work of Jacques-Germain Soufflot and Giovanni Nicolo Servandoni, the architects of the Church of St-Sulpice in Paris. The frescos of the dome and high altar were the work of Franz Anton Maulbertsch, one of the most brilliant Baroque fresco painters in Central Europe. The other important religious buildings centered around the cathedral are the BISHOP'S PALACE; the SEMINARY; the PIARIST CHURCH, SCHOOL AND MONASTERY; and the former FRANCISCAN CHURCH (on Géza Király tér). The DOMINICAN CHURCH (which has a Rococo interior), the former SERBIAN ORTHODOX CHURCH, the PROVOST'S PALACE, the TOWN HALL and the INSTITUTE FOR THE DEAF AND DUMB constitute another group of Baroque buildings, around Március 15 tér.
TRIUMPHAL ARCH This structure, the only one of its kind in Hungary, was the work of Isidore Canevale (the architect of the cathedral). Bishop Migazzi had it erected in 1764, on the occasion of a visit by the Empress Maria Theresa. Since 1855 the THERESIANUM has been a prison; originally it was an academy for young aristocrats, founded by the empress. Among the many political prisoners incarcerated within its walls after the 1956 uprising ● 36 were the historian István Bibó ◆ 282 and Árpád Göncz, the current President of Hungary.

VISEGRÁD

Visegrád is one of the jewels of the Danube Bend. The abundant natural resources of this region rich in water and forests have been exploited since the Stone Age. They were strategically exploited by the Romans who founded the town of Pone Navata, which the Slavs renamed Vise Grad ('high fortress'). The early Hungarian kings built a fortress, church and monastery here. Visegrád enjoyed two golden ages: the first during the reign (1308–42) of Charles Robert of Anjou (Charles I) ● 28, when Visegrád was the capital of the kingdom of Hungary, and the second during the reign of Matthias Corvinus (1458–90) ●, 32.

CHURCH OF ST ANDREW (Izbég) Once a self-contained Serbian village, Izbég is now part of Szentendre. The CHURCH OF ST ANDREW (Szent András templom), built by the Serbs in 1738, has been a Roman Catholic church since 1948. The double commemorative cross of the Serbian calvary is mounted on a Doric column and surrounded by wrought ironwork.

SKANZEN OF OPEN-AIR VILLAGE MUSEUM (Szabadtéri Néprajzi Múzeum) Founded in 1967, this will, when complete, present an overview of the vernacular architectural of ten Hungarian regions. Extending over nearly 115 acres, it will comprise more than 300 re-erected buildings: houses, workshops, mills, churches and other buildings associated with Hungarian village life. At present only four regions are represented.

THE RUINED PALACE OF KING MATTHIAS
The capture of Visegrád by the Turks marked the beginning of the decline of the palace. It was completely destroyed in the 18th century, when Serbian immigrants used it as a 'quarry' to build their houses. In 1934 János Schulek discovered the remains of the palace. About a third of it has now been excavated.

SOLOMON'S TOWER Built around 1250 in late-Gothic style, this tower was originally the keep of the lower fortress. The King Solomon after whom the tower is named never saw it: he was in fact imprisoned from 1081 to 1083 in another tower in Visegrád by King László I. The tower did, however, have a royal occupant: Vlad Tepes (Vlad the Impaler, better known as Count Dracula), Prince of Wallachia, who was imprisoned there until 1476. Apart from its defensive functions, the tower was used to accommodate the royal court, the guests and, of course, the royal guard. The tower has been restored and extended, and now houses the KING MATTHIAS MUSEUM (Mátyás Múzeum). As well as tracing the history of the reconstruction work at Visegrád, the museum includes such items as a fountain from the Angevin period and marbles from the reign of King Matthias ● *32* – among them the Hercules Fountain (on which the demigod is depicted fighting the Hydra) and the Visegrád Madonna.

THE HISTORY OF THE ROYAL PALACE In 1316 Charles Robert of Anjou ● *28*, ▲ *235* took up residence in Visegrád. He built a royal palace, one of the most beautiful of its time, between the lower fortress and the town. In 1335 the palace hosted the Visegrád Congress, when the kings of Hungary, Bohemia and Poland and the leaders of the Teutonic Order agreed to ensure the free passage of Hungarian merchandise to the west and north. Under Louis the Great of Anjou (1342–82) the edifice became a tripartite structure – with the Royal Palace to the north, the queen's palace to the south, and the chapel in between. Sigismund of Luxembourg (1387–1437) ● *28* extended the complex toward the Danube. Further construction was carried out between 1474 and 1486, during the reign of Matthias Corvinus. It was begun by Saxon craftsmen from Transylvania in late-Gothic style, and completed in Renaissance style under the direction of the Italian architect Chimenti Camicia.

**DETAIL OF THE
LION FOUNTAIN**
According to
historical records,
during royal
receptions the
two lion's-head

gargoyles spewed
forth wine (one
red, the other
white), instead of
water.

THE PALACE TODAY The palace was built on several
levels, on a series of terraces. The first level is occupied
by the main courtyard and steps. On the second are the
remains of a Gothic Ambulatory surrounding the
courtyard (where the red-marble Hercules Fountain,
by the Italian sculptor Tommaso Fiamberti, was
discovered). On the third level are the remains of the
ROYAL APARTMENTS, of which a balustrade and balcony
can still be seen. Also on this level was the CHAPEL,
to which King Matthias added a sculpted ceiling,
alabaster altars and, above the entrance, the relief
known as the Visegrád Madonna. The royal baths and
the king's private garden – with its LION FOUNTAIN,
a masterpiece of Hungarian Renaissance
sculpture – occupy the fourth level.

THE CITADEL (Fellegvár) The Citadel was built
between 1245 and 1255 by Maria Lascaris, wife of Béla IV,
to protect nuns and orphans in the event of renewed Mongol
attacks. Charles Robert of Anjou lived there from 1323 until
the completion of his palace in 1330, and constructed a
number of buildings within the walls. It subsequently became
a royal treasury, where the Hungarian royal insignia and,
under Louis the Great, the Polish crown were housed. In 1440
Elizabeth of Luxembourg (daughter of King Sigismund) had
her governess steal the Hungarian crown from the treasury,
so that she could crown her son, László V. Matthias Corvinus
had further work carried out on the citadel, then in 1543 it
was occupied by the Turks. During the course of the next
hundred years it changed hands several times. Finally, in 1702
the Emperor Leopold I, fearing an initiative on the part of
Ferenc Rákóczi's independence movement, had it dismantled.

NAGYMAROS AND ZEBEGÉNY

Nagymaros, at the foot of the Börzsöny Hills, is an extremely
popular resort with a splendid view of Visegrád. Zebegény
occupies an elevated position on the left bank of the Danube,
overlooking a bend in the river, and also offers some truly
magnificent views. A row of Slovakian peasant houses in the
center of the village acts as a reminder of the
immigrants who founded the present community
in the 18th century. In 1920 the great landscape
painter István Szőnyi (1894–1960) came
to live in the village.

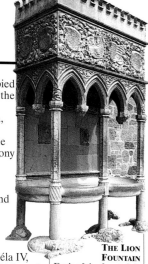

**THE LION
FOUNTAIN**
Each of the fountain's
five hexagonal
columns rests on a
prostrate lion. The
ceiling is decorated
with the coat of arms
of the Hunyadi
dynasty and inscribed
with the year
(incomplete) of
the fountain's
construction
(probably 1473).
The frieze around the
canopy is decorated
with the arms of the
territories conquered
by Matthias Corvinus.

**THE VISEGRÁD
GROUP**
On February 15, 1991
– 656 years after the
alliance signed by
Charles Robert at the
Visegrád Congress –
the presidents of
Czechoslovakia
(Václav Havel),
Poland (Lech Walesa)
and Hungary (Árpád
Göncz) met in
Visegrád at the
instigation of the
Hungarian prime
minister, József
Antall ▲ *215*. His aim
was to create a strong
Central-European
alliance and
coordinate the steps
leading to the three
countries joining the
European Union.
This tripartite
alliance, known as
the Visegrád Group,
was recognized by
Brussels.

THE BASILICA OF ESZTERGOM
The Cathedral of the Assumption was built in 1822–69 in neoclassical style, according to plans by

the architects Pál Kühne, János Packh and József Hild. It stands inside the walls of the old fortress and is the largest church in Hungary.

Chapel of the Royal Palace in Esztergom.

A large part of Szőnyi's work was devoted to views of the Danube. His house has now been transformed into a museum (the garden still contains the 'Zebegény bench', immortalize in one of the artist's best-known paintings). The village becomes particularly animated in the summer, when open workshops introduce would-be artists of all ages to various branches of the arts. The interior and exterior of the CATHOLIC CHURCH are a fine example of Hungarian Secessionist architecture. It was built in 1908–9 by Károly Kó ▲ 176 and Béla Jánsky, who were inspired by the work of Transylvanian architects. The NAVIGATION MUSEUM in the VINCE FARKAS HOUSE, named after a former river pilot, trace the history of navigation on the Danube.

ESZTERGOM

Situated about 40 miles north of Budapest, the town of Esztergom was the cradle of the Hungarian state and for the last thousand years has been the seat of the Roman Catholic Church in Hungary. The Magyar leader Prince Géza, grandson of Árpád ● 27, transferred his residence to the tow in 972. Previously it had been the site of Solva, an important military camp on the fortified boundary (limes) of the Roma Empire and, several centuries later, of Österringen, the easternmost fortress of the empire of Charlemagne. Géza's son Vajk was born in Esztergom, where he was later baptized and given the name Stephen. And it was in Esztergom, on January 1, 1001, that he became the first king of Hungary.

> 'Esztergom appeared, a strange silhouette: a cube and a dome supported by many columns.'
>
> Le Corbusier

His coronation was a key event in the nation's history since it marked Hungary's incorporation into Western Europe and the creation of the Hungarian state. With the consent of Rome, the future Saint Stephen divided the country into ten sees. The Archbishop of Esztergom was made primate of Hungary, with the status of a prince, and throughout kingdom's history was responsible for crowning the kings of Hungary.

THE ROYAL PALACE The construction of Hungary's oldest royal residence – which later became the archbishop's palace – was begun by Prince Géza in the late 10th century. Its remains include the former cathedral and its Porta speciosa; the study (the Chamber of Virtues) of the Humanist primate János Vitéz; and an 11th-century chapel with frescos, depicting lions and the Tree of Life, that reflect the influence of Byzantine art.

BASILICA The monumental interior contains some memorable treasures. The BAKÓCZ CHAPEL, built in 1506–11 by Archbishop Tamás Bakócz to commemorate his own glory, is a masterpiece of Hungarian Renaissance architecture. The ALTAR was sculpted in Carrara marble by the Florentine artist Andrea Ferrucci (1465–1526). The CHAPEL is the only part of the 11th-century Cathedral of St Adalbert to have survived intact, and was dismantled and reinstalled in the new basilica. The CATHEDRAL TREASURY contains crosses, chalices, calvaries, bishops' crooks, and other religious objects, many of them crafted in gold or silver, ranging from the Middle Ages to the 17th century. Particularly worthy of note are the richly decorated Portable Calvary of King Matthias, the Cross of Canon Böjthe, decorated with diamonds and enamel animals, and remarkable embroidered chasubles. The CRYPT contains the tombs of the bishops of Esztergom. In 1991, sixteen years after his death, the remains of Cardinal Mindszenty ● 37, ▲ 135 were interred in the crypt.

MUSEUM OF CHRISTIAN ART (Keresztény Múzeum) ★ This is one of Hungary's most splendid museums. It was founded in the 19th century by two devoted collectors, Archbishop János Simor and Bishop Arnold Ipolyi. As well as Hungarian art from the 15th and 16th centuries (including polyptychs by Tamás Kolozsvári and Master M. S. ▲ 194) and the extraordinary Holy Tomb of Garamszentbenedek (from a Benedictine Monastery in what is now Slovakia), it has a rich collection of about a hundred Italian paintings from the 13th and 14th centuries, including works by Duccio and his school and a beautiful Lady with Unicorn tapestry. The Austrian, German, Spanish and Flemish sections (the latter has a painting of Christ on the Cross attributed to Hans Memling) are also of great interest.

UPS AND DOWNS OF A RELIGIOUS CITY
For over two hundred years Esztergom was the capital of the kingdom of Hungary. In 1242, after the Mongol invasion, Béla IV transferred the royal residence to Buda. However, that did not prevent religious colleges and institutions from flourishing in this seat of Hungarian Catholicism and cradle of the Renaissance. In 1543 the Turkish occupation brought this golden age to an end, and the archiepiscopal see was not reinstated until 1820. The Communist regime conducted an unremitting campaign against Esztergom, its priests and, above all, its archbishop, Cardinal József Mindszenty, who became a national martyr.
Above: Víziváros Parish Church, Esztergom (18th century).

The statue of the Empress Elizabeth ● *30*, ▲ *182* st
stands at the center of the park that bears her nam

VISITING GÖDÖLLŐ
The domes and shaped pediment, the grand staircase and the high windows of the great hall make the Royal Palace at Gödöllő one of the finest country residences in Hungary ● *71*. Since 1985 it has been rebuilt and the apartments refurbished in their original style. It now houses the ROYAL PALACE MUSEUM.

GÖDÖLLŐ PALACE

In 1733 Count Antal Grassalkovich (1694–1771), president of the Chamber of Deputies and confidant of the Empress Maria Theresa, embarked on an ambitious project in the village of Gödöllő, about 19 miles from Pest. Between 1744 and 1749 a Baroque country residence was built according to plans by the great architect András Mayerhoffer. The empress herself stayed there in 1751. During the second phase of construction undertaken by Count Grassalkovich – which was continued by his son Antal II and grandson Antal III (1771–1841) – the mansion assumed the form of a double 'U'. When the male line of the family ended with Antal III, the estate passed to the female line and, in 1850, was sold to Baron György Sina. It was then bought by the Hungarian state, in 1867, and modified by Miklós Ybl ● *76* before being presented the palace to the Emperor Franz Joseph and Empress Elizabeth as a coronation gift. The new queen of Hungary was particularly fond of the palace, which became the summer residence of the imperial family, and took every opportunity to stay there The Emperor Charles I (King Károly IV) ● *96* stayed at the palac just before the collapse of the Austro-Hungarian monarchy. Two years later it became the summer residence of Miklós Horthy (regent of Hungary 1920–44). From 1945 to 1990 the Russian Army used Gödöllő as a military base and totally devastated the estate.

ERZSÉBET
KIRÁLYNÉNK

BUDAPEST
PRACTICAL INFORMATION

THINGS TO KNOW BEFORE YOU GO

In the US

EMBASSY OF THE
REPUBLIC OF HUNGARY
3910 Shoemaker St,
N. W.
Washington, D. C.
20008
Tel: (202) 362 6730
Fax: (202) 966 8135

223 East 52nd Street
New York, NY 10022
Tel: (212) 752 0669
Fax (212) 755 5986

11766 Wilshire Bld,
Suite #410
Los Angeles,
CA 90025
Tel: (310) 473 9344
Fax: (310) 479 6443

HUNGARIAN NATIONAL
TOURIST OFFICE
150 East 58th St
New York
NY 10155-3398
Tel: (212) 355 0240
Fax (212) 207 4103
email:
hnto@gotohungary.com

In the UK

HUNGARIAN EMBASSY
35 Eaton Place
London SW1X 8DY
Tel: 020 7235 5218
General Information
line: 0891 171204

HUNGARIAN TOURIST
OFFICE
46 Eaton Place
London SW1X 8AL
Tel: 020 7823 1032

In Budapest

US EMBASSY
V. Szabadsag ter 12
Tel (36 1) 267 4400
Open Mon–Fri
8.30–11am
email:
webmaster@usis.hu

BRITISH EMBASSY
V. Harmincad utca 6
Tel : (36 1) 266 2888
Open Mon–Fri
9.30–noon, 2.30–4pm

HUNGARIAN NATIONAL TOURIST OFFICE

H-1024 Budapest,
Margit körút 85.
Tel: (36 1) 355 1133
Fax: (36 1) 375 3819
email: htbudapest@
hungarytourism.hu

FORMALITIES

If you have a British,
US, Canadian, or
European passport
(but not from Turkey
or Albania) you do
not need a visa.

You will be granted
access for 90 days.
The passport must
be valid for a further
6 months.

EXCHANGE RATE

Approx: 380 Forint to
the £, and 243 Forint
to the US$.
(see also p. 250)

TIME ZONE

Budapest is one hour
ahead of the UK and
six hours ahead of
the East coast of the
United States.

PHONING BUDAPEST

Dial 00 36 1 from the
UK
Dial 011 36 1 from
the US
(see also p. 252)

CUSTOMS

On entering Hungary,
the tax free limit of
goods is 250,000 Ft
per person. On
leaving Hungary:
items purchased or
received as a gift
worth up to an
individual value
of 30,300 Ft and
a total value of
303,000 Ft are not

subject to custom
fees.
Warning: these
figures are subject
to constant change.
You must keep all
receipts of purchase
which if exceeding
the limit need to be
declared at
Tourinform ◆ 251.

HEALTH

No special
vaccinations are
required.

BANK HOLIDAYS IN HUNGARY

• Jan 1: New Year's
Day
• March 15: National
Day
• Easter Monday
• May 1: Labour Day
• Whitsun Monday
• August 20:
Constitution Day
• October 23:
Republic Day
• December 25-26:
Christmas, Boxing
Day
Working days may
be changed into
weekend holidays
and vice versa to
gain long weekends

BUDAPEST CARD

(see also page 246)
For three days one
can enjoy unlimited
use of public
transportation
and visit almost all
the museums in
Budapest for free!
The card can
be purchased in
Hungary upon
arrival but also
in the USA from:
INTERTICKET Hungary
Tel: (781) 275 5724
Fax:(781) 271 0914
E-mail: usa@
interticket.com
Website:
www.interticket.com

Also available from:
TRADESCO TOURS
Tel: (800) 833 3402
Fax: (310) 649 5852
E-mail: tradesco@
ix.netcom.com

BY AIR
FROM THE US

MALÉV Hungarian Airlines offers the only daily non-stop service from New York/JFK to Budapest, in code sharing with Delta Airlines.

◆ MALÉV New York
30 Fifth Avenue,
Suite #1900
New York, NY 10111
Tel: (800) 223 6884
or (212) 757 6480
Email:
newyork@malev.hu

◆ MALÉV Chicago
11 East Wacker
Drive, Suite # 306
Chicago, IL 60601
Tel: (800) 877 5429
or (312) 819 5353
Email:
chicago@malev.hu

◆ MALÉV Los
Angeles
1888 Century Park
East, Suite # 410
Los Angeles, CA
90067
Tel: (800) 262 5380
or (310) 286 7980
Email:
losangeles@malev.hu

◆ MALÉV Toronto
175 Bloor St East
Toronto, Ontario
M4W 3R8
Tel: (416) 944 0093
Fax: (416) 944 0095
Email:
toronto@malev.hu

For other airlines departing from other US cities contact:
◆ Delta Airlines
Tel: (800) 241 4141
◆ Northwest Airlines KLM
Tel: (800) 447 4747

◆ Lufthansa
Tel: (800) 645-3880
◆ Air France
Tel: (800) 237 2747
◆ British Air
Tel: (800) 247 9297

TRAVEL AGENCIES
◆ Molnar Travel
Agency
245 East 81st Street
New York, NY 10028
Tel: (212) 744 2967
Fax: (212) 535 3681

BY TRAIN
FROM THE US
EURAIL PASSES can be purchased for 15, or 21 consecutive days, 1, 2 or 3 months. Examples:
◆ Eurailpass provides unlimited first-class travel by train in Hungary and 16 other European countries.
◆ Eurail Saverpass, with a discount for two or more people traveling together, is ideal for couples or small groups.
◆ Eurail Youthpass entitles under 26 years olds to second-class travel in Hungary and 16 other European countries.
All Eurail passes must be purchased in North America, prior to departure. They cannot be purchased in Europe.
– For information on train schedules and booking in the US:

RAIL EUROPE
Tel: (800) 4 EURAIL
Fax: (800) 432 1 FAX
– For information and booking in Canada:
Tel: (800) 361 7245
Fax: (905) 602 4198
Website:
www.raileurope.com

BY AIR
FROM THE UK
Only 3 airlines from both Heathrow and Gatwick airports in London:
◆ British Airways
Tel: 0345 222111
From £219 return + £35 airport tax. Regular daily flights from Heathrow.
◆ British Midland
Tel: 0870 2407034
From £219 return + £35 airport tax. 1 flight per day from Heathrow.
◆ Malév (Hungarian Airlines)
Tel: 020 7439 0577
From £148 return + £35 airport tax. 3 flights per day: 2 from Heathrow, 1 from Gatwick. Check www.cheapflights.com for update on cheapest fares.

The cheapest deals will probably be organised deals inclusive of accommodation available through travel agencies. These deals range from B&B – 1 person £199 inclusive of flight, accommodation, and food – to 2 ★ hotel £275 all inclusive.

BY TRAIN
FROM THE UK
INTERNATIONAL TRAIN CENTRE:
Hudsons Place,
Victoria, London SW1
Tel: 020 7834 2345
EUROSTAR from
Waterloo – Paris
(Gare du Nord)

Standard economy: £129 return. If booked 7 days in advance: £89 return. Stay over a Saturday night: £99 return.

Connect to: Paris Gare de l'Est. Trains depart daily at 5.49pm, arrive in Budapest 12.03pm.

IN BUDAPEST
International Train Information:
Tel: (36 1) 461 55 00

TRAVEL AGENCIES
IN LONDON
◆ Budapest Breaks:
Tel: 020 7831 7626
◆ Danube Travel
Tel: 020 7724 7577

BY BUS
FROM THE UK
EUROLINE from
Victoria Station,
London.
– Depart from Victoria at 10am on Thu, arrive Budapest at noon on Fri.
Depart from Budapest at 10am on Sat, arrive at noon on Sun in Victoria Station.
Fare: over 25 years, £100
Under 25 years, £90
Tel: 020 7372 0470

BUDAPEST-VIENNA
ON THE DANUBE
From April to end October a hydrofoil service operates daily on the Danube between Budapest and Vienna, with a stop at Bratislava.
JOURNEY TIME:
4 hrs Vienna-Budapest, 5 hrs Budapest-Vienna.
FOR INFORMATION please contact MAHART Tours in Hungary:
District V
Belgrád rakpart
Tel: (36 1) 318 17 43
or (36 1) 318 15 86

TRAVELING TO BUDAPEST BY CAR:
DISTANCES

Paris–Budapest	905 miles
Brussels–Budapest	887 miles
London–Budapest	1144 miles
Rome–Budapest	775 miles
Prague–Budapest	353 miles
Vienna–Budapest	155 miles

◆ Getting about

(From the airport to the city center, city transport)

Budapest has a comprehensive and efficient transport system (BKV). Buses, trams, trolleycars and the subway run through the city from 4.30am to 11pm. Tickets are on sale at underground stations, tobacconists, newsagents, hotels and travel agencies. It is a good idea to buy a Budapest Card (Budapest Kártya ◆ 246) which offers free travel for three days on all local public transport.

From the Airport into Town

The airport is 15 miles from the city center.

FERIHEGY AIRPORT
DEPARTURE
INFORMATION
Tel: 296 70 00
ARRIVAL INFORMATION
Tel: 296 80 00
GENERAL INFORMATION
Tel: 296 96 96

MALÉV/DELTA flights depart from and arrive at Ferihegy Terminal 2A. All other airlines use Terminal 2B.

BUS
CENTRUM-BUSZ
This goes to Erzsébet tér (the central bus station)
DEPARTURES
Every 30 mins, from 5.30am to 9pm.
PRICE
600 Ft per passenger.
JOURNEY TIME
45 mins

AIRPORT MINIBUSZ
A shared taxi takes passengers wherever they want to go in the city and surrounding suburbs.
PRICE
1200 Ft per passenger. Tickets can be purchased at the service desk located in the passenger halls of both terminals.
RESERVATIONS
Tel: 296 85 55

TAXIS
RESERVATIONS
Tel: 282 22 22
PRICE
The cost is according to zone, and displayed at the taxi rank by the airport exit.

City transport

Bus, trams, trolleycars

• Public transport starts around 4.30am and finishes around 11pm. There is a limited night bus network: fifteen bus routes and two tram routes offer a service on the main lines.
• One ticket is valid for one journey on either the bus, the tram, the trolley or the subway but you cannot change from subway to tram or tram to bus with the same ticket. You will have to buy another one unless you have a day pass
Watch out! When the rail journey crosses the limits of the urban sector, the ticket is no longer valid. You should purchase an HÉV (suburban train) ticket; its price varies according to the destination.

TICKET OPTIONS
• Single ticket (1 journey) 90 Ft
• One-day ticket *(egy napi bérlet)* 700 Ft
• Three-day tourist ticket 1400 Ft

• Seven-day ticket *(egy heti bérlet)* 1650 Ft
• 14-day season ticket *(két heti bérlet)* 2250 Ft
• Monthly season ticket *(egy havi bérlet)* 3400 Ft
• No ticket necessary for children under 6 years old, traveling with an adult.

Things to remember
• Tickets cannot be purchased while traveling i.e. on board the transport system, and must be canceled (franked) on entering the vehicle.
• Fines have been increased: inspectors are sharp-eyed, and do not wear a uniform, only showing their official badge at the last minute.

SUBURBAN TRAINS
For suburban destinations, use HEV trains. For Szentendre, take the train from Batthyány tér; for Gödöllő, take the train from Örs vezér tere.

Our favorite tram routes
• Tram line no. 2 runs which along the bank of the Danube.
• Tram lines nos. 4 and 6 which follow the inner circle (Nagykörút ▲ 164), which encompasses the center of Pest over more than 2.5 miles between the Margit and Petőfi bridges.

Subway

The network is 18 miles long and has three lines, distinguished by a number and a color:
Line 1, yellow;
Line 2, red;
Line 3, blue.
All lines intersect at Deak tér station.
The yellow line (known as the 'little subway') is the oldest in continental Europe

SUBWAY TICKETS
Unless you hae a day, week or month pass valid throughout the whole transport network, make sure that you buy the right subway ticket. These vary according to the distance and complexity of the journey.

CITY TICKET
This is valid only for travel on a single line for a journey of up to half-an-hour's duration and with a maximum of three stops.
Ticket price: 60Ft

CHANGE TICKET
This is valid for up to 1 hour on all lines, should it be necessary to change.
Ticket price: 135 Ft

ZONE-CHANGE TICKET
This is valid for up to one hour, including one change of lines before five consecutive stops.
Ticket price: 90 Ft

BUDAPEST TRANSPORT SYSTEM (BKV)
Information
Tel: 117 55 18 or 342 23 35

◆ GETTING ABOUT IN BUDAPEST
(Trains, scenic trips, the Budapest Card)

TRAINS
INTERNATIONAL
Budapest has three main-line railway stations:
- **KELETI PÁLYAUDVAR** (EAST STATION) Baross tér, VIII Tel: 313 68 35
- **NYUGATI PÁLYAUDVAR** (WEST STATION) Nyugati tér, XIII Tel: 349 01 15
- **DÉLI PÁLYAUDVAR** (SOUTHERN STATION) Krisztina körút, XII Tel: 322 78 60 or 375 62 93

INFORMATION
Mon-Fri: 6am-8pm
Tel: 342 91 50 or 322 40 52
8pm-6am in the rail stations.
RAIL PRICES
Tel: 322 90 35
REDUCTIONS
Available with Inter Rail, BLJ, Euro Domino, and Euro Mini Group railcards.
LEFT LUGGAGE
Available at all stations.

DOMESTIC TRAIN SERVICES
For domestic rail travel, intercity non-stop trains – besides other scheduled trains from Budapest's three railway stations – ensure rapid and reliable connections between Budapest and the main cities of Hungary.
INFORMATION
Tel: 461 54 00

RAIL-BUS
A 12-seater minibus, run by Hungarian Railways, links rail stations with travelers' destinations. It stops outside all stations throughout Hungary.
RESERVATIONS
Available on all Intercity lines throughout Hungary, and on board the train next to the guard.
FREE BONUS
Tickets delivered to your home on request (Budapest only).
INFORMATION
Tel: 353 27 22

SCENIC TRIPS
FUNICULAR (*sikló*)
This is on Clark Ádám tér, in the Buda Castle district (I). Its old-fashioned wagons (1870) climb up from the end of the Chain Bridge, which is the zero kilometer marker for all Hungary.
JOURNEY TIME
A few minutes only
OPENING TIMES
Every day (closed every other Mon) 7.30am–10pm
ACCESS
Bus no. 4 red, and no. 16; tram no. 19
FIACRES
Horse-drawn trips round the old city start from the Funicular exit.

CHAIR-LIFT (*libegő*)
From Zugliget up János Hill, suspended 8m above the ground over a rise of 262m.
JOURNEY TIME
15 mins
OPENING TIMES
May 16-Sep 15 9am–5pm (closed every other Mon); Sep 16-May 15, 9.30am–4pm
ACCESS
Bus 158 from Moszkva tér

Cog or rack-railway
Opened in 1874, this is the third cog-driven railroad to be built in Europe.
LOWER TERMINUS
Budapest Hotel (Szilágyi Erzsébet fasor 47)
UPPER TERMINUS
Széchenyi Hill
OPENING HOURS
Every day 4am–midnight
ACCESS
Tram no. 18 and 56

NOSTALGIA TRAINS
Nostalgia Train excursions to the Danube Bend are available from Budapest to Szob. Departure from Nyugati Station in the morning and return to Budapest in the evening.
FOR FURTHER INFORMATION:
MÁV Nosztalgia Travel Agency 1056 Budapest, Belgrád rkp. 26 Tel 317 16 65

BUDAPEST KÁRTYA
The Budapest Card, on sale in tourist offices, travel agencies, most hotels, museums and subway stations, gives unlimited access for three days to the city's public transport system.
Added bonus
Free entry to 55 museums and other public places of interest; reduced admission prices for guided tours, entry to thermal baths, and some sports centers. savings in certain shops, and on meals in some restaurants, on minibus fares to the airport, car hire etc
PRICE
Adults and children over 14:
2450 Ft (2 days)
2950 Ft (3 days).

ON THE DANUBE

THE DANUBE BEND
Throughout the year, boats belonging to the MAHART cie serve the towns along the Danube Bend.
Tel: 318 18 80
Fax: 318 77 40

TO VISEGRÁD AND SZENTENDRE
DEPARTURE TIMES
Every day at 10am (tickets on sale at the landing-stage).

TO ESZTERGOM
Weekends at 8am, leaving from Vigadó tér.

When driving in Budapest, make sure you understand all the regulations and find out what parking signs mean, for the police are ruthless in their pursuit of motorists who park illegally. Better to use taxis for getting around town. On the other hand, rent a car if you want to go further afield.

BY CAR

TAXIS FARES
All taxis have yellow license plates.
FARES
MINIMUM CHARGE
80-100 Ft
PRICE PER KILOMETER
95-160 Ft
WAITING
22-35 Ft/min.
DAYTIME CHARGE
200 Ft maximum (hire charge + 1km)
NIGHTTIME CHARGE
280 Ft maximum (hire charge + 1 km)
WARNING
Always agree the price before setting off.

TAXI COMPANIES
• AIRPORT TAXI
Tel: 282 22 22
(reservations may be made in English or German)
• CITY TAXI
Tel: 211 11 11
(reservations may be made in English or German)
• RÁDIÓTAXI
Tel: 377 77 77
(reservations may be made in English or German)
• VOLÁNTAXI
Tel: 366 66 66
(reservations may be made in English)

• BUDATAXI
Tel: 233 33 33
(reservations may be made in English)
• FOTAXI
Tel: 222 22 22
(reservations may be made in English)
• TAXI 2000
Tel: 200 00 00
(reservations may be made in English)
• TELE 5 TAXI
Tel: 355 55 55
(reservations may be made in English or German)

CAR RENTAL
All the main international companies have agencies here.
• AVIS
Szervita tér 8, V
Tel: 318 42 40
Or 318 41 58
Fax: 318 48 59
International reservations:
Tel: 318 46 85
Airport Terminal 2
Tel/fax: 296 72 65
• BUDGET
Krisztina krt 41-43, district XII
Tel: 214 04 20
Or 214 04 21
Airport Terminal 2
Tel: 296 84 81

GOOD DRIVING
• Seat belts obligatory in front seats.
• Speed limits of 50 kph in towns, 80 kph on departmental roads, 100 kph on national roads, 120 kph on motorways.

• Driving expressly forbidden if there is the slightest trace of alcohol in the blood.
• Dipped headlights must be switched on (even in daytime) outside built-up areas.

• HERTZ
Apáczai Csere János u. 4, V
Budapest Marriott Hotel
Tel/fax: 266 43 44
Airport terminal 2
Tel: 296 69 88
• EUROPCAR
Üllői út 60-62, IX
Tel: 313 14 92
Airport terminal 2
Tel: 296 66 10
NOTE
Some companies offer reductions to Budapest Card-holders.

PARKING LOTS
MULTI-STORY
• Szervita tér, V
• Aranykéz u. 4-6, VII
• Nyár u. 20, VIII (at the corner of Üllői út and Baross u.)
• Fűtő u. 52, XVIII
PARKING METERS
Parking in city center for maximum of 2 hours, 8am–6pm

Coins accepted: 5, 10, 50, 100, 200 Fts.

GAS STATIONS
Many gas stations belong to the Hungarian company MOL. All the main international companies are represented.
• WARNING
Not all gas stations accept credit cards.
FUEL
91 (lead-free)
95 (lead-free)
98 (super or lead-free)
Diesel

USEFUL ADDRESSES
HUNGARIAN AUTOMOBILE CLUB
Tel: 212 29 38
Fax: 212 38 90

HUNGARIAN AUTOMOBILE CLUB BREAKDOWN SERVICE
Tel: 212 28 21
Fax: 212 29 38

YELLOW ANGELS
Tel: 088

POLICE COMPLAINTS DEPARTMENT
Deák Ferenc u. 16-18, V
Jun 1-Sep 1
(English and German spoken)
Tel: 212 28 21

Choose a taxi company from the list above.

◆ Walks and excursions

City Walks

Gellért Hill
(752 feet)
Districts I and XI.
This is a protected conservation site.
Access
Bus 27; tram no. 18, 19, 47, 49

Margaret Island
In the heart of the city, between Margaret Bridge (*Margit híd*) and Árpád Bridge (*Árpád híd*). Free admission, though cars are not allowed. Car park (paying) available at Árpád Bridge.
Access
Bus no. 26; tram no. 4 and 6 Bicycles for hire, also 'pedal-rickshaws' (*bringóhintó*) for tours of the island.

City Park
District XIV, between the Dózsa György and Ajtósi Dürer avenues, Hermina street and the railroad embankment.
Access
Subway 1 (yellow), Széchenyi Fürdő station; bus 4 (red), 20, 30, 105; trolley 71, 74, 75 79. The lake in the park becomes a skating-rink in winter.
Városligeti Műjégpalya
Tel: 343 82 11

Excursions

Individual tours by minibus
Cityrama Private Tours
Minibuses with guides are available for tourists throughout the year at any time.
Information
Tel: 302 43 82

Individual tours by boat
Mahart
The Mahart company runs a regular servic along the Danube Bend, daily from May to September.
Information
Apáczai Csere János u. 11, district ' Tel: 318 18 80
Fax: 318 77 40

Guided tours

Tickets
Available on board
Duration
3 hrs
Information
IBUSZ
Tel: 318 11 39 or 318 10 43
Reduction for Budapest Card-holders (◆ 246).

● Budatours
Several times a day, in 12 languages.
Departure
Roosevelt tér 5 District V (Gresham Casino).
Tickets
Available on board
Duration
2 hrs
Information
Budatours
Tel: 353 05 58 or 331 15 85 or 312 40 37

● Queenybus
Twice daily, in English, French, German Italian, Spanish and Russian.
Departure
Bus station at Erzsébet tér, Queenybus bay
Tickets
Available on board
Duration
3 hrs
Information
Queenybus
246 47 55

Boat trips
● Duna Bella
A 1 hr cruise thrice daily. Guided commentary in 17 languages. Reduction for Budapest Card-holders (◆ 246).

● Duna Legenda
A 1 hr cruise with *son et lumière*, every evening. Guided commentary in 17 languages.
Embarkation
Landing-stage at Vigadó tér, V, exits no. 6 & 7
Information
Tel: 317 22 03

● Riverboats
May 1-Aug 31, Thu–Sun, 9am– 5pm
Route
From Boráros tér to Római Fürdő, with numerous stops where passengers may board or disembark.
Information
BKV Hajózási Szolgáltató krt
Tel: 369 13 59

Bus trips
● IBUSZ
Several tours daily, with English and German-speaking guides.
Departure
Bus station at Erzsébet tér, district V, bays no. 1 and 2

● Guided tours Cityrama
Thrice daily April-Oct, twice daily Nov-March in English, French, German, Italian and Spanish.
Duration
3 hrs
Reservations
Cityrama
Tel: 302 43 82

N-Bus
City tour with stops. Audio translations in English and German.
Tickets
Available on board, either for the entire day or for certain sections
Duration
1 hr 30 mins
The length of the trip depends on whether you take advantage of the frequent stops to get off and explore, then catch the next bus round.
Buses circulate all day from 9am–6pm. Times are displayed at the bus-stops.
Information
Tel: 369 90 89

Organized trips The Danube bend
By bus or boat, a whole day, visiting Szentendre, Visegrád, Esztergom etc.
Agencies
IBUSZ and Cityrama.

Organized trips Visiting Gödöllő
By bus.
Agencies
Cityrama.

Organized trips Lake Balaton
By bus. Europe's largest fresh water lake offers yachting, sailing, fishing, and scheduled boat services.
Agencies
IBUSZ and Cityrama.

Reservations
IBUSZ
Tel: 318 11 39
Or 318 10 43
Cityrama
Tel: 302 43 82

Boat tours of the city
These leave from Batthyány tér, Gellért tér, and Petőfi tér, every day throughout the holiday season from 9am–8pm.

Although the locals will gladly try to help you out in German or English, it is always useful for the tourist (confused, perhaps, by the simple fact that in Hungary the surname comes before the Christian name, for example) to get to know a little of this exotic language (● 38-40). What's more, Hungarians feel flattered if you make the effort. Remember to pronounce 'a' like the 'o' in hot; 'ö' like 'ur' as in pleasure; 'u' as in pool; 'sz' as in sat; 'cs' as in such; 'gy' as 'dee'.

ON THE STREET

- *Állomás, megálló* ('allomash, maygallo') stop, halt station
- *Áruház* ('aruazz'): store, shop
- *(Autó)busz* ('(outo)boos'): bus
- *Bástya* ('bashtio') or torony ('toronya'): tour
- *Bejárat* ('bayarot'): entrance
- *Bolt* ('bolt'): small shop
- *Cím* ('seem'): address
- *Domb* ('dombe'): hill
- *Duna* ('doono'): Danube
- *Folyó* ('foeeo'): river
- *Földalatti* ('ferldolotti'): the 'Little Subway'
- *Fürdő* ('foorder'): baths
- *Gang* ('gung'): open landing
- *Ház* ('haz'): house, building
- *Hegy* ('heddy'): hill
- *Híd* ('heed'): bridge
- *Kijárát* ('keearat'): exit
- *Körút* ('keroot'): street, boulevard

- *Lakás* ('lockash'): apartment
- *Név* ('név'): name
- *Pályaudvar* ('payoodvor'): train station
- *Rakpart* ('rokpor'): platform
- *Szálloda* ('sallodor'): hotel
- *Színház* ('sinharz'): theater
- *Templom* ('tameplome'): church
- *Tér* ('tare'): town square
- *Udvar* ('oodvor'): courtyard
- *Uszoda* ('oosoda'): swimming pool
- *Utca* ('ootsa'): street
- *Út, sugárút* ('oot, shugaroot'): avenue
- *Vár* ('var'): castle, palace
- *Város* ('varosh'): town
- *Vendéglő, éterrem* ('vendaygler, ayterrem'): restaurant
- *Villamos* ('villomoash'): tramway
- *Vonat* ('vonot'): train
- *Zárva* ('zarvo'): closed

WORDS USED IN CONVERSATION

- *Bocsánat* ('boachanot'): pardon, sorry, excuse me
- *Bor* ('bore'): wine
- *Csókolom* ('chokolom'): good day (from a man to a woman)
- *Fizetek* ('fizzaytake'): please bring me the bill
- *Igen* ('eegain'): thank you
- *Jó* ('yo'): good
- *Jó estét* ('yo estate'): good evening
- *Jó reggelt* ('yo raygailt'): good morning
- *Kávé* ('cavay'): coffee
- *Kenyér* ('kainyair'): bread
- *Köszönöm* ('kersernerm'): thank you
- *Most* ('moast'): now
- *Nem* ('name'): no
- *Sör* ('ser'): beer
- *Tea* ('tayo'): tea
- *Tudja, merre van a...* ('tootya, merray von o'): Can you tell me the way to...?
- *Viszontlátásra, viszlát* ('vissontlatashra, visslat'): goodbye

DAYS OF THE WEEK

- Monday: *hétfő* ('hetfer')
- Tuesday: *kedd* ('ked')
- Wednesday: *szerda* ('sairdo')
- Thursday: *csütörtök* ('chuterterk')
- Friday: *péntec* ('paintek')
- Saturday: *szombat* ('somboht')
- Sunday: *vasárnap* ('vozhanop')

HOURS AND TIMES OF DAY

- *Délben* ('dailben'): noon, mid-day
- *éj* ('ayi'): night
- *Év* ('ev'): year
- *Hét* ('hate'): week
- *Holnap* ('hoalnop'): tomorrow
- *Ma* ('maw'): today
- *Most* ('most'): now
- *Nap* ('nop'): day
- *Óra* ('erer'): hour
- *Perc* ('pairk'): minute
- *Reggel* ('raygel'): morning
- *Tegnap* ('taignop'): yesterday

NUMBERS

- One: *egy* ('aydi')
- Two: *kettő* ('kayter')
- Three: *három* ('harome')
- Four: *négy* ('naydi')
- Five: *öt* ('ert')
- Six: *hat* ('hot')
- Seven: *hét* ('hate')
- Eight: *nyolc* ('nyok')
- Nine: *kilenc* ('keelents')
- Ten: *tíz* ('teez')
- Twenty: *húsz* ('hoose')
- Thirty: *harminc* ('hormints')
- Forty: *negyven* ('naydiven')
- Fifty: *ötven* ('ertven')
- Sixty: *hatvan* ('hotvon')
- Seventy: *hetven* ('hate-ven')
- Eighty: *nyolcvan* ('nyokvon')
- Ninety: *kilencven* ('keelentsven')
- Hundred: *szár* ('sar')
- Thousand: *ezer* ('ayzare')

◆ PRACTICAL INFORMATION
(Money, banks, tipping)

FINDING YOUR WAY

URBAN GEOGRAPHY
THE CITY
• Budapest extends over approximately 203 sq miles (15.5 miles north-south, 18 miles east-west).

V. Kerület, Belváros
Deák Ferenc tér
5 ➝ 4

Reading street-signs: The Roman numeral on the left indicates the district. If a person's name is used, it is customary to put the surname before the Christian name. This is followed by the appropriate word such as 'street' or 'square'. The arrow denotes the direction in which the house numbers run.

• The highest point is János Hill (1,686 ft).
DISTRICTS
Budapest is divided into 23 districts, which are given in addresses and on street-signs using a Roman numeral.

THE DANUBE (Duna)
• This runs through the city from north to south, dividing it into two unequal parts: on the right bank is Buda with Óbuda to the north-west, while on the left bank is Pest. These two sections together make up the modern city.
• The river has three islands in the city: Óbuda Island (Óbudai-sziget), Margaret Island (Margit-sziget), and Csepel Island (Csepel-sziget).
• Its lowest point is 307 ft below sea-level.

• The river is crossed by 7 road-bridges and two rail-bridges.
PRINCIPAL CENTERS OF COMMUNICATION
In Buda: Moszkva tér and Batthyány tér. In Pest: Deák tér, Ferenciek tere, and Blaha Lujza tér.
HOUSE NUMBERING
Even numbers on one side, and odd on the other. Names and abbreviations
• u. (for utca): street
• út: avenue
• krt (for korut): boulevard
• tér: square
• sétány: lane

MONEY, BANKS AND TIPPING

MONEY
HUNGARIAN MONETARY UNIT
• This is the forint (Hungarian abbreviation: Ft; international abbreviation: HUF).
• One US dollar is worth around 243 Ft; one pound sterling is worth around 380 Ft.
• The forint is divided into 100 fillérs.
CURRENCY IN CIRCULATION
• There are bills of 50, 100, 500, 1000, 5000 and 10,000 fts.
• There are coins of 1, 2, 5, 10, 20, 50, 100 and 200 forints.
• There are coins of 10, 20 and 50 fillérs.
BUREAUX DE CHANGE (pénzváltás)
• The forint has been a convertible currency since 1996.
• Unofficial money-changing in the street is illegal, unsafe, and scarcely worth the risk anyway.
• Have your passport with you when you carry money, and keep the change receipts. You may have to show these when you leave the country.
WHERE TO CHANGE MONEY
Banks, bureaux de

change (there are 100 of these), some post offices, travel agencies, hotels, big stores, and 300 automatic machines distributed throughout the city.
BEST RATES
Mezőbank (corner of Párizsi u. and Petőfi Sándor u. district V)
WEEKENDS
Most bureaux de change in district V and around the Castle are open all day.
AUTOMATIC EXCHANGE MACHINES operating round the clock:
– Margit körut 43-45
– Harrer Pál u. 3
– Károly körút 20
– Váci u. 40
– Andrássy út 49
PAYMENTS AND WITHDRAWALS
Payments are generally made in cash or with an international bankers' card.
INTERNATIONAL BANKERS CARDS
Those accepted: Visa, Eurocard, American Express, Diners Club and Carte Blanche. Some hotels and shops accept travellers' cheques.
POSTAL ORDERS
These may be cashed at branches

of Postabank.
BANKS (bankok)
A wide number of banks carry out various financial operations:
• AMERICAN EXPRESS
Deák Ferenc u.10
1052 Budapest
Tel: 266 86 70 or 266 86 80 or 266 86 86
Fax: 267 20 28
• CITYBANK
Vörösmarty tér 4
1052 Budapest
Tel: 268 88 88
Fax: 266 98 95
• CREDITANSTALT
Alkotmány u. 4
1054 Budapest
Tel: 260 08 12
Fax: 269 45 44
• EUROPEAN COMMERCIAL BANK
Váci út 81
1056 Budapest
Tel: 328 48 00
Fax: 328 48 01
• HYPO BANK HUNGARIA
Nagymező u. 44
1065 Budapest
Tel: 269 04 00
Fax: 269 03 98
• IBUSZ BANK
Ajtósi Dürer sor 10
1145 Budapest
Tel: 251 16 66
Fax: 251 41 63
• INTER EUROPA BANK
Szabadság tér 15
1054 Budapest
Tel: 269 18 55
Fax: 302 33 73

• KERESKEDELMI ÉS HITELBANK
Károly körút 70-90
1075 Budapest
Tel: 267 96 26
Fax: 267 89 99
• OTP BANK
Nádor u. 16
1051 Budapest
Tel: 353 14 44
Fax: 312 68 58
• POSTABANK
József nádor tér 5
1051 Budapest
Tel: 318 08 55
Fax: 317 13 69
BANKS OPENING TIMES
The commercial banks are open Mon–Thu 8am–2pm and Fri 8am–1pm. Branches of the OTP Bank are open Mon–Thu 8am–4pm and Fri 8am–1pm. All banks are closed on Saturdays and Sundays. Automatic currency exchange machines and automatic teller machines operate as well
TIPPING
Tipping is customary throughout Hungary.
• In restaurants and taxis it should be about 10% of the bill.
• In hotels, quite generous tips are usual for room service and carrying baggage.

tour**i**nform

INFORMATION

TOURINFORM BUDAPEST
National information center and tourist office. It is the best place to obtain information and the staff are very helpful and friendly.
INFOLINE:
From abroad:
(36) 60 55 00 44
From Hungary:
(06) 80 66 00 44
MAIN OFFICE:
• 100 yards from Deák tér subway station:
Sütő u. 2
1052 Budapest
Tel: 317 98 00
Fax: 317 9656
E-mail: tourinform@mail.hungarytourism.hu
or
hungary@tourinform.hu
English, French, German, Italian and

Russian spoken.
Open Mon–Fri 9am–7pm; Sat–Sun 9am–4pm.

ALSO:
• 1062 Nyugati Pályaudvar
Tel/fax: 302 85 80
E-mail
Info@budtour.hu
English, French and Italian spoken.
Open daily from May-Oct 8am–8pm; Nov-Apr 9am–6pm
• 1077 Király u. 93
Tel: 352 1433
Fax: 352 9804
• Budaörs,
2040 AGIP Complex (M1 & M7 motorways)
Tel: 06 (from inside Hungary) 23 417 518
English, French, German and Italian spoken.

HEALTH

The Hungarian health service is one of the best in Eastern Europe. Although most people will speak English, it may be wise, in case of an emergency, to go to the hospital's casualty department with a Hungarian speaker.
HOSPITALS
(*kórházak*)
SZENT ISTVÁN KÓRHÁZ
Nagyvárad tér 1, VIII
Tel: 216 035
SZENT JÁNOS KÓRHÁZ ÉS INTÉZMÉNYEI
Diósárok köz, XII
Tel: 356 11 22
DOCTORS
(*orvosok*)
A list of doctors speaking foreign languages is available at the embassies (◆ 242).
EMERGENCY MEDICAL SERVICES
FALCK SOS HUNGARY
Kapy u. 49/b, district II
Tel: 200 01 00
Ambulances available.
SOS SZEMÉLYI ORVOSI SZOLGÁLAT
Csalogány u. 4/b, district I

Tel: 318 82 88 / 82 12 / 80 12
This private emergency service has doctors who speak English.
PHARMACIES
(*patika* or *gyógyszertár*) are generally open 8am–6pm or 8am–8pm and on Saturday morning.
OPEN 24 HOURS
• Széna tér 1, I
Tel: 202 15 82
or 202 18 16
• Rákóczi út 86, VIII
Tel: 322 96 13
• Frankel Leó út 22, II
Tel: 315 82 90
• Teréz krt 41, VI
Tel: 311 44 39
• Alkotás u. 1/B, XII
Tel: 355 46 91
DENTISTS
(*fogorvosok*)
PROFIDENT
Károly krt 1, VII
Tel: 342 69 72
SOS DENTAL SERVICE
Király u. 14, VI
Tel: 322 06 02

CENTRAL POST OFFICE
Petőfi Sándor u. 13–15, V
Open Mon–Fri 8am–7pm,
Sat 8am–1pm.

Budapest mailbox.

MAIL

STAMPS
(*bélyegek*)
These are on sale in post offices.
PRICE
(subject to alteration)
A stamp for a postcard to the US costs 85 Ft, and 65 Ft within Europe.

INTERNATIONAL COURIERS
DHL INTERNATIONAL
Rákóczi út 1-3, VII
Tel: 06 / 40 45 45 45
Fax: 266 26 40
TNT EXPRESS WORLDWIDE
Fertő u. 5, X
Tel: 431 31 31
Fax: 431 30 96

251

◆ PRACTICAL INFORMATION
(Main telephone numbers, opening hours)

TELEPHONE

INTERNATIONAL CALLS

To Budapest from the US
Dial 011 36 1 followed by the number you wish to call (seven digits).

To Budapest from the UK
Dial 00 36 1 followed by the number you wish to call.

Calling abroad from Budapest
Dial 00 plus the code of the country you are calling, followed by the town or area code, then the number of your correspondent.

NATIONAL CALLS

Calling Budapest within Budapest
Dial the number you wish to speak to.

Calling another town in hungary from Budapest
Dial 06, followed by the town or area code, then the number of your correspondent.

International directory enquiries
Tel: 199

International operator (English spoken)
Tel: 190

Inland operator
Tel: 191

Inland directory enquiries
Tel: 198

To send a telegram by phone:
Tel: 192

To order wake up service:
Tel: 193

PUBLIC TELEPHONES
These accept coins (10, 20 & 50 forints), and cards.

PHONE CARDS
These are on sale in kiosks, post offices, hotels, travel agencies, gas stations, and newsagents. There are two types of card: 50 or 100 units.

EMERGENCIES

AMBULANCE (*mentők*) Tel: 104 or In English 311 16 66
FIRE BRIGADE (*tűzoltók*) Tel: 105
POLICE (*rendőrség*) Tel: 107
POLICE INFORMATION AND ASSISTANCE
Central Police Station, Andrássy út 12, district VI
Tel: 318 08 00
You may request the services of a qualified interpreter.
TRAFFIC ACCIDENTS
Tel: 343 08 48
POLICE HEADQUARTERS Deák Ferenc u. 16-18, V
YELLOW ANGEL (AID SERVICE ON THE ROAD):
Tel: 088
LOST PROPERTY (*talált tárgyak*)
Akácfa u. 18
1072 Budapest
Tel: 322 66 13

OPENING HOURS

OFFICES
Open Mon–Fri, 8am–5pm

BANKS
See page 250.

POST OFFICES (*postahivatal*)
• Open Mon–Fri 8am–7pm, Sat 8am–1pm
• Post offices work day and night at the Eastern Station (Keleti) and the Western Station (Nyugati), but are open to the public Mon–Fri 8am–5pm.

BUSINESS HOURS
Mon–Fri 10am–6pm,

Sat 9am–1pm
• **FOOD STORES** (*áruház, bolt*)
Open Mon–Fri 7am–7pm, Sat 7am–2pm.
• **DEPARTMENT STORES**
Open Mon–Fri 10am–6pm (several have late-night shopping on Thursdays until 8pm).
• **COVERED MARKET**
Fővám tér 1-3, district IX
Open Tue–Fri 6am–6pm, Sat 6am–4pm Mon 6am–5pm
• **SHOPPING MALLS**
Open on Sundays too.
– DUNA PLAZA

Váci út 178, district XIII
– EUROPARK Üllői út 201, district XIX
– POLUS CENTER Szentmihályi út 131, district XV
– CORA At Torokbalint in the suburbs, near M7 motorway.
• **TOBACCONISTS, BAKERS AND FLORISTS**
Open additionally Saturday afternoons and Sunday (as a rule).

OPEN 24 HOURS (*éjjel-nappali*)
• **PHOTO PROCESSING**
SOOTER'S DEÁK

Ferenc krt 23, district IX
• **FOOD**
– NONSTOP ABC Hegedűs Gyula u. 20/A, XIII
- BUDAI NONSTOP Margit krt 62
• **FLORIST**
GYÖRGYI FLEUR Erzsébet tér, V
1052 Budapest, at the bus station.

RESTAURANTS (*vendéglő étterem*)
As a rule, these are open every day.

MUSEUMS (*múzeum*)
Open Tue–Sun 10am–6pm.

FOREIGN BOOKSHOPS

BESTSELLERS
*Október 6 u., V
Open Mon–Fri
9.30am–6.30pm
Sat 10am–6pm*
The largest selection of English language contemporary fiction in Budapest. Also magazines and newspapers.

IROK BOLTJA
*Andrássy út 45, VI
Open Mon–Fri
10am–6pm;
Sat 10am–1pm from May to Sep only*
The Famous Writer's Bookshop (▲ 144). It may not have the widest choice of English books, but it is still worth going, for the charming atmosphere. Café, art books, magazines.

LITEA BOOKSTORE AND CAFE
*Hess András Tér 4, District I
Open daily
10am–6pm*
Guidebooks, art books, books on architecture, prints

and postcards, magazines and newspapers, the choice is wide. Also sells coffee.
• Secondhand bookshop fanatics should explore Múzeum korút, particularly **KÖZPONTI ANTIKVÁRIUM** *at no. 15 Múzeum krt
Open Mon–Fri
10am–6pm,
Sat 10am–2pm*
Postcards, old prints, rare Hungarian books and the best selection of secondhand English ones.

MEDIA

PRESS
FOR TOURISTS
A number of free newspapers with business and tourist information are available at the airport, a and in hotels and tourist offices

• MONTHLY MAGAZINES
Budapest Panorama (official listings of events in English, Italian and Russian).
Programmes in Hungary (lists programmes in English and German)
Where Budapest (English-language magazine)
• QUARTERLY MAGAZINES
Downtown (update on city life, in English)
Budapest Pocket Guide (English-language guide to the city).

HUNGARIAN PAPERS IN FOREIGN LANGUAGE EDITIONS
These are available at newsstands and the airport, as well as in the big hotels.
IN ENGLISH
Budapest Sun, *Budapest Business Journal* and *Budapest Week*.

OFFICIAL LISTINGS MAGAZINES
Two weeklies:
Pesti Műsor and *Pesti Est* (free) – appear each Wednesday.

TELEVISION
Two national channels. Several hotels are fitted with a dish to receive international channels.

RADIO
• Bartók: FM, jazz and classical music station.
• Sláger: FM, specializes in chart hits of the 1970s.
• The two most popular national stations for news and music are Petőfi and Kossuth.
• HUNGARIAN RADIO (shortwave 39.75 and 60.25) broadcasts news in English daily at 9pm and 11pm.

◆ NIGHT AND DAY
(Swimming pools, children, ticket offices)

SWIMMING POOLS (uszoda)

Swimming is a favorite pastime in Budapest, and its popularity is reflected in the number of pools, both open and covered. Remember that most pools require bathers to wear a swimming-cap, though these may be hired on the way in. A selection of public swimming pools is given below:

CSÁSZÁR-KOMJÁDI USZODA
Árpád fejedelem u. 8
1023 Budapest
Tel: 326 14 78
ACCESS
Bus 6, 60, 86;
tram 17
Suburban train (HÉV) to Szentendre.
OPENING TIMES
Daily 6am–8pm

CSEPELI STRANDFÜRDŐ
Hollandi út 14
1213 Budapest
Tel: 277 65 76
ACCESS
Bus 71, 71/A
OPENING TIMES
May 15-Aug 20:
8am–7pm;
Aug 21-Sep 10:
8am–6pm

CSILLAGHEGYI STRAND-USZODA
Pusztakúti út 3
1038 Budapest
Tel: 250 15 33

ACCESS
Bus 42
Suburban train (HÉV) to Szentendre.
OPENING TIMES
May 1-Aug 20:
7am–7pm;
Aug 21-Sep 30:
8am–7pm

HAJÓS ALFRÉD SPORTUSZODA
Margit-sziget
1138 Budapest
Tel: 311 40 46
ACCESS
Bus 26
OPENING TIMES
Mon–Fri 6am–5pm,
Sat–Sun 6am–6pm

KISPESTI USZODA
Simonyi Zsigmond u. 31
1191 Budapest
Tel: 280 60 95
Or 208 40 26
ACCESS
Bus 48, 51, 68;
subway line 2 (blue)
OPENING TIMES
Mon–Fri 6am–5pm,
Sat–Sun 6am–6pm

NYÉKI IMRE USZODA
Kondorosi út 14
1116 Budapest
Tel: 208 40 25
Or 208 40 26
ACCESS
Bus 3, 7/A, 14, 114;
tram 18, 41, 47
OPENING TIMES
June 1-Aug 31:
Mon–Fri 6am–8pm,
Sat–Sun 6am–7pm;
Sep 1-May 31:

Mon–Fri 6am–8pm,
Sat 6am–6pm,
Sun 6am–5pm

PALATINUS STRANDFÜRDŐ
Margit-sziget
1138 Budapest
Tel: 312 30 69
ACCESS
Bus 26
OPENING TIMES
May 1-Aug 3:
8am–7pm daily;
Sep 1-15:
10am–6pm daily

PASKÁL STRANDFÜRDŐ
Egressy út 178
1141 Budapest
Tel: 252 69 44
ACCESS
Trolley 77, 82
OPENING TIMES
May 1-Aug 31:
9am–7pm daily

PÜNKÖSDFÜRDŐ STRAND
Királyok útca 272
1039 Budapest
Tel: 338 66 65
ACCESS
Bus 34
OPENING TIMES
May 15-Aug 31:
9am–7pm

RÓMAI STRANDFÜRDŐ
Rozgonyi Piroska u. 2
1031 Budapest
Tel: 388 97 40
ACCESS
Bus 34, 42;
Suburban train (HÉV) to Szentendre
OPENING TIMES
May 1-Aug 31:
8am–7pm;
Sep 1-15: 10am–6pm

GOING OUT
TICKET OFFICES
FOR THEATER, OPERA & SHOWS
• MUSIC MIX
Váci u. 33
Budapest district V
Tel: 317 77 36
• NEMZETI FILHARMÓNIA
(National Philarmonics)
Vörösmarty tér 1
or Mérleg u. 10
Budapest district V
Tel: 318 02 81
• SZINHAZAK KOPONTI JEGYIRODAJA
(Central Theater ticket office)
Andrássy út 18
Budapest district VI
Tel: 312 00 00
• SZABAD TER SZINHAZ
Hollán Ernő u. 10
Budapest district XII
Tel: 311 42 83
• PUBLIKA
Erszébet krt 6
Budapest district VII
Tel: 342 75 83
• TICKET EXPRESS
Jokai u. 40
Budapest district VI
Tel: 353 06 92
• VIGADÓ
Vigadó u. 5
Budapest district V
Tel: 318 99 03
• SPRING FESTIVAL BOOKING OFFICE
Rákóczi út 65
Budapest district VIII
Tel: 210 27 92

CHILDREN'S RAILROAD

ÚTTÖRÖ VASÚT (OR GYERMEK VASÚT)
Known as the 'Pioneers' Railroad', this was built in 1948. Its 7½ miles of narrow-gauge track runs through the wooded hills. All the staff (except for the driver) are children aged from 10-14.
TICKETS
On sale at the terminus.

• Single ticket: 120 Ft
• Return ticket: 200 Ft
• Children under 4 yrs: 60 Ft
• Children aged 4-14: 100 Ft

TERMINUS
Hűvösvölgy
Tel: 376 56 04
Széchenyi-hegy
Tel: 395 54 20
Open daily (except Mon in low season)
8.45am–5pm.

SOME THEATERS AND CONCERT HALLS

ÁLLAMI BÁBSZÍNHÁZ	*(puppets)*	Vörösmarty u. II
INTERNATIONAL BUDA STAGE	*(shows with English audio translation)*	Tárogató út 2-4, district II
MAGYAR ÁLLAMI OPERAHÁZ	*(National Opera)*	Andrássy út 22, II
VIGSZÍNHÁZ	*(musical shows)*	Szent István krt 14
BARTÓK EMLÉKHAZ		Csalán út 29, II
DUNA PALOTA	*(classical concerts)*	Zrinyi 1-5
PETŐFI CSARNOK	*(vaudeville)*	Zichy Miklós út
PESTI VIGADÓ	*(large-scale shows)*	Vigadó tér 1, V
ZENEAKADÉMIA	*(classical concerts)*	Liszt Ferenc tér 8

NIGHTLIFE

CASINOS
There are 10 gambling casinos in Budapest. With the exception of the Hilton (which is in the Castle district), all casinos in the city are in the center of Pest. Here are a few:
HILTON
Hess András tér 1-3, I
Tel: 214 30 00
VÁRKERT
Miklós tér 9-11, I
Tel: 202 42 44
LAS VEGAS CASINO
Atrium Hyatt Hotel
Roosevelt tér 2, V
Tel: 317 60 22
Open daily 5pm–5am
LIDO
Szabad sajtó út 5, V
Tel: 318 24 04
Open daily 1pm–4am

CAFÉS
CAFÉ INCOGNITO
Liszt Ferenc tér 3, VI
Tel: 267 02 39
Open Mon–Fri
10am–midnight,
Sat–Sun:
noon–midnight
Beers and sangria.
The staff speak
English and Spanish.
Music.
CAFÉ MIRÓ
At the corner of Úri u.
and Szentháromsag
u., district I.
Décor inspired by
Miro's paintings.
Literary and
musical events
in the evenings.
CAFÉ PIERROT
Fortuna u.14, I
Tel: 375 6971

Open 11am–1am
Piano bar.
• JAZZ CAFÉ
Balassi Bálint
u. 25, district V
Tel: 269 55 06
Open Mon–Fri:
11am–3am
Sat–Sun: 6pm–3am
Jazz every night
(except Sun).

BARS
• BUDA CENTER PUB
Csalogány u. 23, I
Tel: 201 72 17
Open 24 hrs a day
• COLUMBUS IRISH PUB
Vigadó tér, district V
Tel: 266 90 13
Open noon–3am
• GÖSSER
Régi posta u. 4, V
Tel: 318 26 08
Open daily
10am–9pm
• ANDRÁSSY CLUB
Andrássy út 19, VI
Tel: 322 78 96
Open 11am–midnight
• FAT MOS MUSIC CLUB
Nyáry Pál u. 11, II
Tel: 267 31 99
Open daily noon–2am
except Sat:
10am–2am

WINE BARS
(borozó)
Increasingly popular
night spots.

• GRINZINGI
Veres Pálné u. 10, V
• TORTILLA BORBÁR
Budai Nagy Antal u. 3
district XIII
• MUMM CHAMPAGNE
BÁR
Kristóf tér 8, district V

NIGHT-CLUBS
Establishments
featuring live nude
shows.
• HOROSZKÓP BÁR
Krisztina krt 41-43, XII
Hôtel Mercure Buda
Tel: 356 63 33
Open Mon–Sat
9pm–3am
Caribbean setting.
Admission free.
• IRIS BÁR
Árpád fejedelem útja
94, district III,
Aquincum Hotel
Tel: 250 33 60
Open 10pm–4am
Guitar & piano.
• TROCADERO CAFÉ
Szent István krt 11, V
Tel: 311 46 91
Open 8pm–4am
Latin-American
music.

DISCOTHEQUES
• ÁRKÁDIA MULATÓ
Váci u. 33, VI
Tel: 266 99 37
• EZRES KLUB
Irinyi János u. 9-11,
XVI
Tel: 463 29 22
KEPI BLANC CLUB
Üllői út 45-57, IX
Tel: 217 41 00
UNDERGRASS DANCE
Liszt Ferenc tér 10, VI
Tel: 322 08 30

SHOPPING

SOUVENIRS
• MAJOR FOLK STORES
Váci u. 14, V
and József krt 78
EMBROIDERY AND
PORCELAIN
Look in the shops in
the Castle district and
Vaci utca, in the
markets and flea
markets, and in
boutiques on Szent
István korut or near
Blaha Lujza Square.
• HEREND PORCELAIN
To be found in the
Amfora chain of
shops, and at József
nádor tér 11, district V.

MUSIC
• RÓZSAVÖLGYI MUSIC
STORE
Szervita tér 5, V
• MCD AMADEUS
Tel: 318 66 91
Open
9.30am–9.30pm
• ZENEI ANTIKVÁRIUM
Múzeum krt 17
(scores, books on
music etc)
• WAVE LEMEZBOLT
Bajcsy-Zsilinszky út
15/D, district VI
• UNDERGROUND
RECORDS
Kiraly u. 54, VI
(latest records)

ANTIQUES
• ANTIK BAZAR
Váci u. 67, district V
• AANTIK DISKONT
Falk Miksa u. 22, V
• ANTIK UDVAR
Szent István krt 1, V
• DARIUS
Falk Miksa u.24-26, V
• BÁV
Falk Miksa u. 21, V
• POLGAR GALÉRIA
Kossuth L. u. 3, V
• QUALITAS ANTIQUITAS
Kígyó u. 5, V
• OPERA ANTIKVARIUM
Hajós u. 7, district VI
• ROYAL ANTIKVITAS
Wesselényi u. 34,
district VII

WINES
• LA BOUTIQUE
DES VINS
József Attila u. 12, V

◆ FESTIVALS AND EVENTS

Public holidays: *hivatalos ünne,*
New Year's Day: *újé*
Christmas: *Karácson*

SPRING

BUDAPEST SPRING FESTIVAL Info: BUDAPESTI FESZTIVÁLKÖZPONT KHT ☎ 210 27 92 fax 133 20 75	• *March 12-28* *Cultural events in and around Budapest. International artists, music, dance, theater etc.*
INTERFOLKTÁNC (BUDAPEST) Info: TÁNCFÓRUM ☎ 201 87 79 fax 201 51 28	• *March 13-28* *Folk dance festival.*
HUNGARIAN MARATHON (BUDAPEST) Info: MAGYAR MARATHON KLUB ☎ 367 32 34 fax 387 34 06	• *April 25* *Race for sportsmen and amateurs (distance of over 26 miles)*
INTERNATIONAL MUSIC DAY	• *June 21*
BÚCSÚ (BUDAPEST)	• *June 24* *One of the biggest street festivals, celebrating the departure of Russian Forces. Music and other events.*
LABOR DAY *(a munka ünnepe)*	• *May 1* *Celebrations in the City Park and Tabán district.*

SUMMER

SUMMER IN SZENTENDRE Info: SZENTENDRE TEÁTRUM ☎ 312 657	• *June-August* *Theater festival (Szentendre Teatrum)*
FERENCVÁROS CELEBRATIONS (BUDAPEST) Info: FERENCVÁROSI NYÁRI JÁTÉKOK KHT ☎ 215 79 05 fax 218 31 00	• *mid-June to mid-July* *In Bakáts Square: opera, classical & rock concerts.*
WORLD PENTATHLON CHAMPIONSHIP (BUDAPEST) Info: ÖTTUSA VB SZERVEZŐ BIZOTTSÁGA ☎ 464 00 23 fax 209 02 28	• *July 12-18* *Men and women's competition.*
INTERNATIONAL CASTLE FESTIVAL (VISEGRÁD) Info: NAGYKÖZSÉGI ÖNKORMÁNYZAT ☎ (36 26) 398 255 fax (36 26) 398 163	• *mid-July* *Jousting and troubadour music in the royal castle of Visegrad.*
ANNE CELEBRATIONS (BALATONFÜRED) Info: ÖNKORMÁNYZAT ☎ (36 87) 343 255 / 247 fax (36 87) 343 457	• *July 24* *Celebration dating back to the Reformation: beauty contest, Chamber music etc*
ISLAND FESTIVAL (BUDAPEST) Info: SZIGET KULTURÁLIS MENEDZSERIRODA KFT ☎ 372 06 50 fax 372 06 51	• *August* *International youth festival on Óbuda Island. Hundreds of shows and events.*
SUMMER OPERA AND BALLET FESTIVAL (BUDAPEST) Info: VIP. ARTS MANAGEMENT ☎ 302 42 90 fax 332 48 16	• *August 6-18* *Opera 'proms'.*
SZENT ISTVÁN ÜNNEP *(St Stephen's Day)*	• *August 20.* *One of the two most important national holidays.*
FORMULA 1 GRAND PRIX (MOGYORÓD) Info: OSTERMANN FORMULA-1 KFT. ☎ 317 28 11 fax 317 29 63	• *Late August*
BUDAPEST INTERNATIONAL WINE FESTIVAL Info: MAGYAR SZŐLŐ-ÉS BORKULTÚRA ALAPÍTVÁNY ☎ 355 18 47 fax 202 23 90	• *September 7-12* *Auction of vintage wines, Harvest Ball, wine, music, food and dancing.*

AUTUMN/WINTER

BUDAPEST AUTUMN FESTIVAL Info: BUDAPESTI FESZTIVÁLKÖZPONT KHT ☎ 133 20 75	• *October 16-November 1* *Contemporary arts festival. Competition for young composers.*
ANNIVERSARY OF THE REVOLUTION *(56-as forradalom évfordulója)*	• *October 23* *Commemorates the 1956 uprising.*
ST NICHOLAS' DAY *(Mikulás)*	• *December 6*
MASKED BALL AT THE OPERA HOUSE (BUDAPEST) Info: VIP. ARTS MANAGEMENT ☎ 302 42 90 fax 332 48 16	• *December 31*
NEW YEAR'S CONCERT (BUDAPEST) Info: INTEROPERETT ☎ 317 50 67	• *January 1* *Operetta concert given in the Royal Palace, with an ensemble of 100 violins.*
CLASSICAL MUSIC SERIES (BUDAPEST) Info: MUSA - MUSICA SACRA BT. ☎ 365 22 93	• *February 19-December 31* *Concerts held in the Matthias Church at Buda Castle.*
NEMZETI ÜNNEP *(public holiday)*	• *March 15. Celebrates the day in 1848 when Hungary was proclaimed a republic.*

múzeum: museum   *palota*: palace
templom: church   *vár*: castle

DISTRICT I

ARANY SAS PATIKAMÚZEUM
Tárnok u. 18
☎ 375 97 72
Access: bus 16; várbusz (Castle bus)

GOLDEN EAGLE PHARMACY MUSEUM
Open Tue–Sun 10.30am–5.30pm
• *History of pharmacy from the Middle Ages to the 17th century*

HADTÖRTÉNETI MÚZEUM
Tóth Árpád sétány 40
☎ 356 95 86
Access: bus 16; várbusz (Castle bus)

MILITARY HISTORY MUSEUM
Open Apr 1–Sep 30: Tue–Sun 10am–6pm;
Oct 1–Mar 31: 10am–4pm
Guided tours in English & German;
• *weapons, uniforms, medals, flags etc.*

▲ 202

HALÁSZBÁSTYA
Szentháromság tér
Access: bus 16; várbusz (Castle bus)

FISHERMEN'S BASTION
• *Lookout tower; free visits Mon and evenings; also crypt of St Michael's Chapel.*
Open Apr–Oct: 10am–6pm; Nov–March: 10am–4pm

▲ 203
▲ 204

KERESKEDELMI ÉS VENDÉGLÁTÓIPARI MÚZEUM
Fortuna u. 4
☎ 375 62 49
Access: bus 16; várbusz (Castle bus)

COMMERCE & CATERING MUSEUM
Open Wed–Fri 10am–5pm, Sat–Sun 10am–6pm
• *A look at hotels & restaurants in turn-of-the-century Budapest.*

▲ 204

KIRÁLYI VÁR
Budavári palota
Access: bus 5, 16, 78; várbusz (Castle bus); tram 18; funicular.

ROYAL PALACE
• *The Castle district is forbidden to automobiles.*

▲ 183
▲ 190

MAGYAR NEMZETI GALÉRIA
Wings B, C, D of the Royal Palace
Disz tér 17
☎ 375 79 92 / 423

HUNGARIAN NATIONAL GALLERY
Open Tue–Sun 10am–6pm. Free on Wed. Guided tours (English, Russian) to Crypt of Archduke Joseph.

▲ 194

LUDWIG MÚZEUM
Wing A of the Royal Palace
☎ 375 91 75

LUDWIG MUSEUM
Open Tue–Sun 10am–6pm
• *American Pop Art, & art of the 1980s.*

▲ 199

MÁTYÁS KÚT
In NE Courtyard of the Royal Palace

MATTHIAS FOUNTAIN

▲ 198

BUDAPESTI TÖRTÉNETI MÚZEUM
Wing E of the Royal Palace
Szent György tér 2
☎ 375 88 49

BUDAPEST HISTORY MUSEUM *Open Mar 1–May 15:*
Wed–Sun 10am–6pm; May 16–Sep 15: Mon–Sun 10am–6pm; Sep 16–Oct 31: Mon, Wed–Sun 10am–6pm; Nov 1–Feb 28: Mon, Wed–Sun 10am–4pm

▲ 192

NÁDOR KRIPTA
Access via National Gallery

THE HABSBURG ROYAL CRYPT

▲ 199

ORSZÁGOS SZÉCHÉNYI KÖNYVTÁR
Wing F of the Royal Palace
☎ 375 75 33

NATIONAL SZÉCHÉNYI LIBRARY
Open Mon–Sat 9am–5.30pm. Free admission.
• *Medieval manuscripts.*

▲ 199

KÖZÉPKORI ZSIDÓ IMAHÁZ
Táncsics Mihály u. 26
☎ 355 87 64
Access: bus 16; várbusz (Castle bus)

MEDIEVAL JEWISH PRAYER HOUSE
Open May 1–Oct 31: Tue–Fri 10am–2pm,
Sat–Sun 10am–6pm
• *Jewish tombs, manuscripts etc from Old Buda.*

▲ 205

MÁRIA MAGDOLNA TORONY
Kapisztrán tér 6
Access: bus 16; várbusz (Castle bus)

MARY MAGDELENE TOWER
Open Mon–Sun 10am–6pm
• *Medieval church tower with a peal of 24 bells that ring every 30 mins.*

▲ 205

MÁTYÁS TEMPLOM, OR BUDAVÁRI NAGYBOLDOGASSZONY TEMPLOM
Szentháromság tér 2
Access: bus 16; várbusz (Castle bus)

MATTHIAS CHURCH (BUDA CHURCH OF OUR LADY)
• *Contains a magnificent treasury.*
(tel: 355 56 57)
Open Feb 18–Jan 12: Mon–Sat 9.30am–5pm,
Sun 11.30am–5pm

▲ 202

PANOPTIKUM
Szent György tér 1–2 Sándór palota
Access: bus 16; várbusz (Castle bus); funicular

BUDA CASTLE WAXWORKS
Open March–Oct: Tue–Sat 10am–6pm.

▲ 202

SEMMELWEIS ORVOSTÖRTÉNETI MÚZEUM
Apród u. 1–3
☎ 375 35 33
Access: bus 5, 7, 78, 86; tram 18, 19

SEMMELWEIS MUSEUM OF MEDICAL HISTORY
Open Tue–Sun 10.30am–6pm
Guided tours in English, French & German.
• *Housed in the birthplace of Ignac Semmelweis, the museum traces the history of medicine.*

▲ 214

TELEFÓNIA MÚZEUM
Úri u. 49
☎ 201 81 88
Access: bus 16; várbusz (Castle bus)

TELEPHONE MUSEUM
Open Apr 1–Oct 31: Tue–Sun 10am–6pm;
Nov 1–March 31: Tue–Sun 10am–4pm.
Guided tours in English & German.
• *Collection housed in an old telephone exchange.*

Addresses and opening times

múzeum: museum   *palota:* palace
templom: church   *vár:* castle

VÁRBARLANG (corner of Dárda u.) Access via Úri u. 9 ☎ 214 31 21	CASTLE LABYRINTH *Open Tue–Sun 10am–6pm. Guided tours only (in English, French and German).* • *The Labyrinth is part of the Buda Castle Waxworks.*
ZENETÖRTÉNETI MÚZEUM In the Erdődy Palace Táncsics Mihály u. 7 ☎ 214 67 70 Access: bus 16; várbusz (Castle bus)	MUSIC HISTORY MUSEUM ▲ 204 *Open March 15-Oct 31: Tue–Sun 10am–6pm; Nov 1-March 14: Tue–Sun 10am–5pm.* • *Collection of historical musical instruments, rare manuscripts etc.*

DISTRICT II

BARTÓK BÉLA EMLÉKHÁZ Csalán út 29 ☎ 276 21 00 Access: bus 5, 29	BARTÓK MEMORIAL HOUSE *Open Tue–Sun 10am–5pm* • *The composer's house, arranged to display his life and work.*
GÜL BABA TÜRBE Turbán u. 11 ☎ 355 87 64 Access: bus 91	TOMB OF GÜL BABA ▲ 210 *Open July 1-Sep 30: Tue–Sun 10am–6pm;* ▲ 211 *Oct 1–31: Tue–Sun 10am–4pm* • *Muslim chapel and place of pilgrimage.*
SZENT ANNA TEMPLOM Batthyány tér Access: subway line 2 (red) to Batthyány tér	SAINT ANNE'S CHURCH ▲ 186 • *Baroque masterpiece.* ▲ 207

DISTRICT III (ÓBUDA)

AQUINCUMI MÚZEUM ÉS ROMTERÜLET Szentendrei út 139 ☎ 368 82 41 Access: bus 42, 134; suburban train HÉV to Aquincum	AQUINCUM MUSEUM ▲ 227 *Open Apr 15-Mar 30 & Oct 1-31: Tue–Sun 9am–5pm;* ▲ 228 *May 1-Sep 30: Tue–Sun 9am–6pm.* • *Remains of Roman villa, with other archeological finds.*
HERCULES-VILLA Meggyfa u. 19-21 ☎ 250 16 50	HERCULES VILLA ▲ 227 • *3rd-century mosaic floor, with Roman sarcophagi in the gardens.*
KISCELLI MÚZEUM Kiscelli u. 108 ☎ 388 85 60 Access: bus 60, 165; tram 17	KISCELL MUSEUM ▲ 223 *Open Apr 1-Oct 31: Tue–Sun 10am–6pm;* ▲ 224 *Nov 1-March 31: Tue–Sun 10am–4pm* • *Part of Budapest History Museum. A fine mixed collection including contemporary Hungarian art.*
KUN ZSIGMOND GYŰJTEMÉNY Fó tér 4 (opp. Zichy Mansion) ☎ 368 11 38 Access: bus 86	ZSIGMOND KUN FOLK ART COLLECTION ▲ 226 *Open Tue–Fri 2–6pm, Sat–Sun 10am–6pm* • *Museum of folk arts & crafts.*
VARGA IMRE GYŰJTEMÉNY Laktanya u. 7 ☎ 250 02 74 Access: bus 6, 86; suburban train HÉV to Árpád híd	IMRE VARGA GALLERY ▲ 227 *Open Tue–Sun 10am–6pm Guided tours in German.* • *Standing collection of the work of the sculptor Varga.*
ZICHY PALOTA Fő tér 1 Access: bus 6, 86 (red), 86; tram 1; suburban train HÉV to Árpád híd	ZICHY MANSION ▲ 226
KASSÁK LAJOS EMLÉKMÚZEUM ☎ 368 70 21	KASSÁK MEMORIAL MUSEUM ▲ 226 *Open March 16-Oct 31: Tue–Sun 10am–6pm; Nov 1-March 15: Tue–Sun 10am–5pm*
ÓBUDAI HELYTÖRTÉNETI GYŰJTEMÉNY ☎ 250 10 20	OBUDA LOCAL HISTORY MUSEUM ▲ 226 *Open Tue–Fri 2pm–6pm, Sat–Sun 10am–6pm*
VASARELY MÚZEUM ☎ 250 15 40 Access: bus 6, 86 (red), 86; tram 1; suburban train HÉV to Árpád híd	VASARELY MUSEUM ▲ 226 *Open March 15-Oct 31: Tue–Sun 10am–6pm; Nov 1-March 14, Tue–Sun 10am–5pm. (Free on Wed)* • *Guided tours in English.* *400 works of the 'father' of pop-art, Victor Vasarely.*

DISTRICT V

ADY ENDRE EMLÉKMÚZEUM Veres Pálné u. 4-6 ☎ 337 85 63 Access: subway line 3 (blue) to Ferenciek tere; bus 8, 15; tram 2	ADY MEMORIAL MUSEUM *Open March 1-Oct 31: Wed–Sun 10am–6pm; Nov 1-Feb 28: Wed–Sun 10am–4pm.* • *Home of the poet Endre Ady.*
BELVÁROSI PLÉBÁNIA TEMPLOM Március 15. tér Access: subway line 3 (blue) to Ferenciek tere; tram 2	INNER CITY PARISH CHURCH • *Splendid building begun in 12th century, and* ▲ 120 *completed in a whole mixture of styles.*

CONTRA AQUINCUM Eastern side of Március 15. tér Access: bus 7, 78 (Ferenciek tere stop), 5, 8 (Március 15. tér stop)	AQUINCUM CAMP • Ruins of 3rd-century Roman fort.	▲ 220 ▲ 221
EGYETEMI TEMPLOM Egyetem tér (University Square) Access: bus 7, 78 (Ferenciek tere stop), 5, 8 (Március 15. tér stop)	UNIVERSITY CHURCH • The city's most beautiful baroque church.	
FÖLDALATTI VASÚT MÚZEUM Deák Ferenc téri aluljáró (underground passage) ☎ 317 24 11 / 41 103 Access: subway lines 1 (yellow), 2 (red), 3 (blue) to Deák tér; bus 9, 16, 105; tram 47, 49	UNDERGROUND RAILWAY MUSEUM Open Sun–Tue 10am–6pm • With carriages dating from 1896.	▲ 123
GÖRÖKELETI TEMPLOM Petőfi tér Access: bus 7, 78 (Ferenciek tere stop), 5, 8 (Március 15. tér stop)	GREEK ORTHODOX CHURCH • 17th-century church with rococo façade.	▲ 118
MAGYAR TUDOMÁNYOS AKADÉMIA Roosevelt tér Access: bus 105 (József Nádor tér stop); tram 2 (Roosevelt tér stop)	HUNGARIAN ACADEMY OF SCIENCES • Statues of famous scientists on 2nd floor.	▲ 137
NATIONAL LUTHERAN MÚZEUM Deák Ferenc tér 4-5 ☎ 317 41 73 Access: subway lines 1 (yellow), 2 (red), 3 (blue) to Deák tér; bus 9, 16, 105; tram 47, 49	NATIONAL LUTHERAN MUSEUM Open Tue–Sun 10am–6pm Guided tours in English & German. • In the presbytery of the Lutheran church, with Martin Luther's original Bible.	▲ 123
NÉPRAJZI MÚZEUM Kossuth Lajos tér 12 ☎ 312 48 78 Access: subway line 2 (red) to Kossuth tér; bus 15; tram 2; trolley 70, 78	ETHNOGRAPHICAL MUSEUM Open Mar 1-Oct 30: Tue–Sun 10am–6pm; Dec 1-Feb 28: 10am–4pm. (Free on Tue.) • Hungarian peasant life at the turn of the century.	▲ 134
ORSZÁGHÁZ Kossuth Lajos tér 1-3 ☎ 268 49 04 et 268 44 15 Access: subway line 2 (red) to Kossuth tér; bus 15; tram 2; trolley 70, 78	PARLIAMENT Guided group visits available Tue–Sun at 10am (in English), 11am (in German). Apply to Door X. • Parliamentary Library: Mon–Thur 9am–8pm, Fri 9am–2pm, Sat 9am–6pm. Entrance Door XXV, by the river.	▲ 127 ▲ 186
PESTI VIGADÓ Vigadó tér 2 Access: subway 1 (yellow) to Vörösmarty tér, 2 (red) and 3 (blue) to Deák tér; tram 2	CONCERT HALL • No visits, except for performances. There is an art gallery on the ground floor, open Tue–Sun 10am–6pm.	▲ 118 ▲ 183
PETŐFI IRODALMI MÚZEUM Károlyi Mihály u. 16 ☎ 317 36 11 Access: subway line 2 (red) to Astoria, line 3 (blue) to Ferenciek tere; bus 5, 8, 15, 112; tram 47, 49	PETŐFI MUSEUM OF LITERATURE Open March 1-Oct 31: Tue–Sun 10am–6pm; Nov 1-Feb 28: 10am–4pm. • Introduction to the great Hungarian writers.	▲ 122
SZENT ISTVÁN TEMPLOM Szent István tér ☎ 317 28 59 Access: subway line 3 (blue) to Arany János u.	ST STEPHEN'S BASILICA • Houses the basilica treasury, which includes examples of 19th-century religious art. Open Apr 1-Sep 30: 9am–5pm; Oct 1-31: 10am–4pm.	▲ 136
DISTRICT VI		
ERNST MÚZEUM Nagymező u. 8 ☎ 341 43 55 Access: subway line 1 (yellow) to Oktogon; trolley 70, 78	ERNST MUSEUM Open Apr 1 –Oct 31: Tue–Sun 10am–6pm • Temporary exhibitions housed in an art nouveau building.	
HOPP FERENC KELET-ÁZSIAI MŰVÉSZETI MÚZEUM Andrássy út 103 ☎ 322 84 76 Access: subway line 2 (red) to Bajza u.; bus 4, 105	FERENC HOPP MUSEUM OF EAST ASIAN ART Open Apr 1-Oct 31: Tue–Sun 10am–6pm; Nov 1-March 31: Tue–Sun 10am–5pm	▲ 148

◆ PLACES TO SEE
Addresses and opening times

múzeum: museum   *palota:* palace
templom: church   *vár:* castle

KODÁLY ZOLTÁN MÚZEUM Kodály körönd 1 ☎ 342 84 48 Access: subway line 1 (yellow) to Kodály körönd; bus 4, 105	ZOLTÁN KODÁLY MUSEUM *Open Wed 10am–4pm, Thur–Sat 10am–6pm,* *Sun 10am–2pm* • *The composer's home, showing aspects of his life and work.*
LISZT FERENC MÚZEUM Vörösmarty u. 35 ☎ 342 73 20 Access: subway line 1 (yellow) to Vörösmarty utca	FRANZ LISZT MUSEUM ▲ 145 *Open Jan 1-July 15 & Aug 21-Dec 31:* *Mon–Fri 10am–6pm, Sat 9am–5pm.* • *The composer's last home, with displays of his life and work.*
MAGYAR ÁLLAMI ÓPERAHÁZ Andrássy út 22 ☎ 332 81 97 Access: subway line 1 (yellow) to Ópera; bus 4	HUNGARIAN STATE OPERA HOUSE ▲ 141 ▲ 142 *Guided visits every day at 3 and 4pm (English, French, German, Italian & Spanish).*
POSTAMÚZEUM Andrássy út 3 ☎ 269 68 38 Access: subway line 1 (yellow) Bajcsy–Zsilinszky út, lines 2 (red) and 3 (blue) to Deák tér; bus 4, 105	POSTAL MUSEUM ▲ 141 *Open Apr 1-Oct 31: Tue-Sun 10am–6pm;* *Nov 1-Mar 31: 10am–4pm* *Guided tours in English & German.* • *History of the mail service in Hungary.*
RÁTH GYÖRGY MÚZEUM Városligeti fasor 12 ☎ 342 39 16 Access: subway line 1 (yellow) to Bajza utca; bus 4, 105; trolley 78, 79	GYÖRGY RATH MUSEUM ▲ 149 *Open June 26-Oct 31: Tue-Sun 10am–6pm,* *Nov 1-Mar 31: 10am–5pm. Free Tue.* *Guided tours in English, German & Mongolian.* • *Collection of Chinese and Japanese art.*

DISTRICT VII

BÉLYEGMÚZEUM Hársfa u. 47 ☎ 341 55 26 Access: tram 4, 6; trolley 74	STAMP MUSEUM *Open Apr 1-Oct 31: Tue-Sun 10am–6pm,* *Nov 1-Mar 31: 10am–4pm*
ZSIDÓ MÚZEUM Dohány u. 2 (entrance also on Wesselényi u.) ☎ 342 23 53 Access: subway lines 1 (yellow), 2 (red), 3 (blue) to Deák tér; tram 47, 49;	THE NATIONAL JEWISH MUSEUM ▲ 167 *Open Mon-Fri 10am–5pm, Sun 10am–1pm* • *Part of the Synagogue (Zsinagoga). Jewish history, with displays labeled in English.*

DISTRICT VIII

MAGYAR NEMZETI MÚZEUM Múzeum krt 14-16 ☎ 338 21 22 Access: subway line 2 (red) to Astoria, line 3 (blue) to Kálvin tér; bus 9; tram 47, 49	HUNGARIAN NATIONAL MUSEUM ▲ 123 ▲ 124 *Open Apr 15-Oct 15: Wed–Sun 10am–6pm;* *Oct 16-Apr 14: Wed–Sun 10am–5pm* • *History of Hungary, including the Crown Jewels.*
MAGYAR TERMÉSZETTUDOMÁNYI MÚZEUM Ludovika tér 2 ☎ 333 06 55 Access: subway line 3 (blue) to Klinikák	MUSEUM OF NATURAL SCIENCES *Open Mon, Wed–Sun 10am–6pm;* *Free on Fri, 1pm–6pm*

DISTRICT IX

IPARMŰVÉSZETI MÚZEUM Üllői út 33-37 ☎ 217 52 22 / 171 Access: subway line 3 (blue) to Ferenc körút; tram 4, 6	MUSEUM OF APPLIED ARTS ▲ 171 ▲ 172 *Open Tue–Sun 10am–6pm* *Free on Tue.*
JÓZSEF ATTILA MÚZEUM Gát u. 3 ☎ 218 01 93 Access: tram 4, 6, 30	ATTILA JÓZSEF MUSEUM *Open Tue–Sun 10am–6pm. Admission free.* • *The poet's home, with a collection of his manuscripts.*

DISTRICT XIV

ÁLLATKERT City Park Állatkerti körút 6-12 Access: subway line 1 (yellow) to Széchenyi fürdő; bus 4	BUDAPEST ZOO ▲ 160 *Open May 1-Aug 31: Mon–Sun 9am–7pm;* *Sep1-Apr 30: 9am–5pm*
KÖZLEKEDÉSI MÚZEUM Városligeti körút 11 (City Park)	TRANSPORT MUSEUM *Open May 1-Sep 30: Tue-Fri 10am–5pm, Sat–Sun*

☎ 343 05 65 Access: tram 1; trolley 70, 72, 74	10am–6pm; Oct 1-Apr 30: Tue–Fri 10am–4pm, Sat–Sun 10am–5pm. Free on Wednesdays. • Old vehicles of all kinds, and many models.	
MAGYAR FÖLDTANI INTÉZET Stefánia út 14 ☎ 267 14 27 Access: subway line 2 (red) to Népstadion; bus 7; trolley 75	THE INSTITUTE OF GEOLOGY Open Jan 2-Dec 23: Thur, Sat–Sun 10am–4pm • The building is a masterpiece of the Hungarian Secession.	▲ 162
MŰCSARNOK Hősök tere 1 ☎ 343 74 01 Access: subway line 1 (yellow) to Hősök tere; bus 4 (red), 20, 30, 105; trolley 75, 79	THE PALACE OF ARTS Open Tue–Sun 10am–6pm • Hungary's biggest art gallery space is a fin-de-siecle masterpiece.	▲ 148
KÖZLEKEDÉSI MÚZEUM Zichy Mihály u. 14 (City Park) ☎ 343 05 65 Access: subway line 1 (yellow) to Széchenyi fürdő; trolley 70, 72, 74	AVIATION MUSEUM Open May 15-Sep 30: Tue–Fri 10am–5pm, Sat–Sun 10am–6pm. Free on Wednesdays. • Aircraft ancient & modern, with many models.	
SZÉPMŰVÉSZETI MÚZEUM Dózsa György út 41 (City Park) ☎ 343 97 59 Access: subway line 2 (red) to Hősök tere; bus 4, 20, 30, 105; trolley 75, 79	THE MUSEUM OF FINE ARTS Open March 1-Oct 31: Tue–Sat 10am–4pm; March 16- Dec 31: Tue–Sat 10am–6pm • Magnificent mixed collection, rich in Spanish old masters.	▲ 149 ▲ 152 ▲ 153
VAJDAHUNYAD VÁRA Városliget (City Park)	VAJDAHUNYAD CASTLE • Roman chapel & gothic tower in the castle's gardens.	▲ 161
MEZŐGAZDASÁGI MÚZEUM ☎ 343 05 73 Access: subway line 1 (yellow) to Széchenyi fürdő; bus 4 (red), 20, 30, 105; trolley 75, 72, 75, 79	MUSEUM OF AGRICULTURE Open March 1-Oct 31: Tue–Fri 10am–5pm, Sat–Sun 10am–6pm; Nov 1-Feb 28, Tue–Fri 10am–4pm, Sat–Sun 10am–5pm.	▲ 161
DISTRICT XXII		
SZOBORPARK At the corner of Balatoni út ☎ 227 74 46 Access: bus 50	STATUE PARK Open March 15-Nov 15: Mon–Fri from 10am, Sat–Sun from 8am • A fascinating oddity: the last resting-place of all the Communist statues that used to adorn the city streets.	
AROUND BUDAPEST		
ESZTERGOM		2000
BASILIQUE Szent István tér 1, Esztergom	THE BASILICA OF ESTERGOM (WITH TREASURY)	▲ 238
KERESZTÉNY MÚZEUM	MUSEUM OF CHRISTIAN ART	▲ 239
VÁRMÚZEUM Szent István tér ☎ (33) 317 243 & (33) 315 986	PALACE MUSEUM	
GÖDÖLLŐ		2100
GRASSALKOVICH KASTÉLY ☎ (28) 410 124 & (28) 410 402	ROYAL PALACE MUSEUM Open Apr 1-Oct 31: Tue–Sun 10am–5pm; Nov 1-March 31: Tue–Sun 10am–4pm.	▲ 240
SZENTENDRE		2500
ANNA MARGIT-AMOS IMRE MÚZEUM Bogdányi u. 10/b	March 1-Oct 31: Tue–Sun 10am–4pm; Nov 1-Feb 28: Fri–Sun 10am–4pm	▲ 234
BARCSAY MÚZEUM	BARCSAY MUSEUM Open March 1-Oct 31: Tue–Sun 10am–4pm; Nov 1-Feb 28: Fri–Sun 10am–4pm	▲ 232
CZÓBEL MÚZEUM Templom tér 1	BÉLA CZÓBEL MUSEUM Open March 1-Oct 31: Tue–Sun 10am–4pm; Nov 1-Feb 28: Fri–Sun 10am–4pm	▲ 233
FERENCZY KÁROLY MÚZEUM Fő tér (main square) 6	FERENCZY MUSEUM Open March 1-Oct 31: Tue–Sun 10am–4pm; Nov 1-Feb 28: Fri–Sun 10am–4pm	▲ 231
KOVÁCS MARGIT MÚZEUM Vastagh György u. 1	MARGIT KOVÁCS MUSEUM Open Tue–Sun 10am–6pm	▲ 232
VADJA LAJOS MÚZEUM Hunyadi u. 1	LAJOS-VADJA MUSEUM Open March 1-Oct 31: Tue–Sun 10am–4pm; Nov 1-Feb 28: Fri–Sun 10am–4pm	▲ 233

Budapest has no less than thirty thermal baths, fed by hot springs which surface here and there, particularly on the bank of the Danube ● *62*. More than ten of them are remedial centers recommended for the prevention and treatment of certain disorders. If the water sometimes appears cloudy (it is constantly renewed), this is due to its high mineral content. Be careful: to simply bathe, make sure to obtain the right ticket, *csak fűrdő* ('bathing only').

DAGÁLY GYÓGYFÜRDŐ, USZODA, STRANDFÜRDŐ
Népfürdő u. 34-36
1138 Budapest
Tel: 320 22 03
ACCESS
Bus 133; tram 1
OPENING TIMES
May 1-Sep 30:
6am–7pm
Oct 1-Apr 30:
Mon–Fri 6am–7pm,
Sat–Sun 6am–5pm
BATHS
Covered bathing pool, two thermal baths at 33ºC (91ºF) and 36ºC (96ºF), and a children's pool.
TREATMENTS
Articulatory disorders, rheumatic and arthritic, and related injuries.
SERVICES
Hydromassage, massage, swimming lessons, sauna, restaurant and snack bar, football pitch, games area, toboggan, beautician, solarium, chiropody.

KIRÁLY GYÓGYFÜRDŐ
Fő u. 82-84
1027 Budapest
Tel: 201 43 92
ACCESS
Bus 60, 86
OPENING TIMES
Mon–Fri 6.30am–7pm
Sat 6.30am–7pm
THERMAL SERVICES:
Mon, Wed, Fri for men; Tue, Thu, Sat for women.
BATHS
4 pools, at 26ºC (79ºF), 32ºC (90ºF), 36ºC (96ºF) and 40ºC (104ºF).
TREATMENTS
Rheumatic and arthritic disorders, spinal distortion, slipped disc,

neuralgia, decalcification, related injuries.
SERVICES
Hydromassage, massage, dry and humid steam rooms, double Finnish sauna, snack bar, hairdresser, chiropody.

LUKÁCS GYÓGYFÜRDŐ és USZODA
Frankel Leó út. 25-29
1027 Budapest
Tel: 326 16 95
ACCESS
Bus 6, 60, 86;
tram 4, 6, 17;
suburban train (HEV) to Szentendre
OPENING TIMES
May 1-Sep 30:
Mon–Fri 6am–7pm,
Sat 6am–7pm,
Sun 6am–5pm
Oct 1-Apr 30:
Mon–Fri 6am–7pm,
Sat–Sun 6am–5pm
BATHS
2 swimming pools, 4 thermal baths at 24ºC (75ºF), 32ºC (90ºF), 36ºC (96ºF)

and 40ºC (104ºF), mud bath, footbath.
TREATMENTS
Rheumatic and arthritic disorders, spinal distortion, slipped disc, decalcification, neuralgia, related injuries, digestive and respiratory diseases.
SERVICES
Hydromassage, massage, physiotherapy, thermal aquatic therapy, natural medicine, dry and humid steam rooms, mud baths, Finnish sauna, swimming lessons, sun-tanning, refreshments, beautician, hairdresser, chiropody.

DANDÁR GYÓGYFÜRDŐ
Dandár u. 5-7
1095 Budapest
Tel: 215 70 82
ACCESS
Bus 23, 54; trams 2, 23, 24, 30

GELLÉRT GYÓGYFÜRDŐ

Kelenhegyi út 4-6
1111 Budapest
Tel: 366 6166
ACCESS
Bus 7, 7/A, 86;
tram 18, 19, 47, 49
OPENING TIMES
Mixed bathing daily: 6am–7pm,
Sat–Sun 6am–5pm
Live music July-Aug 8pm–midnight.
BATHS
Gaseous thermal pool, open pool with wave machine, 4 thermal baths at 26ºC (78ºF), 35ºC (95ºF), 36ºC (96ºF) and 38ºC (100ºF), open children's pool.

REMEDIAL TREATMENT
Degenerative arthritic disorders, joint inflammation, slipped disc, neuralgia, cardio-vascular problems.

SERVICES
Hydromassage, massage, inhalation, dentist, seated baths, physiotherapy, dry & humid steam rooms, sauna, naturist sun-tan area on terrace, snack bar, restaurant, hairdresser, beautician, chiropody.

OPENING TIMES
Mon–Fri 6am–7pm,
Sat 6am–noon
BATHS
3 thermal baths, at 20ºC (68ºF), 36ºC (96ºF) and 38ºC (100ºF).
TREATMENTS
Rheumatic and arthritic disorders, slipped disc, neuralgia.
SERVICES
Hydromassage, massage, sauna, snack bar, chiropody.

PESTSZENTERZSÉBE JÓDOS-SÓS GYÓGYFÜRDŐ, STRANDFÜRDŐ
Vizisport út 2
1203 Budapest
Tel: 283 08 74
ACCESS
Bus 48, 51, 59;
suburban train (HEV) to Soroksár
OPENING TIMES
Mon–Fri 7am–4pm,
Sat 7am–3pm
THERMAL STEAM FACILITIES:
Tue, Thu, Sat for men; Mon, Wed, Fri for women.
BATHS
3 thermal baths at 28ºC (82ºF), 36ºC (96ºF) and 39ºC (102ºF), pool with wave machine, children's pool.
TREATMENTS
Rheumatic and arthritic disorders, slipped disc, neuralgia, gynecological disorders.
SERVICES
Hydromassage, massage, dry & humid steam rooms, refreshments, games room, beach volleyball.

AZ ÉG ÁLDÁSÁT KÉREM E NAGYSZERŰ HATÁSÚ FÜRDŐRE, MELYBEN SÚLYOS BAJOMTÓL GYORSAN SZABADULTAM MEG. 1902 AUGUSZTUS 5. REISMANN JOZEFA TASNÁD.

...ÁC GYÓGYFÜRDŐ
...adnagy u. 8-10
...013 Budapest
...el: 356 10 10
ACCESS
...us 5, 8, 78, 86, 112;
...am 18
OPENING TIMES
...on–Sat
...30am–7pm
THERMAL FACILITIES:
...ue, Thur, Sat for
...en; Mon, Wed, Fri
...or women.
BATHS
...thermal baths at
...°C (82°F), 32°C
...0°F), 36°C (96°F)
...nd 38°C (100°F).
TREATMENTS
...heumatic and
...rthritic disorders,
...ipped disc,
...euralgia.
SERVICES
...ydromassage,
...assage, dry &
...umid steam rooms,
...ness room,
...airdresser,
...eautician, solarium,
...hiropody.

...UDAS
...YÓGYFÜRDŐ,
...s USZODA
...öbrentei tér 9
...013 Budapest
...el: 375 83 73
ACCESS
...us 7, 7/A, 86;
...am 18, 19
OPENING TIMES
...on–Fri 6am–6pm,
...at–Sun 6am–1pm
THERMAL FACILITIES
...or men only:
...on–Fri 6am–7pm,
...at–Sun 6am–1pm
BATHS
...wimming pool, 6
...hermal baths at 16°C
...60°F), 28°C (82°F),
...0°C (86°F), 33°C
...91°F), 36°C (96°F)
...nd 42°C (107°F).
TREATMENTS
...heumatic and
...rthritic disorders,
...ipped disc,
...euralgia,
...ecalcification,
...igestive and
...espiratory
...omplaints.
SERVICES
...ydromassage,
...assage, thermal
...ater therapy,
...atural medicine,
...hysiotherapy, dry &

humid steam rooms,
swimming lessons,
sun-tanning,
chiropody.

AQUINCUM
CORINTHIA HOTEL
Árpád fejedelem u. 94
1036 Budapest
Tel: 250 33 60
ACCESS
Bus 106; tram 1; train
suburban train (HEV)
to Szentendre
OPENING TIMES
Remedial facilities
available 7am–9pm
daily
BATHS
3 thermal baths,
gaseous thermal
pool.
TREATMENT
Spinal disorders and
injuries, post-surgical
therapy to motor
system.
SERVICES
Inhalation, hot & cold
shower, Turkish bath,
electrotherapy,
sauna, hairdresser,
beautician.

SZÉCHENYI
GYÓGYFÜRDŐ
Állatkerti krt 11
1146 Budapest
Tel: 321 03 10
ACCESS
Trolley 72;
subway line 1
(yellow)
OPENING TIMES
Mixed bathing and
thermal steam rooms:
May 1-Sep 30:
6am–7pm daily;
Oct 1-Apr 30:
Mon-Fri 6am–7pm
Sat-Sun 6am–5pm
BATHS
• Swimming pool,
thermal pool at 38°C
(100°F);
• 5 mixed thermal
baths at 20°C (68°F),
34°C (93°F), 35°C
(95°F), 36°C (96°F)
and 37°C (98°F);
• 4 thermal baths for
women at 30°C
(86°F), 34°C (93°F),
36°C (96°F) and 38°C
(100°F);
• 3 thermal baths for
men at 25°C (77°F),
34°C (93°F) and 38°C
(100°F).
TREATMENT
Rheumatic and

arthritic disorders
and related injuries,
digestive complaints.
SERVICES
Hydromassage,
massage, thermal
water therapy,
natural medicine,
physiotherapy,
underwater gym, dry
and humid steam
rooms, sauna,
swimming lessons,
naturist sun-tanning
area, refreshments,
chiropody.

ÚJPESTI
GYÓGYFÜRDŐ
ÉS USZODA
Árpád út 114-120
1042 Budapest
Tel: 369 31 94
ACCESS
Bus 20, 25/A, 96,
104, 120
OPENING TIMES
Pool:
Mon-Fri 6am–7pm,
Sat-Sun 6am–1pm
THERMAL STEAM ROOM
(mixed):
Mon, Wed, Fri
6.30am–7pm;
Sat, Sun
6.30am–1pm
BATHS
Swimming pool,
children's pool
(summer only),
3 thermal baths at
20°C (68°F), 34°C
(93°F), and 38°C
(100°F).
TREATMENT
Rheumatic and
arthritic disorders
and malformation,
orthopedic conditions
and related injuries.
SERVICES
Hydromassage,
massage, dry and
humid steam rooms,
swimming lessons,
sun-tanning,
refreshments,
chiropody.

DANUBIUS THERMAL
HOTEL HELIA
Kárpát u. 62-64
1133 Budapest
Tel: 270 32 77

arthritic disorders,
digestive complaints.

ACCESS
Bus 7, 7/A, 86;
trams 18, 19, 47, 49
OPENING TIMES
7am–10pm daily
BATHS
4 pools.
TREATMENT
Locomotor system
disorders, treatment
of fractures, sporting
injuries, therapy
following orthopedic
surgery, articulatory
deterioration.
SERVICES
Orthopedic and
cardiovascular
investigation,
hydromassage,
massage, mud &
cream baths, natural
medicine,
electrotherapy,
inhalation, manicure,
chiropody, solarium,
sauna, gaseous
thermal baths,
steam baths,
solarium, beautician,
fitness room, tennis,
sun-tanning.

DANUBIUS
THERMAL HOTEL
MARGIT-SZIGET
Margit-sziget
1138 Budapest
Tel: 311 10 00
ACCESS
Bus 26
OPENING TIMES
7am–8pm daily
BATHS
Swimming pool,
4 thermal baths.
TREATMENT
Rheumatic and
arthritic disorders,
muscular trouble,
digestive and
nervous system
complaints.
SERVICES
Medical center,
dental clinic, sauna,
solarium, fitness
room, bars,
restaurants, tea-
room, beautician,
hairdresser, souvenir
shops.

◆ HOTELS AND RESTAURANTS

◆ Prices are not included here since they vary from one season to another. Additionally, in a fast-developing country such as Hungary, prices can alter radically in the wake of improvement schemes and the restructuring of tax systems.

Hotel categories in Hungary were revised in July 1998, and the new classification will come into effect at the end of 1999.

It is to be noted, therefore, that some hotels may change category after having been inserted in this guide. Travelers are urged to study the prices on display at restaurants, and to ask for them if they are not given.

As a rule, it is a good idea to be suspicious of an establishment where prices are not on display.

District I

HOTELS

MERCURE BUDA HOTEL ★★★★
Krisztina krt 41-43
Tel: 356 63 33
Fax: 355 69 64
E-mail
mercurebuda@
pannoniahotels.hu
A little way from the city center, the building is typical of central European hotels of the 1960s. The staff are attentive and helpful, and there is a fine view overlooking the old city of Pest and its castle. Good restaurant, with regional specialities and local wines. Bar, bureau de change, hotel taxis, babysitting.
� P ⛽ ▢ ☎ ⚅

RESTAURANTS

ALABÁRDOS
Országház u. 2
Tel: 356 08 51
Open Mon–Sat noon–

4pm, 7–11pm.
Closed Sunday
Close to the Matthias Church, set in an ancient cellar of old Buda, and with live guitar music. Alabardos specializes in Hungarian and Transylvanian cuisine. Specialties: gigot of lamb with huckleberries, stewed venison with galuska (a sort of gnocchi), potatoes or pasta, and excellent wild boar.

ARANYKAVIÁR
Ostrom u. 19
Tel: 201 67 37
Open daily 6pm–midnight.
A corner of old Russia, where you can try all the different kinds of caviar complemented by shots of assorted vodkas. Zakuski, borsch, shashlik, vareniki and other Russian specialties, with the authentic flavor of the mother-country even in this Hungarian 'isba'. Music, friendly atmosphere, and nostalgia.

ORIENT EXPRESS
Vérmező út
Tel: 213 01 22
Open daily
11am–1am
If you're hoping to climb aboard the fabled mysterious train, forget it! The restaurant is a former depot of a railroad company, tastefully refurbished. The service and the menu are both straightforward, featuring both

★ LE DOMINICAIN
Hess András tér 1-2
Tel: 214 30 00
Fax 356 02 85
Open daily
noon–3pm,
6pm–midnight.
On the heights of Buda, the modern and elegant Hilton hotel overlooks Pest, the Parliament, and the majestic sweep of the Danube. It blends in perfectly with its historical setting, and it shares one of its walls with a Jesuit cloister next door! Its panoramic restaurant, Le Dominicain, offers a gastronomic feast at affordable prices. There is a huge dining-room with large and elegant tables – choose one near the window if you can, the best spot to enjoy the view – first-class service, and generous helpings of excellent food. Try the braised foie gras with a glass of Tokay Aszu no.3. Unforgettable!

Hungarian and international dishes.

II District

RESTAURANTS

NÁNCSI NÉNI
Ördögárok u. 80
Tel: 397 27 42
Open daily
noon–11pm
Aunt Nancy serves delicious traditional and unpretentious food: bean soup (bableves), game, fromage blanc (túrógombóc). Goulash bubbling straight from the pot is superb, and the beer is excellent too. In summer you can eat outside on the terrace. Book in advance.

REMIZ KAVÉHÁZ ÉS ÉTTEREM
Budakeszi út 5
Tel: 275 13 96
Fax 394 18 96
Open daily 9am–1am
Make sure to book a table here, where the clientele includes artists, diplomats and businessmen. The word Remiz means warehouse or depot, so the owners have installed some yellow ironwork from a 1930s tramway to add to the atmosphere. The extensive menu includes many regional specialities, such as goulash with palacsintas.

	City center	🅿	Parking
	Credit cards accepted		Swimming pool
	Air-conditioning	☎	Rooms with telephones
	Live music	📺	Television
	Garage	✝	Terrace
	Garden		

★ MARGITKERT

Margit u. 15, II
Tel: 335 47 91
Daily noon–midnight.
This centuries-old inn is one of the most

ancient in Budapest. Here you can sample authentic dishes from the Puszta and other Hungarian specialties: cabbage stuffed with meat and rice;, mushrooms with sheep's cheese; the great classic dishes of the country. The garden and dining-rooms echo to the sound of gypsy music. On the wall are photos of the famous who have dined here. Make sure to book, and gentlemen should wear a tie (except for outside in the garden during

III District

HOTEL

CORINTHIA THERMAL HOTEL AQUINCUM
★★★★★
Árpád fejedelem u. 94
Tel: 250 33 60
Fax 436 41 56
E-mail cor.hot@aqu.hu
Located on the way out of Budapest on the right bank of the
Danube opposite Margaret Island, on the site of a Roman settlement. Bureau de change, babysitting, restaurant, bar.
🅿 🚗 📺 ☎ ⊗ ≈

RESTAURANTS

KÉHLI VENDÉGLŐ
Mókus u. 22
Tel: 250 42 41
Open Mon–Fri 5pm–midnight, Sat–Sun

noon–midnight.
Kéhli is one of the oldest restaurants in Óbuda, once a favorite haunt of the writer and gourmet Gyula Krúdy. The place could be the setting for a romantic novel at the turn of the century, enhanced by the evocative photos and prints on the wall. Traditional cuisine in an atmosphere of great charm. Try goose livers with mashed potato, or one of the many turkey specialties.

KISBUDA GYÖNGYE
Kenyeres u. 34
Tel: 368 64 02
Open daily except Sun noon–midnight.
The decor of this fine restaurant is rustic, comfortable and homely, with violin music adding to the charm. Hungarian specialties such as venison with Transylvanian mushrooms can be followed by Somloi galuska, an irresistible confection of biscuit, chocolate, vanilla and crème Chantilly.

★ VADRÓZSA

Pentelei Molnár u.15
Tel: 326 58 17
Open daily noon–3pm, 7pm–midnight
'The Wild Rose' is housed in a beautiful baroque villa in the residential quarter of Buda. Its luxurious interior boasts elegant fabrics and hangings, Louis XV chairs and crystal chandeliers. The cuisine too is sumptuous, specialties being foie gras, and breast of goose stuffed with truffles and cheese.
The extensive and select wine list includes some splendid Tokays, Rieslings, Sauvignons Chardonnays, and Cabernets. A pianist plays each evening.

UDVARHÁZ

Hármashatárhegyi út 2
Tel: 388 87 80
Open daily 11am–11pm
The effort of getting here is well rewarded by a magnificent view over the city. Fresh fish is prepared at your table, or try breast of veal stuffed with rice and mushrooms. Your visit may also be enhanced by live traditional music.

VALENTINE RESTAURANT

Miklós tér 9
Tel: 202 42 44
Fax 202 67 64
Open daily 7pm–2am
This delightful 19th-century restaurant is on the bank of the river near the Varkert Casino, with helpful staff who speak several languages, and pretty red tablecloths. The menu leans toward classic cuisine, such as pork chops with cream sauce and mushrooms, medaillon de boeuf with geen peppers, chocolate crepes, and various strudels.

V District

HOTELS

BUDAPEST MARRIOTT HOTEL ★★★★★
Apáczai Csere János u. 4
Tel: 266 70 00
Fax 266 50 00
E-mail pako@pronet.hu
This immense building on the left bank of the Danube has 362 luxurious rooms overlooking the river. The way down to the river bank is past terraces lined with souvenir and craft shops. Bureau de change, hotel taxis, babysitting, restaurant, bar.
🅿 🚗 📺 ☎ ⊗

ERZSÉBET HOTEL ★★★
Károlyi Mihály u. 11

◆ HOTELS AND RESTAURANTS

Tel: 328 57 46
Fax 328 57 63
E-mail
budarz@euroweb.hu
Close by the traffic-free pedestrian center of Budapest, the Erzsébet Hotel dates back to 1872. It has recently been modernized to make it even more comfortable than it was before. Its restaurant, Janos Pince, specializes in regional dishes such as goulash and fondues.

⛅ ☎ 🔲 ⚙ 🎵

HOTEL INTERCONTINENTAL BUDAPEST *****
Apáczai Csere János u. 12-14
Tel: 327 63 33
Fax 327 63 56
E-mail
budapest@interconti.com
Large modern hotel on the left bank of the Danube, with river views, near the Chain Bridge. In the lobby

★ ASTORIA
Kossuth Lajos u 19-21
Tel: 317 34 11
Fax 318 67 98
Open daily
7am–11pm
This historic restaurant is situated on hallowed ground! It was here that the country's first democratic government was formed, following the collapse of the Austro-Hungarian Empire in 1918. It is also a gem of Hungarian art nouveau, standing out from the faceless modern buildings that surround it. Sit back

stands a statue of the writer and politician József Eötvös, with the inscription 'Erected by the people of Hungary'. Good restaurant, bar and coffee lounge, Le Café Viennois.

🔆 🅿 🚗 🔲 ☎ ⚙ 🎵 📶

HYATT REGENCY BUDAPEST *****
Roosevelt tér 2
Tel: 266 12 34
Fax 266 91 01
E-mail
atriumhyatt@pannoniahotel.hu
Early in the 1980s the left bank of the Danube became the home of huge new hotels, boasting more than 1000 first-class rooms to cater for the international clientele. This establishment, with 350 rooms, belongs firmly in the new class of hotels. Every detail that can enhance a visitor's stay here has been carefully

and feast your eyes, while you enjoy a drink in one of the bar's comfortable club armchairs. Out of the window is a panorama of the modern city, with lifts gliding up and down the futuristic high-rise buildings. The interior features granite columns with mahogany panels picked out in brass and copper. The Empire-style rooms have recently been refurbished to cater for an increasingly international clientele. Close to the city center, with parking (payable) nearby.

thought out: there is a café with south-facing terrace, a gastronomic restaurant, Le Gourmet, a nightclub, a casino, and a fitness center. Bureau de change, hotel taxis, babysitting etc.

🅿 🚗 🔲 ☎ ⚙ 📶

KEMPINSKI HOTEL CORVINUS BUDAPEST *****
Erzsébet tér 7-8
Tel: 429 37 77
Fax 429 47 77
E-mail
hotel@kempinski.hu
The ultra-modern design of this hotel has made it one of the city's new curiosities, with its giant windows and a lobby flooded with light. It could be the last word in luxury, elegance, and style! There are 369 rooms. Bureau de change, hotel taxis, babysitting, restaurant and bar.

🅖 🚗 🔲 ☎ ⚙ 📶

MERCURE KORONA HOTEL ****
Kecskeméti u. 14
Tel: 317 41 11
Fax 318 38 67
E-mail
mercurekorona@pannoniahotels.hu
Its central location, between the Covered Market and the pedestrian precinct, has confirmed this hotel's popularity. Its two buildings on either side of the street are linked by a footbridge decked with flowers. 433 rooms. Bureau de change, hotel taxis, babysitting, restaurant and bar.

🅖 🅿 🚗 🔲 ☎ ⚙ 📶 🏊

TAVERNA HOTEL ****
Váci u. 20
Tel: 338 49 99
Fax 318 71 88
E-mail
hotel@hoteltaverna.hu
The most central of city center hotels! Access is via the pedestrian Váci u. and Petőfi u. Behind its façade of

columns decorated with sculptures are 227 well-appointed rooms thoughtfully arranged around the complex. The architects and interior designers have exercised their imagination to optimum effect to ensure the hotel's comfort and practicality. Its gastronomic restaurant is renowned: this is one of the best addresses in the city. The reception area also has a comfortable coffee lounge, bar, brasserie, bowling alley and sauna. Bureau de change, hotel taxis.

🚗 🔲 ☎ ⚙

RESTAURANTS

ADMIRAL
Belgrád rakpart 30
Tel: 318 07 23
Open daily
noon–11pm
With its wood-paneled walls, the interior of this restaurant on the left bank of the Danube resembles an old-fashioned schooner. The international dishes on its menu (notably Chinese) allow the diner to travel the world without leaving his comfortable chair. In summer a terrace planted with flowers enhances the diner's enjoyment, lending a romantic charm that is typical of Budapest's welcome.

AMADEUS
Apáczai Csere János u. 13
Tel: 318 46 77
Open daily
noon–midnight.
The Amadeus has become one of the most fashionable venues in the capital. In a modern designed setting, a large blackboard displays the day's menu, based on choice produce from the market. Specialties include a selection of char-grilled meats served with a variety of salads.

★ APOSTOLOK
Kígyó u. 4-6
Tel: 267 02 90
Fax 318 36 58
Open daily
noon–midnight.
The Apostolok is almost 100 years old, and looks like a chapel. The main dining-room is divided into a dozen pew-like compartments, each bearing the name of one of the apostles, and the sturdy square tables add to the monastic atmosphere. The walls of the smaller dining-room (called the Trianon), are decorated with murals depicting the towns of old Hungary and with portraits of the country's heroes. At the back of the room, above a large china pot, is a stained-glass window depicting King Istvan I making an offering to the Virgin, a copy of an original in St Stephen's Basilica. On fine days, eat on the terrace and watch the city go by.
At Apostolok, to the sound of gypsy violins, you can try delicious specialties such as soup with Tokay and a grilled fillet of fish from Lake Balaton.

BIARRITZ
Balassi Bálint u. 2
Tel: 302 39 43
Open daily
11am–midnight.
Light meals, notably salads, are the specialties at the Biarritz. Its attractive terrace becomes packed as soon as the warm weather begins.

CYRANO
Kristóf tér 7-8
Tel: 266 30 96
Open 11am–5pm, 5.30pm–midnight.
Easy to spot, with its huge flag fluttering in the breeze, Cyrano is right in the heart of Pest, in a pedestrian street. It owes its name to having leant its chandelier for use in the motion picture Cyrano de Bergerac, starring Gérard Depardieu. There are also attractive little balconies, and a large terrace where you may sample such delicacies as veal with paprika and gnocchi, or a fillet of pike-perch.

KÁRPÁTIA
Ferenciek tere 7-8
Tel: 317 35 96
Open daily
11am–11pm.
Richly decorated in the Gothic style with painted vaulting and attractive tables, Kárpátia also has gypsy violins to charm your ear as well. To seduce your palate, try stuffed cabbage the way it is prepared at Christmas in Transylvania: the fermented cabbage leaves are spread with a mixture of minced pork, rice and spices, and accompanied by sauerkraut and smoked meat in a cream sauce. The finished dish is then sprinkled with dill. The regional wine list is outstanding.

LÉGRÁDI & TÁRSA
Magyar u. 23
Tel: 318 68 04
Open Mon-Sat
6pm–midnight.
White walls, pictures, antique furniture and silver, and Chinese vases create an air of elegant opulence in this stylish restaurant.

★ GERBEAUD CUKRÁSZDA
Vörösmarty tér 7
Tel: 318 13 11
Open:
winter 9am–8pm
summer 9am–10pm

Gerbeaud's sign has been on the wall here since 1870, when a Swiss industrialist called Emil Gerbeaud bought the place from Henrik Kugler. It is one of the most famous coffee-houses in Budapest, and is decorated in the 1920s style typical of central Europe. Mouthwatering cakes are invitingly displayed in the window, tempting passers-by to self-indulgent acts of gluttony! Try pogacsa, a savoury brioche, and dobstorta, a rich creamy gateau.

★ LÉGRÁDI ANTIQUE
Bárczy István u. 3-5
Tel: 266 49 93
Open Mon–Fri
noon–3pm,
7pm–midnight
Sat noon–midnight
This fashionable and discreet restaurant is tucked away at the back of an antique shop. Beautiful old furniture and decoration are a feature here, and the tables are candlelit. The specialties are dishes from the north

of Hungary, such as goose offal with Heves rice, served with crackling from the bird, carrots, baby turnips, celeriac and mushrooms. The enchanting atmosphere is enhanced by a group of gypsy musicians. Best to book in advance.

◆ HOTELS AND RESTAURANTS

The kitchen spares no effort in its preparation of authentic traditional dishes, such as paloc (a hearty soup of vegetables and shoulder of mutton enriched with sour cream and sprinkled with parsley). The restaurant is open only in the evenings. It is advisable to book.

MARCO POLO
Vigadó tér 3
Tel: 338 33 54
Everyone who's anyone in Budapest knows Marco Polo, which serves high-class Italian food seasoned with fresh herbs from the Adriatic and around Florence. The wine list is comprehensive, ranging from down-to-earth vins de pays to the great vintages.

NAUTILUS ÉTTEREM
Váci u. 72
Tel: 338 48 30
Nautilus is a restaurant in a cellar, which ingeniously resemble the interior of a submarine. The specialty here is seafood.

PILSNER URQUELL SÖRFORRÁS
Váci u. 15
Tel: 318 38 14
Open daily
11am–11pm
A popular rendezvous which serves a range of dishes in generous portions, accompanied by Pilsner beer and the music of a jazz band. Chicken with paprika, a national dish, is prepared here in simple but authentic fashion, unlike the fussy attention which it is given in so-called gourmet establishments.

LOU LOU
Vigyázó Ferenc u. 4
Tel: 312 45 05
Open Mon–Fri
noon–3pm,
6pm–midnight
Sat 6pm–midnight.
The decor in this bistro is traditional French. There are prints of old Paris on the walls, and in the small dining-room Napoleon looks proudly down on its eight tables. Booking is essential, since the high quality of Lou Lou's Italian food is renowned throughout the city.

District VI

HOTELS

K+K HOTEL OPÉRA **
Révay u. 24
Tel: 269 02 22
Fax 269 02 30
A quiet hotel, located between the Hungarian State Opera and St Stephen's Basilica. The decor is unassuming, but its 205 rooms are very comfortable. Bureau de change, hotel taxis, babysitting, bar.
🅿 ☐ ☎ ☻

RADISSON SAS BÉKE HOTEL BUDAPEST **
Teréz krt 43
Tel: 301 16 00
Fax 301 16 15
E-mail
sales@
budzh. rdsas.com
Its imposing façade overlooks the ring boulevard of the city. There are 239 rooms, recently refurbished.

The staff are attentive and courteous, and on the floor above the imposing lobby there is a wide range of gifts and souvenirs for sale. The Shakespeare restaurant is dominated by a large mural illustrating the playwright's works, and offers a good selection of national dishes ◆ 269, together with excellent wines of the region. The Zsolnay Café is hung with mirrors and chandeliers: a good place to relax and listen to the pianist. Bureau de change, hotel taxis, babysitting.
🅒 🅿 🚗 ☐ ☎ ☻ 🍴

RESTAURANTS

ARTICSÓKA
Zichy Jenő u.17
Tel: 302 77 57
Open daily
8am–10pm
A good place to sit outside on the terrace, and sample the flavor of fine paprika, which is typical of the cuisine of Southern Hungary.

⭐ **BELCANTO ÉTTEREM**

Dalszínház u. 8
Tel: 311 84 71
Open daily
6am–2am
The arias you can hear are not issuing from the Opera house opposite, but are the voices of the waiters singing Bellini as they go about their work in this handsome restaurant. Naturally enough, the cuisine is Italian too: such delights as seafood risotto, spaghetti with anchovies and Venetian ratatouille are accompanied by a good range of Italian wines.

BARROKK
Mozsár u. 12
Tel: 317 89 42
Open daily noon – midnight.
To go down into the cellar that houses the Barrokk is to take a step back in time. The staff are dressed as 17th-century flunkeys, with decor to match. The cuisine is traditional Hungarian: try Bakony mushroom salad, hot tomatoes stuffed with cottage cheese and dill, and the delicious cherry gateau.

CHEZ DANIEL
Szív u. 32
Tel: 302 40 39
Fax 311 66 70
French cuisine rather than Hungarian dominates the menu at Chez Daniel. The menu is of the encouraging

268

sort that changes daily according to the availability and quality of produce in the market. Clever use made of local specialties used in classic dishes, executed with sensibility, imagination and flair. Booking essential.

MŰVÉSZINAS
Bajcsy-Zsilinszky út 9
Tel: 268 14 39
A popular eating-house with the locals, serving generous portions of traditional specialties. The menu is extensive, and also includes many classic European dishes.

★ MŰVÉSZ KÁVÉHÁZ
Andrássy út 29
Tel: 267 06 89
& 267 02 06
In summer you can relax on the terrace of this elegant old coffee-house, just across the street from the National Opera. In winter, the mirror-lined interior features work by local artists. By the door is a superb display of cakes and pastries, especially strudels. Francia kremes is a delicious cream gateau, while the sublime Esterhazy kocka is a rich old-fashioned confection with walnuts.

VII District

HOTELS

GRAND HOTEL HUNGARIA ★★★★
Rákóczi út 90
Tel: 322 90 50
Fax 352 18 58
E-mail
grandhun@
hungary.net
Ten minutes' walk from the central pedestrian precinct, the Hungaria is a luxurious hotel with 511 rooms (all of them light and peaceful), completely refurbished in 1985. The name of the figure on horseback at the entrance is Fiaker Sorozo, and this is also the name of the hotel's excellent restaurant. Bureau de change, hotel taxis, babysitting, bar.

🚗 ☐ ☎ ⚘

RESTAURANTS

FÉSZEK MŰVÉSZKLUB
Kertész u. 36
Tel: 322 60 43
Open daily
noon–1am

★ FAUSTO'S RISTORANTE
Dohány u. 5
Tel: 269 68 06
Open daily
noon–3pm,
7pm–midnight
Fausto's *has become one of the landmarks of*

Budapest. Its cheerful Italian decor seems just right for the Tuscan cuisine and chianti for which it is renowned: bollito misto, fegato alla veneziana, risotto, vitello alla pizzaiola, tiramisu and much, much more. Or try Fausto's excellent fresh pasta, such as fettuccini genovese, tortellini alla ricotta or spaghetti alla napoletana, all served with fresh basil and parmesan.

It takes a while to read the entire menu here, it is virtually an encyclopedia of Hungarian cuisine! It is a haunt of actors and artists, who love to sit in its shady courtyard in summer, and in winter crowd its medieval dining-room. The food is classic Hungarian, and the restaurant is located inside a theater. Booking advisable.

District VIII

HOTEL

PANNONIA HOTEL NEMZETI ★★★
József krt 4
Tel: 303 93 10
Fax 314 00 19
E-mail nemzeti@
pannoniahotels.hu
The Nemzeti is located near Blaha L. Tér subway station. Behind its attractive 'Transylvanian blue'

★ CAFÉ NEW YORK
Erzsébet krt 9-11
Tel: 322 38 49
or 322 16 48
Open daily
9am–midnight.
Located on the ground floor of the New York Palace (built in the 1890s for an American insurance company), this café is a beautifully preserved gem of the great coffee-houses that flourished here between the wars. Its gilding, brasswork and sparkling mirrors are a nostalgic echo of times past . Formerly this was one of the great literary meeting-places of Budapest, and pens and paper are still on offer. Sample the local cuisine here, and listen to the haunting music of its gypsy orchestra.

façade are 80 comfortable, air-conditioned bedrooms, recently refurbished. The old-fashioned dining-room is a masterpiece of gilding, glasswork and art deco furnishing. Restaurant, bar, bureau de change.

⊆ ⌂ □ ☎ ♨

District IX

HOTEL

IBIS HOTEL CENTRUM **
Ráday u. 6
Tel: 215 85 85
Fax 215 87 87
126 brand new rooms (summer 1998). Plain decor. Restaurant.

⊆ ℗ 🚗 □ ☎ ♨

RESTAURANT

★ MÚZEUM KÁVÉHÁZ
Múzeum krt 12
Tel: 338 42 21
Open Mon–Sat noon–1am
This elegant, high-ceilinged coffee-house dates back to 1885, and still has the original murals painted by Karoly Lotz. It is also a brasserie and restaurant, renowned among Budapest gourmets. The menu is a skilful blend of traditional dishes and more modern cuisine, and the salads are excellent. The wine list is outstanding. A good place to eat after a visit to the Hungarian National Museum across the street.

XI District

HOTELS

DANUBIUS HOTEL GELLÉRT ****
Szent Gellért tér 1
Tel: 385 22 00
Fax 366 66 31
E-mail
resoff@gellert.hu
The Géllert is a temple of art nouveau, frequented by those coming to take the cure at the adjoining thermal baths. There is also a medical center. This famous hotel shows its age here and there, but it is an establishment of unique charm and the rooms are undergoing renovation. At the back is a swimming pool with wave-machine. Bureau de change, hotel taxis, babysitting, restaurant and bar.

℗ □ ☎ ♨ ♒

PARK HOTEL FLAMENCO BUDAPEST ****
Tas Vezér u. 7
Tel: 361 22 50
Fax 365 80 07
E-mail
budfla@hungary.net
The Flamenco enjoys magnificent views, set in a park with a lake, in the foothills of Buda. It is only ten minutes on foot to the center of Pest, and there are tennis courts for guests. The restaurant has dancing in the evenings, and there is a lively late-night bar, Le Pinot Noir. Rooms are plain but comfortable. Bureau de change, hotel taxis.

℗ ⌂ 🚗 □ ☎ ♨ ♒ ♣ ♒ ♪

XII District

HOTELS

BUDAPEST HOTEL ****
Szilágyi Erzsébet fasor 47
Tel: 202 00 44
Fax 212 2729
E-mail
hhtours@hungary.net
Located at the foot of Castle Hill in Buda, the Budapest is a white 15-story-high tower, with large bay windows in the rooms to help guests enjoy the superb view. There are two restaurants, a bureau de change, and hotel taxis.

℗ □ ☎ ♨

NOVOTEL BUDAPEST CONGRESS ****
Alkotás u. 63-67
Tel: 209 19 90
Fax : 466 56 36
E-mail
novotel-reservation@pannoniahotels.hu
Set beside a little park, and not far from the Southern Railroad Station, the Novotel is ten minutes' walk from the city center. The Pannonia chain of hotels maintains high levels of cleanliness and efficiency, both indispensable to the comfort of the modern traveler. There is a reasonable restaurant, but the hotel's most distinguishing feature is its brasserie-grill, located in the bowling alley. Bureau de change, babysitting.

⌂ ℗ 🚗 □ ☎ ♨ ♒ ♒

RESTAURANTS

CASCADE
Szarvas Gábor út 8/d
Tel: 275 10 39
Open daily noon–1am
Cascade has an unruffled, sophisticated atmosphere with mellow brick walls, paneling and wrought-iron chandeliers. In addition to well-cooked Hungarian dishes, there are Mediterranean specialties as well.

KÉKGOLYÓ
Kék Golyó u. 1
Tel: 212 94 79
Open daily noon–midnight.
Near Deli subway station, this charming restaurant specializes

n fish. As well as soup prepared with fish from Lake Balaton, there is soup from Szeged, with carp, pike-perch and sheatfish (silurus) simmered in a broth of onions, paprika, red peppers and tomatoes. Hearty dishes such as these go well with one of the local red wines.

XIII District

HOTELS

DANUBIUS THERMAL HOTEL HELIA ★★★★
Kárpát u. 62-64
Tel: 452 58 00
Fax 452 58 01
E-mail
helia@
mail.matav.hu
This luxury spa hotel specializes in various fitness programs, and is also equipped for guests with disabilities. Its modern design includes chrome and leather chairs, and attractive blond wood in the bedrooms. Its restaurant serves local specialties, while the Neptunus Café has a number of vegetarian dishes available. Bureau de change, hotel taxis, babysitting.
🅿 🚗 🛄 🕿 🌐

DANUBIUS THERMAL HOTEL MARGIT-SZIGET ★★★★
Margit-sziget
Tel: 329 23 00
or 349 27 69
Fax 329 25 87
E-mail
margotel@
hungary.net
A modern and spacious hotel with package deals for guests wishing to take thermal cures. Massage and fitness facilities are also available. The establishment shares the baths with the Ramada Grand Hotel next door. Bureau de change, hotel taxis, restaurant and bar.
🅿 🚗 🛄 🕿 🌐 🌊

DANUBIUS GRAND HOTEL MARGIT-SZIGET ★★★★
Margit-sziget
Tel: 329 23 00
or 349 27 69
Fax 329 24 29
E-mail
margotel@
hungary.net
The most sought-after rooms in this old fashioned establishment on Margaret Island are those overlooking the park. The hotel has a peaceful setting, only a few minutes from the city center. It shares thermal baths and other remedial facilities with the Danubius Thermal Hotel next door. There is an excellent restaurant, and gypsy musicians play on the terrace. Bar, bureau de change, hotel taxis, babysitting, fitness center, medical consultations.
🅿 🚗 🛄 🕿 🌐 🌊
♨ 🎵 ✝

XIV District

RESTAURANTS

★ GUNDEL
Állatkerti krt 2
Tel: 321 3550
Fax 342 2917
Open daily
noon–3pm,
6pm–midnight.
The most renowned gastronomic restaurant in Hungary, and one of the best table in Eastern Europe. Gundel is run by the country's best-known restaurateur, George Lang, who bought the place in 1991 and gave it a splendid make-over to recreate its former glory. Originally opened in 1894 by János Gundel, it was taken over by his son Károly Gundel in 1910. The Gundel is set in a grand art nouveau mansion by the zoo, with ballroom, terrace, and garden.The dining-room is sumptuous, with fine Zsolnay porcelain on the tables, and 19th-century oil paintings on the paneled walls. Gypsy musicians stroll from table to table, while you enjoy the delights of delicious dishes such as veal cutlets or palacsinta (stuffed pancakes) cooked to perfection. A memorable treat.

★ ROBINSON
Városliget Állatkerti krt
Tel: 343 37 76
Open daily
noon–4pm,
6pm–midnight
Robinson is by Heroe's Square, behind the Fine Arts Museum, on a small island in the lake in the City Park, a romantic setting for a fine restaurant of international renown. Inside, a subdued elegance prevails, while outside guests dine beneath the shade of poplar and willow trees. The cuisine is predominantly light and the menu imaginative, based on choice produce from the day's market: for dessert, try a palacsinta Robinson (a crepe filled with fresh fruit and smothered in vanilla cream) which is accompanied by a glass of pezsgo (a local sparkling wine).

◆ HOTELS AND RESTAURANTS

ESZTERGOM

(zip code 2500)

HOTEL

HOTEL ESZTERGOM DANUBIUS BETA *
Primás-sziget
Tel: 412 555
Fax 412 853
E-mail
hotelesz@
mail.elender.hu
This little gem of a hotel has 36 delightful bedrooms, and runs a program of activities such as exploring the local wildlife, fishing and sailing on the Danube, and pony trekking. Restaurant, bar, bureau de change, fitness center.
🅿 ☐ ☎ ⌂

RESTAURANTS

BELVÁROSI KÁVÉHÁZ
Vörösmarty u. 2
Tel: 417 510
Fax 311 590
Open Mon–Thur
8am–10pm;
Fri–Sat
8am–midnight;
Sun 10am–10pm
A congenial coffee-house with pretty pink walls and blue-framed windows, that dates back to 1896. Inside the old mirrors and chandeliers have been preserved; this is an
ideal place to relax in the comfortable armchairs and enjoy an excellent pot of coffee.

PRÍMÁS PINCE
Szent István tér 4
Tel: 313 495
Fax 313 495
Open daily
10am–10pm
This medieval building was originally the town's first cathedral, as its vaulting, stone columns and flagged floor suggest. Later it became the residence of the archbishop. Now it is an elegant restaurant specializing in regional cuisine.

SZALMA CSÁRDA
Nagy Duna sétány 2
Tel: 315 336
Fax 315 336
Open daily
11am–9pm
The surrounding countryside finds an echo here in the bouquets of wild flowers that decorate the tables. The emphasis here is on the rustic, with terracotta pots, old farm implements and tresses of garlic and paprika hanging from the ceiling. The extensive menu includes dishes of fish from the Danube. The restaurant's unique atmosphere is enhanced by a group of gypsy musicians, and the terrace enjoys a superb view of the river.

SZENTENDRE

(zip code 2000)

HOTEL

BETA HOTEL PROVINCIA *
Paprikabóry
u. 21-23
Tel: 301 081/ 082
Fax 301 085
At the turn of the century artists often left Budapest and settled here in Szentendre, only 11 miles from the city, and the place has lost none of its charm. This small quiet hotel is a haven of peace and comfort, offering excellent service and a variety of activities in an attractive setting. There are 23 rooms. Bureau de change, fitness center, restaurant, bar, car hire.
🚗 ☐ ☎ ⌂

RESTAURANTS

ARANYSÁRKÁNY
Alkotmány u. 1/A
Tel: 311 670
Fax 311 670
Open daily
noon–10pm
Diners come all the way from Budapest to taste the lamb ragout in this friendly small restaurant. The interior is unpretentious: two rows of bistro tables, and a long polished wooden bench against the wall. The warm welcome offered by the family who run the place is friendly and genuine, one of the
secrets of Aranykarny's continued success.

NEMZETI BORMÚZEUM ET LABIRINTUS
Bogdányi u. 10
Tel: 317 054
Fax 317 054
Open daily
10am–10pm
The Museum of Wine here explains the history of winemaking in Hungary and its different vintages in a well laid out series of displays, which also offer an opportunity to taste different Chardonnays, Merlots and Pinots noirs – not forgetting sparkling wines, as well. Its restaurant, housed in an adjacent cellar, features many dishes prepared with Hungarian wine.

RAB RÁBY
Péter Pál u. 1/A
Tel: 310 819
Fax 310 819
From its extraordinary decor, you might think you had come into another museum here instead of a restaurant. Musical instruments, armor, clocks, oil lamps, old radios and a thousand other curiosities jostle for space on the walls and in the corners. Each table is named after a famous personality from the area. The food is fantastic: try fish soup, or leg of goose – and the desserts are out of this world!

◆ HISTORY ◆ CULTURE

◆ BEATON (C.), *The Wandering Years, Diaries 1922-39*, Weidenfeld, 1979
◆ BROOK (S.), *The Double Eagle: Vienna, Budapest, & Prague*, Hamish Hamilton
◆ COOPER (L.R.), KENESI (A.), *Hungarians in Transition : Interviews with Citizens of the Nineties*, Mcfarland and Co., 1993
◆ DENES (M.), *Castles Burning*, Doubleday, 1997
◆ GERŐ (A.) (ed.), *Modern Hungarian Society in the Making*, CEU Press, 1995
◆ GERŐ (A.), *The Hungarian Parliament (1867-1918): A Mirage of Power*, East European Monographs, 1997
◆ HOENSCH (JÖRG. K.), TRAYNOR (K.), *A History of Modern Hungary 1867-1994*, Longman, 1995
◆ KOESTLER (A.), *Arrow in the Blue*, Collins with Hamish Hamilton Ltd 1952
◆ LÁZÁR (I.), *Hungary: A Brief History*, Corvina
◆ LEIGH FERMOR (P.), *A Time of Gifts*, Penguin Books, 1979
◆ LUKÁCS (J.), *Budapest 1900 : A Historical Portrait of a City and Its Culture*, Grove Press, 1990
◆ POGANY BENNETT (P.) CLARK (V.R.), *The Art of Hungarian Cooking*, Hippocrene Books, 1997
◆ TAYLOR (A.J.P.), *The Habsburg Monarchy 1809-1918*, Penguin, 1964

◆ ARTS ◆

◆ CHALMERS (K.), *Bela Bartok (20th-Century Composers)*, Phaidon, 1995
◆ COOPER (D.), *Bartok: 'Concerto for Orchestra'*, Cambridge University Press, 1996
◆ COTIER (J.), *Nudes in Budapest*, Aktok, 1992
◆ ERNYEY (G.), *Made in Hungary: The Best of 150 Years in Industrial Design*, Rubik Innovation Foundation
◆ FODOR (I.) et al, *Baroque Splendor: The Art of the Hungarian*

Goldsmith, Bard Graduate Center, 1995
◆ FRIGYESI (J.), *Béla Bartók and Turn-of-the-Century Budapest*, University of California Press, 1998
◆ GERLE (J.), *The Turn of the Century*, City Hall
◆ HEATHCOTE (E.), *Budapest: A Guide to Twentieth-Century Architecture*, Ellipsis, 1997
◆ KOLBA (J.H.), *Hungarian Silver*, Thomas Heneage, 1998
◆ LORINC, *Budapest Ballet*, Branden Publishing, 1971
◆ LUCY (M.), EVANS (C.), *Hungarian Journeys*, M.Evans, London, 1996
◆ MAGRIS (C.), *Danube*, The Harvill Press, 1999
◆ MANSBACH (S.A.), *Two Centuries of Hungarian Painters 1820-1970*, University Press of America, 1992
◆ MORRIS (J.), *Fifty Years of Europe : An Album*, Penguin, 1998
◆ SOLTI (G.), *Memoirs*, Chatto and Windus, 1997
◆ VARDY (S.B.), *Clio's Art in Hungary and Hungarian -America*, East European Monographs, 1986

◆ LITERATURE ◆

◆ ADY (E.), *Neighbours of the Night: Selected Short Stories*, Corvina
◆ ADY (E.), *Poems*, University Press of America, 1988◆ BIRO (V.), *Hungarian Folk Tales*, Oxford University Press, 1992
◆ CZIGÁNY (L.), *The Oxford History of Hungarian Literature from the Earliest Times to the Present*, Oxford University Press, 1988
◆ ESTERHÁZY (P.), *A Little Hungarian Pornography*, Quartet, 1995
◆ ESTERHÁZY (P.), *She Loves Me*, Quartet, 1997
◆ FISCHER (T.), *Under the Frog*, Penguin, 1993
◆ GATTO (K.), *Treasury of Hungarian Live*, Hippocrene, 1996
◆ GOMORI (G.), SZIRTES (G.), *The Colonnade of Teeth*, Bloodaxe Books, 1996
◆ GYORGYEY (C.), *A Mirror to the Cage: Three Contemporary*

Hungarian Plays, University of Arkansas, 1993
◆ GONCZ (A.), et al, *Plays and Other Writings*, Garland, 1990
◆ JÓZSEF (A.), *The Iron-Blue Vault*, Bloodaxe Books, 1999
◆ KABDEBO (T.), *Life of Attila Jozsef*, Libris, 1995
◆ KERTÉSZ (I.), *Fateless*, Northwestern University Press, 1992
◆ KONRÁD (G.), *The Case Worker*, Penguin
◆ KONRÁD (G.), *The Loser*, Harcourt Brace International
◆ KOSZTOLÁNYI (D.), *Anna Edes*, New Directions, 1992
◆ KOSZTOLÁNYI (D.), *Skylark*, CEU Press
◆ KRUDY (G.) SZIRTES (G.), *The Adventures of Sindbad*, Central European University Press, 1998
◆ LENGYEL (P.), *Cobblestone*, Readers International, 1993
◆ LYNNE (A.), *Safe Houses*, Penguin
◆ MAKKAI (A.) (ed.), *In Quest of the 'Miracle Stag:' An Anthology of Hungarian Poetry from the 13th Century to the Present*, Atlantis-Centaur/Corvina/M. Szivarvany, 1996
◆ NADAS (P.), *A Book of Memories*, Vintage, 1998
◆ NADAS (P.), GOLDSTEIN (I.), *The End of a Family Story*, Jonathan Cape, 1999
◆ NEMES-NAGY (A.) et al, *Agnes Nemes Nagy on Poetry: A Hungarian Perspective*, Edwin Mellen, 1998
◆ NEMES-NAGY (A.), *Between : Selected Poems of Agnes Nemes Nagy*, The Dedalus Press
◆ ÖRKÉNY (I.), *One Minute Stories*, Corvina
◆ ÖRKÉNY (I.) et al, *The Flower Show and the Toth Family*, W.W.Norton, 1982
◆ TIBOR (D.), *The Portuguese Princess*, Calder, 1967
◆ VAJDA (M.) (ed.), *Modern Hungarian Poetry*, Columbia University Press, 1979

◆ CLASSICAL MUSIC ◆

Béla Bartók

◆ *Allegro Barbaro Sz 49, 3 Rondos Sz 84, 3 Hungarian Folk Tunes Sz 66, Romanian Dances Sz 56, 15 Hungarian Peasant Songs Sz 71*, Zoltán Kocsis (piano).
◆ *Cantata Profana Sz 94, Concerto for orchestra Sz 116*, József Réti (tenor), András Faragó (baritone), Budapest Choir and Symphony Orchestra, János Ferencsik (conductor).
◆ *Concerto for orchestra, 3 Village Scenes*, Kossuth... Budapest Festival Orchestra, Iván Fischer (conductor).
◆ *Violin Concerto No.2 Sz 112* (+ *Violin Concerto in D* by Igor Stravinsky), Viktoria Mullova (violin), Los Angeles Philharmonic Orchestra, Esa-Pekka Salonen (conductor), 1 CD Philips 456 542-2
◆ *Gyermekeknek (for Children) Vols. 1–IV*, Zoltán Kocsis (piano).
◆ *Complete works for piano and orchestra (3 concertos), Rhapsody Op.1 Sz 27, Scherzo Op.2 Sz 28)*, Zoltán Kocsis, Budapest Festival Orchestra, Iván Fischer (conductor).
◆ *Complete works by Bartók performed by the composer*, Béla Bartók (piano).
◆ *Kossuth (Symphonic Poem DD75a), Piano Quintet DD77*, Budapest Symphony Orchestra, György Lehel

conductor), Csilla Szabó (piano), Tátrai Quartet.
◆ *Duke Bluebeard's Castle*, Walter Berry (Bluebeard), Christa Ludwig (Judith), London Symphony Orchestra, Kertesz (conductor).
◆ *The Miraculous Mandarin*, Hungarian Peasant Songs, Romanian Dances, Budapest Festival Orchestra, Iván Fischer (conductor).
◆ *The Wooden Prince* complete ballet), Dance Suite.Iván Fischer (conductor).
◆ *Three Piano Concertos*, Géza Anda (piano), Berlin Radio Symphony Orchestra, Ferenc Fricsay (conductor).
◆ *Mikrokosmos Sz 107*, Gyermekeknek (for Children), Dezsö Ránki (piano), Sz 42.
◆ *14 Bagatelles Op.6 Sz 38, 2 Elegies Op.8b Sz 41, 6 Romanian Dances Sz 56, Sonatina Sz 55*, Hungarian Folk Tunes Sz 66, Zoltán Kocsis (piano).
◆ *Six String Quartets*, Takács Quartet.
◆ *Sonata for 2 pianos and 2 percussion Sz 110 (+ Andante and 5 Variations K.501 by Mozart; En blanc et noir by Debussy)* M. Argerich and S. Bishop Kovacevich (pianos), W. Goudswaard, M. de Roo percussion).

Bartók and Kodály
◆ *Cantata Profana* (Bartók), *Psalmus Hungaricus* (Kodály), *Serenade for small orchestra Op.3* (Leo Weiner), Tamas Daroczi (tenor),

Alexandre Agache (baritone), Hungarian Radio & Television Choir, Budapest Festival Orchestra, Georg Solti (conductor)
◆ *Háry János Suite, Dances of Galánta, Dances of Marosszék* (Kodály), *Hungarian Sketches, Romanian Dances* (Bartók), Hungarian Philharmonic Orchestra, Antál Dorati (conductor),
◆ *Sonata for unaccompanied violin* (Bartók), *Duo Op.7 for violin and cello* (Kodály), Gérard Poulet (violin), Christoph Henkel (cello).

Zoltán Kodály
◆ *Solo Cello Sonata Op.8, Sonata for cello and piano Op.4*, Miklós Perényi (cello), Jenő Jandó (piano).
◆ *Te Deum of Budavár, Missa Brevis*, Éva Andor (soprano), Márta Szirmay (contralto), József Réti (tenor), József Gregor (bass), Budapest Symphony Orchestra, János Ferencsik (conductor),

Franz (Ferenc) Liszt
◆ *Concerto No.1 in E Flat Major for piano and orchestra, Totentanz, Concerto No.2 in A Major for piano and orchestra, Hungarian Fantasia for piano and orchestra*, György Cziffra (piano), 2 CDs EMI 7 47640 2
◆ *Mephisto Waltz, Jeux d'eaux à la villa d'Este, Valse-Impromptu, Valse-Caprice No.6, St Francis of Paule Walking on the Waves, Chasse-neige, Ricordanza, Gaudeamus Igitur,*

György Cziffra (piano.
◆ *Rêve d'amour No.3 in A Flat Major, La Ronde des lutins, St Francis of Assisi Preaching to the Birds, Valse oubliée in F Sharp Major*, György Cziffra.
◆ *Hungarian Rhapsody No.2 for orchestra, Fantasia on Hungarian Folk Melodies for piano and orchestra, Hungarian Rhapsody No. 4 for orchestra, Hungarian Rhapsody No.6 "Pest Carnival" for orchestra, Rákóczi March for orchestra*, Jenő Jandó (piano), Szeged Symphony Orchestra, Tamás Pál (conductor); Hungarian National Orchestra, János Ferencsick (conductor, Gyula Németh (conductor).
◆ *Hungarian Rhapsodies* György Cziffra (piano).

Sándor Veress
◆ *Homage to Paul Klee, Concerto for piano, strings and percussion, Six Csardas*, András Schiff (piano), Dénes Varjon (piano), Budapest Festival Orchestra, Heinz Holliger (conductor),

◆ CONTEMPORARY MUSIC ◆

◆ *Contemporary Romanian and Hungarian Music* (Cornel Taranu, Máté Hollós, Adrian Borza, László Dubrovay, Péter Szegö), Anonymus Ensemble, Péter Szegö (conductor).

György Ligeti
◆ *Concerto for cello and orchestra, Chamber Concerto for 13 instruments, Concerto for piano and orchestra* Miklós Perényi (cello), Ueli Wiget (piano), Ensemble Modern, Péter Eötvös.
◆ *Chamber Concerto, Ramifications, String Quartet No.2, Adventures, Lux Aeterna, Manning*, Thomas Pearson, Ensemble InterContemporain, Pierre Boulez (conductor), LaSalle Quartet, Hamburg Radio

Choir, Franz (conductor).
◆ *Études for piano (1st and 2nd books, part of 3rd book)*, Musica Ricercata, Pierre Laurent Aimard.
◆ *String Quartets No.1 "Métamorphoses Nocturnes" and No.2*, Arditti Quartet.
◆ *Horn Trio, Passacaglia ungherrese, Hungarian Rock, Continuum, 3 Pieces (Monument, Selbstporträt, Bewegung)*, Gawriloff, Baumann, Besch, Chojnacka, Ballista, Canino.

György Kurtág
◆ *Jaketok (Games)*, Márta and György Kurtág (piano).
◆ *Music for stringed instruments*, Keller Quartet, Miklós Perényi (cello), György Kurtág (celesta).

◆ TRADITIONAL MUSIC ◆

◆ *Ando Drom* (Gypsies of Budapest) *Phari Mamo.*
◆ *Music from Transylvania Erdélyi Népzene* (traditional music of Romania's Hungarian minorities).
◆ Muzsikás and Márta Sebestyén *Hazafelé* (traditional Hungarian music).
◆ Muzsikás *Szól a Kakas Már* (Jewish folk music from Transylvania).

◆ JAZZ ◆

◆ *Akosh S. Unit Élettér.*
◆ *Seffer (Yochk'o) Rétrospective.*
◆ *Szabo (Gabor) The Sorcerer.*

INDEX